RAGS TO RICHES

THE STORY OF MUNSTER RUGBY

A moment in time – Munster captain Paul O'Connell takes time out to hug his father, Mick, in the crowd after the Heineken Cup final at the Millennium Stadium in 2008.

RAGS TO RICHES
THE STORY OF MUNSTER RUGBY

BARRY COUGHLAN

The Collins Press

For Kaelan

First published in 2009 by
The Collins Press
West Link Park
Doughcloyne
Wilton
Cork

All photographs courtesy of the *Irish Examiner* except for those on
pp 272 and 273, which are courtesy of Keith Wiseman.

British Library Cataloguing in Publication Data

Coughlan, Barry.
Rags to riches : the story of Munster rugby.
1. Munster (Rugby team)—History.
2. Rugby Union football—Ireland—Munster—History.
3. Rugby Union football—Ireland—Munster—Anecdotes.
I. Title
796.3'3362'09419-dc22

ISBN-13: 9781848890190

Design and typesetting by Glen McArdle
www.fairwaysdesign.com
Typeset in Frutiger 10pt

Printed in Malta by Gutenberg Press Limited

Contents

Acknowledgements

I would like to thank The Collins Press for giving me this opportunity to pay tribute to Munster rugby, and I want to highlight the contribution of editor Aonghus Meaney for his vigilance and professionalism.

Former players of great distinction helped me to complete this tale of Munster rugby through their recall of special games and the events surrounding them. Amongst that group are Jim McCarthy, Paddy Reid, Gerald Reidy, Norman Coleman, Tom Kiernan, Noel Murphy, Brian O'Brien, Ken Ging, Liam Hall, Johnny Moroney, Phil O'Callaghan, Colm Tucker, Paul Derham, Ken O'Connell, Terry Kingston, Donal Lenihan, Mick Galwey (*Galwey, The Autobiography* (Dublin 2002)), Anthony Foley (*Axel, A Memoir* (Dublin 2008)) and Ronan O'Gara (*Ronan O'Gara, My Autobiography* (Dublin 2008)).

Statistics supplied by Munster's Honorary Secretary Frank Byford proved to be invaluable; I want to thank him especially – not just for providing the information but for getting it to me quickly when pressure mounted to finish the project. Munster Chief Executive Garrett Fitzgerald provided a valuable insight into the workings of the Munster product; media man Pat Geraghty pointed me in the right direction for information on several occasions while Fiona Murphy and Jennifer Kiernan were also very helpful in aspects of the book's promotion.

My friend and colleague Edmund Van Esbeck, *Sunday Times* journalist Denis Walsh, former English and Lions international Stuart Barnes, Len Dinneen of Limerick Radio fame, and Ian Moriarty also contributed hugely towards the completion of the project, and I thank them for their help.

My special thanks to the *Irish Examiner* owners, the Crosbie family, to Chief Executive Tom Murphy, the Editor Tim Vaughan, and Sports Editor Tony Leen for their encouragement and for putting all the back-up facilities of the company at my disposal.

I would like to thank the library staff at the *Irish Examiner*, especially Anne Kearney, Declan Ryan and Tim Ellard.

I wish to acknowledge the huge contributions of my great friend and long-term colleague Des Barry and two other award-winning photographers and valued colleagues in the *Irish Examiner*, Denis Minihane and Dan Lenihan.

Keith Wiseman from Limerick provided photographs of Munster's Magners League trophy presentation in Thomond Park in May of 2009 and captured images of a unique moment in the club's history – Anthony Horgan's last try for the province on a night when he retired after thirteen years' service. For facilitating supply and delivery of those pictures, I would like to thank well-known press photographer from the *Limerick Leader*, Owen South.

Also on the photographic front, I want to offer my gratitude to both Pat Good and Paddy Barker who waded through a mound of photographs on screen and transferred them to disc or emailed them to the publishers.

Finally, and without meaning to patronise, may I offer praise to successive Munster teams, some of whom I watched as a young supporter and others as a professional observer going back through the decades; for the excitement they generated and for the sheer pleasure they gave hundreds of thousands of people as they strived for, and achieved, excellence in rugby stadiums at home, throughout Britain, Europe and beyond.

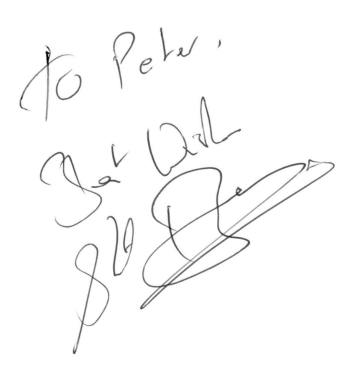

Introduction

The date 31 October 1978 will be forever ingrained in the minds of all Munster rugby fans. One would venture to suggest Leinster, Ulster, Connacht and New Zealand supporters would have cause to remember it as well, having been reminded often enough of its significance by proud Munster men and women.

If was, of course, the day Munster beat the All Blacks at Thomond Park by 12 points to nil, the day New Zealand were told they were lucky to get nil!

That magnificent Munster achievement is enshrined in the annals of the game down south; what isn't quite right, however, is that other noble achievements by different Munster teams over the years have not been given the same due recognition.

It is fair to say that Munster never built a reputation based on what they achieved at home; from the late 1800s they were always playing catch-up behind Ulster and Leinster. And although Munster's standing improved once the Irish Rugby Football Union (IRFU) organised an official senior Interprovincial Championship, held between 1946 and 2000, their record was no better than moderate relative to Ulster and Leinster.

Yes, there were spells of dominance but Munster failed for years to match the 'big two' with successive titles – with Connacht always bringing up the rear – until they made a late gallop to three in a row during the early days of the professional era between 1998 and 2000. They would win one and fade back until the next and they had an average winning sequence of just one title every four years, although the statistics are unbalanced somewhat by Ulster's amazing dominance of the championship between 1984 and 1992.

Yet if Munster had a relatively low profile in domestic rugby, they made up for it when the 'big boys' came to town, namely New Zealand, South Africa and Australia.

Munster even played the Argentinian Pumas once, ironically five years to the day before 1978's giant-killing feat against New Zealand. Despite their prowess in the game, Argentina were the sleeping giants of southern hemisphere rugby, barely recognised by the other major powers, who wanted to protect their cosy cartel. And although there existed close cultural and sporting links between Ireland and Argentina, there was no love lost when the Pumas, on their first visit to Ireland, came to Limerick in 1973. Had it been a football match, the trouble on the pitch might have sparked off riots on the terraces.

Munster secured a 12–12 draw thanks to four penalties from captain Barry McGann. Ulster referee Alex Sturgeon tried hard to keep control of two sides more intent on slugging it out than playing rugby, with Munster responding firmly to Puma provocation from the start of the game.

It is worth noting that, despite its not being a capped game, fourteen of the fifteen Munster personnel had either played for Ireland already or were destined to do so, the exception being Garryowen winger Pat Pratt.

The Munster team that day was: D. Spring (Trinity), P. Pratt (Garryowen), P. Parfrey (UCC), S. Dennison (Garryowen), P. Lavery (London Irish), B. McGann (Cork Constitution) (captain), D. Canniffe (Cork Constitution), G. McLoughlin (Shannon), P. Whelan (Garryowen), P. O'Callaghan (Dolphin), M. Keane (Lansdowne), B. Foley (Shannon), J. Buckley (Sunday's Well), T. Moore (Highfield), S. Deering (Garryowen).

Munster's history against touring teams, however, is better documented by recounting some epic struggles against the All Blacks, the Springboks and the Wallabies; history – and this book – shows they have much more to be proud of than that single victory over New Zealand.

Apart from three matches which can be categorised as calamitous – against New Zealand in 1905 (0–33), South Africa in 1970 (9–25) and Australia in 1996 (19–55) – Munster showed no respect for reputation or achievement when playing touring sides, as reflected in the magnificent 1992 victory over Bob Dwyer's Australia, then the reigning world champions.

Munster played New Zealand eight times, and although the record shows one win (1978), one draw (1973) and six defeats, the Irish side could easily have won three more, not least the classic encounter in the new Thomond Park on 18 November 2008.

South Africa had one facile victory and twice escaped narrowly against determined Munster teams in 1951 and 1960 – but Australia were not so lucky. From the very first of eight matches when a late try at the Mardyke secured a fortuitous 6–5 victory for the touring side in 1947, the Wallabies found Munster too much of a handful on no fewer than three occasions. The Munster record of three wins, a draw and four defeats tells its own tale, although, naturally enough, not the full story.

In the modern era, Munster, once the whipping boys for some of Europe's top sides, first gained a degree of respect before stamping their class and authority all over the northern hemisphere game. In the last decade Munster rugby has been immersed in a wondrous, magical and often fruitful journey of discovery.

This is the story of transition: from rags to riches.

PART 1

Chapter 1:
1905:
THE PIONEERS

Munster v New Zealand
Market's Field, Limerick – 28 November 1905

Munster 0 | New Zealand 33

MUNSTER:

A. Quillinan (Garryowen), A. Newton (Cork County), B. Maclear (Constitution) (captain),
W. Stokes (Garryowen), R. McGrath (Constitution), F. McQueen (Queen's College), J. O'Connor (Garryowen),
J. Wallace (Wanderers and Garryowen), T. Reeves (Monkstown and Garryowen), S. Hosford (Constitution),
W. Parker (Cork County), M. White (Queen's College), R. Welply (Queen's College), T. Acheson (Garryowen),
T. Churchwarden (Cork County).

NEW ZEALAND:

Booth, Smith, McGregor, Hunter, Abbott, Mynott, Stead, Gillet, Newton, Tyler, Mackrell,
Cunningham, Nicholson, McDonald, Glasgow.

1905:
THE PIONEERS

The first player to captain Munster against the All Blacks was the legendary Basil Maclear. A captain in the Dublin Fusiliers, Maclear was instantly recognisable on the rugby field because of his magnificent physique – and his white gloves! However worrying the white gloves may have been to his teammates, they certainly did not prevent him from getting stuck in. So much so, in fact, that he set a record by playing against Dave Gallaher's first New Zealand tourists no fewer than four times in twenty-four days in 1905.

As well as captaining Munster – he was stationed in Fermoy, County Cork and played club rugby with Cork County and Constitution – the English-born Irish international also lined out against the tourists for Blackheath, Bedford and Ireland. He first appeared as a fifteen-year-old from Bedford School for Blackheath and played as a guest for Bedford in their match against the tourists.

Maclear must have been sick of the sight of the All Blacks, because in over five-and-a-half hours against them he never saw his team score a point. Blackheath were beaten 32–0, Bedford fell 41–0, Ireland were overcome 15–0 and Munster succumbed 33–0. Maclear's teams conceded twenty-eight tries in those games, nine of which came via his opposing centre pairings.

Having served in the Boer War (1900–2) and in Aden (1903), Maclear won the first of his eleven Irish caps in 1905. He was one of eight Irish internationals killed during the First World War, dying on 24 May 1915 during the Battle of Ypres.

Maclear was not always a loser on the rugby field, however, nor was his short life without drama and excitement, as this excerpt from an article by E.A. Rolfe in the *Old Bedfordians Year Book* of 1929 illustrates.

He was the youngest of five sons who all served overseas in the First World War, three being killed in action. During his schooldays at Bedford, he

lived with his Mother in the 'Crescent' district of the town.

As a youngster at the Priory School he signalized himself by winning every event in the athletic sports. Entering Bedford School in May 1893, he soon showed promise in the playing fields. At the early age of 15 he played for Blackheath and the records of the time describe him as 'a promising forward, tall, heavy, strong and fast, a resolute tackler and a reliable place-kicker'.

Later, at Sandhurst he represented the College at cricket, rugby football, athletics and shooting and won the Sword of Honour in 1900. He served with

Bandon, the first winners of the Munster Senior Cup in 1886, but it was Queen's College Cork and Garryowen who dominated the competition and provided the bulk of the early Munster teams before Constitution started to make their mark around the time of the 1905 clash with New Zealand.

his regiment in the Boer War from 1900 to 1902 and received the Queen's Medal with 5 clasps. He saw further active service at Aden in 1903 during the operations in the interior. On returning home he resumed his place in the football field.

He was a man of magnificent physique nearly six feet in height and weighing close on 14 stone, yet retaining most of the great speed of his *schooldays and his resolution was equal to his physical powers. A forceful rather than subtle player, he was dangerous in attack and formidable in defence, and particularly noted for the vigour of a well practised hand-off.*

No big game in which he took part could ever be dull. His powerful form, in green jersey, with white kid gloves cut down to mitts; his fair hair and moustache; his evident delight in the fray, together with his great reputation as a daring individualist gave spectators and players alike an exciting sense of anticipation, for there was always the chance that he might, by some unaided effort, some sudden rush, completely change the fortunes of a game.

Rolfe, pointing to Maclear's eligibility – through his Irish-born father – to play for Ireland, took the English Rugby Football Union (RFU) to task for their lack of interest in the player.

For reasons best known to themselves, the authorities of the English Rugby Union in spite of strong recommendations, could not be persuaded to give him a trial – an error of which they no doubt repented when on three occasions, Basil Maclear was one of the chief agents in the defeat of the English team.

The Irish Rugby Union was wiser and in 1905 – for he was qualified both by birth and by residence to play for Ireland – chose him to play against England, Scotland, Wales and New Zealand (the famous first 'All Blacks'); in 1906 against England, Scotland and Wales. Then, unfortunately, knee trouble diverted his energies from Rugby to Hockey, in which game he also excelled.

Of all his international matches, the one by which he is best remembered is, perhaps, that against the South Africans on the Balmoral Ground at Belfast in 1906, at the end of which he almost succeeded in snatching victory from defeat by making his way single-handed from his own '25' through an unusually powerful opposition and securing a historic try. The scene which followed will never be forgotten by any who witnessed it. Such frantic and long-continued excitement has probably never been displayed, even on an Irish football ground. Even after the decisive kick at goal by J.C. Parke had failed, the storm of applause still continued.

In 1912 Maclear joined the staff of the Royal Military College, Sandhurst as inspector of physical training, and won the admiration and affection of cadets and officers alike.

In February 1915 he rejoined his regiment and the following month was sent to France. He took part in all the heavy fighting at Ypres during April and May; until about 8 May he was second in command of his regiment, and for four days in full command in most trying circumstances. Every day, in brief intervals snatched from the fighting, he wrote to his mother, his last letter dated 23 May. The next morning he was killed.

According to Rolfe, he was sadly mourned by thousands of soldiers, who either knew him personally or by reputation.

Those who remember him on the football field can well imagine Basil Maclear in battle – the big, cheery, heartening presence, cool, resolute, formidable, a tower of strength, the born soldier and leader.

One of the thirty-odd survivors of his Battalion wrote of him as follows: 'No words can describe his loss; he was a man every single one of us would have risked our lives to save. There is a blank in our regiment now which will never be filled.' When the news of his death reached England there was not a newspaper or periodical which did not contain some tribute to this great sportsman and soldier, whose personality had made so deep an impression on so many minds.

His name was not forgotten in Ireland either. In 1928 officials from the IRFU and the Irish international players presented to Mrs Maclear a football from an international trial match signed by all the participants in the game.

Basil Maclear's memory lived on in England too, evident in this extract from an article by O. L. Owen (rugby correspondent of *The Times* and editor of *Rugby Football Annual*) that featured in the programme of the England v Ireland match at Twickenham in 1954, just weeks after the All Blacks had played in Ireland for the first time since 1905.

The unique unrivalled Basil Maclear appeared so often on the roll of fame that one sometimes finds it hard to believe that he played in only 11 international matches. But what 11 matches they were! One was against the original All Blacks at Cork, where the New Zealanders had reason to note his formidable running and tackling.

Against the first Springboks a year later (1906), Maclear, picking up in his own '25', scored about the most sensational try ever seen in an international match. He very nearly equalled the effort in the same game, when he made the run which sent in one of his fellows for an equalising try, which forced South Africa into making a desperate recovery in order to win by 15 points to 12. England encountered Maclear three times, and on each occasion Ireland – one very nearly wrote Maclear – won. In those three matches Ireland scored 13 tries to 2.

No sportsman would grudge Ireland their possession of Maclear, son of an Irish father if born in Hampshire, a heroic Dublin Fusilier, a casualty at Spion Kop, and granted a soldier's death in the first Great War.

Chapter 2:
1947: PIPPED AT THE POST

Munster v Australia
The Mardyke – 8 December 1947

Munster 5
(P. Reid, try, conversion)

Australia 6
(McBride, try; Hardcastle, try)

MUNSTER:

J. Staunton (Garryowen), J. O'Sullivan (UCC), P. Reid (Garryowen) (captain), J. Mackessy (Cork Constitution), R. Dennehy (Dolphin), A. McElhinney (Dolphin), H. de Lacy (Harlequins and Garryowen), T. Clifford (Young Munster), J. C. Corcoran (London Irish and Sunday's Well), B. Hayes (Cork Constitution), E. Keeffe (Sunday's Well), P. Madden (Sunday's Well), C. Roche (Garryowen), T. Reid (Garryowen), J. McCarthy (Dolphin).

AUSTRALIA:

Windsor, McBride, Walker, Howell, Bourke, Broad (captain), Cawsey, Davis, Dawson, McMaster, Shehadie, Hardcastle, Winning, Stenmark, Keller.

CHAPTER 2
1947: PIPPED AT THE POST

The world was recovering from the trauma of a long war, shipping lanes had opened up again, commercial air travel was expanding slowly and rugby in its international form was beginning to settle into a new, unbroken routine. The Five Nations Championship was back on the 1946/7 calendar after a lapse of seven seasons.

There was a thirst for travel at this time and a desire to gain new experiences, and the southern hemisphere rugby fraternity were anxious to partake in new challenges. Between July 1947 and March 1948 the Australian national side, known as the Wallabies, embarked on a world tour, playing a total of five Tests and thirty-six tour matches in Ceylon (now Sri Lanka), Britain, Ireland, France and the United States. It was the first such tour since that of the 1927–8 Waratahs, as the 1939 Wallaby tour was thwarted by the onset of war. The 1947–8 side was notable in keeping Ireland, England, Scotland and Wales from scoring tries in the Test matches played.

The nine-month journey was one of the last of that era of epic tours when transport was mostly by ship and when the tourists were wholeheartedly welcomed by rugby fans and townships, civic officials and royalty.

The Australians in those days were still showcasing the new running style of rugby that had not yet been fully embraced in the northern hemisphere. The legacy of previous leaders and the credo of running rugby as played by the Randwick Club in Sydney had something to do with the excitement generated by the presence of the Wallabies.

The new approach to rugby came because of competition in Australia from rugby league that forced the game in Sydney and Brisbane to attempt to match the speed and open play of the thirteen-a-side code. This need was not the same in London, Edinburgh, Dublin or Cardiff where league did not yet pose a serious threat to spectator numbers coming through rugby union turnstiles.

The Munster team that lost in the last minute to Australia at the Mardyke in 1947.
Back row (l–r): C. Roche, B. Hayes, J. C. Corcoran, J. O'Sullivan, J. Staunton,
T. Clifford, T. Reid. Referee: O. Glasgow; middle row (l–r): A. McElhinney, E. Keeffe,
P. Reid, P. Madden, J. Mackessy, J. McCarthy; front (l–r): D. Dennehy, H. de Lacy.

So it was that Australia embarked on that tour, and the Wallabies became the first overseas team to play in Ireland since the All Blacks in 1935. It was to be a challenge they would never forget, for after defeating Ireland at Lansdowne Road on 6 December 1947 with relative ease (16–3), they felt they only needed to turn up at the Mardyke a few days later to win.

Nick Shehadie was an inexperienced prop forward; the fourth youngest of the Australian party, he was thrown in at the deep end against Munster. It was there that, famously, Cork Constitution and Munster prop forward Batt Hayes, setting himself for the first scrum of the game in the opening seconds, looked the 21-year-old Shehadie in the eye and said, 'Son, come on in, you might as well die here as in Sydney!'

Years later when Shehadie led the 1981 Wallabies on a European tour as manager, he recalled those words and admitted, 'That game was surely a baptism of fire.'

Yet, that introduction to the rigours of top-class rugby did young Shehadie no harm; he went on to play thirty Tests for Australia, and captained them on a number of occasions in both tour and Test games. In later years he became a renowned rugby administrator. Indeed, Shehadie was instrumental in changing the face of international rugby when he played a leading role in the organisation of the inaugural World Cup in 1987.

Beyond rugby, he entered politics as an alderman with Sydney City Council and served as the city's lord mayor between 1973 and 1975. On 20 October 1973 he oversaw the official opening of Sydney Opera House by Britain's Queen Elizabeth.

Shehadie had been a member of the Sydney Cricket Ground (SCG) for twenty-nine years when in 1978 he was invited by the New South Wales minister for sport, Ken Booth, to become a trustee. At the time, Shehadie was patron of Randwick Rugby Club and a committee member of Sydney Turf Club. He served as trustee of the SCG from 1978 to 2001 and was chairman from 1990 to 2001. His time as trustee saw the installation of lights at the cricket ground and the building of the Sydney Football Stadium where a stand was named in his honour. In his final year as chairman, a Walk of Honour was opened, commemorating thirty-three sporting champions who performed at the SCG — one of those honoured is Sir Nicholas Shehadie.

In 1981, Shehadie was back in Cork. 'That was the match that launched my international career,' he recalled. 'It was a tough, uncompromising contest and I remember the crowd baying at us throughout the match, but it was a great learning process; I went on to win my first two Australian caps later on that tour.'

Although Munster were defeated by a controversial late try by Phil Hardcastle, they took much of the glory for a performance that had a capacity Mardyke crowd on the edge of their seats throughout a pulsating, confrontational match.

Jim McCarthy, a rising flanker (wing-forward) star with Dolphin and Munster, would go on to win his first cap for Ireland in the Five Nations Championship later that season before adding twenty-seven more in a glittering career that yielded Ireland Grand Slam, Triple Crown and Championship titles

An Australian player is too late to stop Munster scrum half Hugh de Lacy (far right) get the ball away to his backs.

between 1948 and 1951. He was to become the first ever Munster man to captain his country in 1954 towards the end of Ireland's first real golden era of international rugby.

McCarthy was on the Mardyke pitch that day, and over sixty years on still remembers the hairs on the back of his neck bristle as he ran on to the pitch.

I don't think, certainly not up to then, I have ever experienced such an intense, emotional experience on a rugby pitch. The atmosphere was absolutely electric, and the whole place went berserk in the first couple of minutes when a fight broke out.

I can't remember what actually started it, but one of our guys took a fall and we were all in immediately to sort it out. From that to the final whistle, the crowd were on our side; I suppose from an Australian point of view, it was probably very intimidating; even if the supporters were well behaved, they were certainly vociferous and the Aussies would have known who they wanted to win!

Up to then, even playing with Munster, we would only have been used to games being played in front of hundreds rather than thousands. I can't remember how many were there that day, but the place was full to capacity; there were seats on the touchline, so that's how close the supporters were to the action. Running out onto the pitch, we just knew this was going to be something different from what we ever experienced prior to it; I felt like I was running out to play my first international.

We just sensed that it would be a special occasion, and when the row broke out we just said 'f**k this, we don't want to just give these guys a game, we want to beat them out the gate.' Another melee before half time merely confirmed that determination.

I think I remember the first problem began straight after a Garryowen was launched; our guys got up on it and tackled the catcher, somebody took

Australian legend Nick Shehadie is closest to see the drama on the ground unfold in a battle for possession. Jim McCarthy (right of centre) is about to come to the rescue for Munster.

offence to the tackle, threw a punch, and the rest of us waded in to sort it out.
The fans were thrilled with it and from that moment on we didn't take a step
backwards in terms of confrontation. There was no way we were going to be
bullied and it was a real tough match, a game that probably did a huge amount
of good for Munster rugby in the years to come. Subsequent performances
and results proved that no Munster team was going to be pushed around; I
think that lives right to the present day.

A cursory glance at the team sheet should have warned the tourists
that Munster would provide stern opposition, especially as Australia selected
something between a first- and second-choice team.

Paddy Reid, the highly talented Garryowen and Ireland centre, scored and
converted Munster's try to set the scene for some excellent backline play from
the home side, with John McBride responding for the Wallabies. Munster looked
set for victory . . . until those dying seconds and Hardcastle's disputed try.

Reid recalled, 'Their winning try was a travesty, for the ball had been
passed well forward to him before he got in for the score. He admitted as
much when I met him in London some years afterwards.'

Jim McCarthy recalls the build-up differently, but agrees that the try should
not have been allowed. 'From what I remember, the ball was put in crooked to
a line-out and someone knocked it forward before Hardcastle picked it up from
an offside position and dived over. It certainly wasn't a legitimate score and it
was a heartbreaking end to what should have been a great day for us.'

What made Munster's near-miss even more amazing was the fact that
they had only come together a few hours before the kick-off, as McCarthy
explains. 'There was certainly no such thing as a training session, whereas
Australia would have been having sessions every day on tour and working
with and for one another on the training park. There was no coach; in those
days the player that talked the most before the match was the coach!'

But for all that apparent lack of organisation, Munster did the province
and the country proud. McCarthy was not surprised. 'We had a really good
team out that day, fellows that were prepared to put their bodies on the line
for the red jersey. That was ironic in a sense, because the rule in that time was
that you only got one jersey and one cap at the start of the season. If you tore
it, I think the Munster Branch might have paid for the first repair done by a
tailor or seamstress, but anything after that had to be paid for by the player,
and that included buying a new jersey if necessary!'

McCarthy remembers with pride players such as Tom Clifford, J. C. Corcoran,
Tom Reid, Paddy Reid and Batt Hayes, whom he believed would have won several
Irish caps in another era. 'He was around at the wrong time, because John
[Corcoran] was a key figure and an incredible influence in both the Munster and
Irish teams of the time. But Hayes was a real, high-quality player – the type you
would always want to have on your side and not on the opposition.'

Chapter 3:
1951: RUCKED AND BEATEN

Munster v South Africa
Thomond Park – 11 December 1951

Munster 6	**South Africa 11**
(J. McCarthy, try; J. Horgan, penalty)	(Johnstone, try; du Rand, try; Viviers, penalty, conversion)

MUNSTER:

P. Berkery (Lansdowne), M. Quaid (Garryowen), J. Horgan (UCC),
G. Phipps (Rosslyn Park), M. Lane (UCC), J. Roche (Garryowen), J. O'Meara (UCC),
T. Clifford (Young Munster), D. Crowley (Cork Constitution), D. Donnery (Dolphin),
A. O'Leary (Cork Constitution), S. Healy (Garryowen), J. McCarthy (Dolphin) (captain),
G. Reidy (Dolphin), D. Dineen (Bohemians).

SOUTH AFRICA:

Keevy, Saunders, Lategan, Viviers, Johnstone, D. Fry, du Toit, Bekker, Delport,
van der Ryst, Myburgh, Dannhauser, Barnard, du Rand, S. Fry.

1951: RUCKED AND BEATEN

'**B**umps and bruises' is often used by rugby coaches to describe injuries picked up during the course of a game. A particular favourite of Irish legend Willie John McBride, it is a vague description that fails to specify anything in particular. Throughout my years covering rugby, I must have heard the term 'bumps and bruises' a thousand times.

Therefore, Gerald Reidy's description of how he felt when he trooped off the Thomond Park pitch following Munster's galling 1951 defeat to South Africa is enlightening, a brutally honest account of what can happen when the opposition fail to play according to the rules.

In those days, rucking was an art that removed man from ball in the vicinity of where the attacking team wanted to be, i.e. if an opposing player was lying on the ball, it was fairly certain he would end up with a severely scraped and bruised back.

Reidy, a big back-row forward well capable of protecting possession in any way he could, knew that if you lived by the sword, you could also die by it. But this Springbok side, Reidy recalls, was prepared to do serious damage to anyone who got in their way. Although he had survived many tough Munster Cup encounters up to this, he was not prepared for the type of punishment dished out by the touring side.

They came to Ireland with a huge reputation of toughness and they tried their best to live up to it. But they stepped well over the mark. They were close to being savage on the day; I came off that pitch and there wasn't even a small spot on my back that wasn't full of stud marks.

If you ended up on the ground, they would run over you, using your back as a stepping board, not just one of them, but two, three or even four; their whole job was to get the forward, even if they had to let the forward and the ball behind.

Yet, ironically, I got no sympathy; just a bit of recognition from the crowd that I must have been doing my job by going down on the ball and frustrating the opposition. The supporters probably didn't give a s**t whether I got kicked to kingdom come in the process.

Reidy recalls, with a mixture of emotion, the 11–6 defeat against what was generally recognised as the finest team in the world at the time. He looks back with immense pride on the performance of the Munster pack, and the front row of Tom Clifford, Derry 'Starry' Crowley and Derry Donnery in particular.

These boys stood up to South Africa and didn't concede an inch; I think the visitors were genuinely shocked because they didn't expect such a difficult time in the front row.

There was quality right through the team; we had a good second row, a different type of second row from the norm in that Archie O'Leary was a very big man and his partner, Seán Healy from Garryowen, was the lightest forward you could possibly imagine. But he was a fantastic line-out jumper in an era when you could not receive assistance to get in the air. He had a brilliant game that day and put in a fierce amount of tackles. There wasn't a pick on him and next to Archie he looked tiny, but that didn't stop him from playing like a man possessed. All things considered, he would have been my man of the match for producing an inspirational performance that inspired all of us as well.

Reidy concedes he was probably selected for that game based on his ability to jump in the line-out.

That was an important part of my game, and against a team like South Africa it was crucial that we put ourselves in a position to win and retain possession. I think that was the main reason why we ran them so close; the main reason why we felt cheated by losing.

We gave as good as we got up front; they had some great players in the pack but we didn't give them an inch. There is no doubt they had superior ability throughout the team and would possibly have won easily were it not for our level of success in that forward battle. It frustrated them and perhaps that was one of the reasons why they felt they had to resort to other tactics to try and win the game.

They didn't quite like the idea either that we matched them when a punch-up occurred in the first couple of minutes. It all happened after maybe the second scrum of the game when the front rows broke up and all of a sudden there were punches being thrown left, right and centre. I was a bit away from it but I saw a punch headed in my direction and tried to duck out of the way. When I lifted my head again, the guy who had been coming at me was on the ground.

I can't remember how it started, can't remember how it finished, but I'd venture to suggest that Starry [Crowley] and Derry [Donnery] were in the

*thick of it. They were two really tough players who relished the rough stuff;
they mightn't have started anything but they sure would want to be in there
to finish it. Anyway, the referee managed to get it sorted out by warning the
two teams and there wasn't any repeat.*

Despite Reidy's assessment that Jim McCarthy had 'the game of his life',
that Paddy Berkery gave a classic exhibition of crash tackling and that out-
half Jim Roche varied play cleverly, his abiding memory is how Munster were
denied possible victory by Ulster referee Ollie Glasgow.

With the teams locked together at six points apiece, Reidy remembers
how 'Mick Lane picked up a poor clearance and exploded out of the blocks
before finding McCarthy in support. Off they went and the move ended with
a try at the far end. For some reason better known to himself, the referee,
who was yards and yards behind the play, decided it was a forward pass. We
couldn't believe it; nobody could believe it and the crowd started throwing
bricks and stones on to the pitch to show their discontent.'

While Reidy describes the referee as 'quite a bit out of condition ', Jim
McCarthy is more forthright.

*Mick [Lane] threw the ball inside to me just inside the South African half
and kept running alongside me in support. I suppose I had to go about 50
[yards] to the try line and I had a feeling I was going to be caught – the
Springbok fullback was closing in – so I managed to get the ball away again
to Mick; I actually handed it to him rather than passed. The referee, who was
grossly unfit, was way back in the distance and couldn't possibly have come
up with a forward pass based on vision. He whistled us back for scrum and
the Springboks cleared.*

*My reaction was to call him a fat something b****x and he just turned to
me and said, 'You open your mouth again, and I'll put you off the field.' I just
had to keep quiet, although there were a lot of things that I felt like saying; I
would have called a lot of things into question given the chance . . .*

That lost opportunity was clearly the turning point, for South Africa struck
in the dying minutes – just as Australia had done four years previously at the
Mardyke – scoring a converted try to secure victory, one of thirty out of the
thirty-one match tour of Britain, Ireland and France.

For the Munster players, it was back to work. Gerald Reidy, who worked
with National Cash Registers, moved from Cork to Dublin to take up a new
position following an eight-month training programme in London. The trip
from England required an overnight stay in a Limerick hotel prior to the South
Africa game and the cost of that was covered by the Munster Branch.

But in those days, amateurism was king and players had to adhere to the strict
rules and regulations, sometimes imposed in a vigorous manner by the officials.
Some time later, on a visit home, Reidy called to the office (Lawsons' shop in
MacCurtain Street, Cork) of the honorary secretary of the Munster Branch, the

late Bill O'Brien, to be reimbursed for the cost of the hotel he had personally paid for (the bill had been submitted by post to the branch).

He was surprised to find that he was left 1s 6d short from his original bill. 'I brought the matter up, suggesting that perhaps a mistake had been made, that I had been left short. I wasn't prepared for what happened next, for what was probably the first real confrontation of my life in rugby.'

He was met with a furious response. O'Brien read him the riot act, highlighting the fact that the additional charge was for a telephone call home to Cork (to inform his family that he had arrived safely after eight months in

Mick Lane (left), who was a member of Ireland's Triple Crown winning side in 1949 and championship victors in 1951, pictured with his nephew Michael Kiernan, who won Triple Crowns with Ireland in 1982 and 1985. Lane played against the 1951 Springboks; Kiernan, son of another former Munster player, Jim, and nephew of Tom, went on to play against Australia in 1981 and 1984 and New Zealand in 1989.

London) and that he was not entitled to any such allowances and how dare he even think he was. 'I didn't know where to look, but my eye wandered over to where another person was standing. It was a well-known Cork-based Irish selector of the time, who just shuffled away and kept out of it. I think he was really embarrassed by the bellow of abuse I was getting.'

Chapter 4:
1954: SUCKER-PUNCHED AGAIN

Munster v New Zealand
The Mardyke – 13 January 1954

Munster 3
(G. Kenny, try)

New Zealand 6
(Wilson, try; Tanner, try)

MUNSTER:

P. Berkery (Lansdowne), G. Kenny (Sunday's Well), N. Coleman (Dolphin), R. Godfrey (UCD), B. Mullen (Cork Constitution), D. Daly (Sunday's Well), J. O'Meara (Dolphin), G. Wood (Garryowen), D. Crowley (Cork Constitution), T. Clifford (Young Munster), T. Reid (Garryowen), M. Madden (Sunday's Well), J. McCarthy (Dolphin) (captain), G. Reidy (Dolphin), B. Cussen (UCC).

NEW ZEALAND:

Kelly, Tanner, Fitzgerald, Freebairn, Wilson, Haig, Bevan, Clarke, Woods, Skinner, Jones, Dalzell, Bagley, Oliver, Stuart.

CHAPTER 4

1954: SUCKER-PUNCHED AGAIN

If Gerald Reidy sported welts on his back for weeks after South Africa's victory in Limerick, there was hardly a blemish on his body following his second appearance against a major touring side three years later at the Mardyke.

Munster, yet again, fell victim to a late sucker punch and lost to New Zealand by six points to three. This time, however, Reidy and his colleagues had no issue with the result.

Sure, they were disappointed, but for Jim McCarthy, who was creating a unique record by having played against all three of the southern hemisphere rugby giants, it was less galling than the previous two defeats. He was in full agreement with Reidy's assessment that 'the visiting side probably deserved to win'. Reidy recalls the difference between the touring sides.

It was disappointing to lose in the final few minutes when they got in for a try, but there wasn't any controversy; everything about the game was legitimate, it was rough, tough but played very fairly and the All Blacks were a really decent crowd as we experienced for a couple of hours after the match.

There was an official dinner for the South African game a few years before but they made no attempt to mix or socialise with us. We were interspersed at mixed tables, but they seemed intent on talking Africaans between themselves; anyway, we couldn't understand the few guys who made some attempt to speak English.

Unfortunately, there was no dinner in honour of the All Blacks because they were getting the boat to England later that night. We met up for a couple of hours in the Mardyke Pavilion, had tea and sandwiches and then went our separate ways. We had to make our own way back into town and I remember that Starry [Dermot] Crowley picked up a horse and cart outside the ground with a friend of his and tried to charge it to the Munster Branch. I doubt if he got his money back, though, given the circumstances at the time.

The New Zealand team visiting Blarney Castle on their visit to Cork in 1954 – note that none of them appears to have suffered from vertigo!

Reidy remembers playing rugby in front of a handful of supporters.

Maybe you would get a big enough crowd for a Munster Cup game, but friendly matches really only attracted the proverbial dozen fans and a dog. In those days there was very little recognition from the public; I don't ever remember getting praised for anything we achieved with Munster although the supporters were probably appreciative. They certainly turned up in force that day against the All Blacks and they gave us their full voice for the duration of the game. But that was an era when there was little or no interchange with selectors; you got selected, you played and hoped that you got another chance, but in all my days playing at that level I never actually spoke to a selector, and they never spoke to any of us.

Jim McCarthy, meanwhile, was completing a tour of duty against the southern hemisphere giants and to this day regrets not being part of at least one winning side. 'It was all very disappointing, but we couldn't have any argument about the New Zealand result. It was very close, and we came within a whisker of getting a draw, but they were the better side and there wasn't any controversy, to be fair.'

He was proud of the Munster performance, highlighting the contributions made by Norman Coleman, Boyle Cussen, Paddy Berkery, Tom Reid and Tom Clifford. Coleman famously won a Munster Senior Cup medal with Dolphin, aged eighteen, having played just two senior matches, and McCarthy believes the centre could have played for Ireland – 'if he got the lead out of his arse and put his mind to it'.

Coleman was to take the comment, made by one of the greatest players ever to play for Christian Brothers College Cork and Dolphin, as a compliment. Reminded of it some years later, a smiling Coleman responded, 'Tell him he's one son of a b***h.'

Coleman's elevation to the Munster team for the game against the All Blacks remains among his most precious career memories, especially considering that Munster were later sensationally beaten by Connacht in the Irish Interprovincial Championship.

Coleman was working in the Cork Milling Company at the time, happy to be in a good, dependable job that would provide him with a guaranteed pension later in life.

I didn't think too much of being selected against the All Blacks initially; the people in the Cork Milling Company, particularly Frank Moore, my boss, who was a huge rugby fan, seemed more excited than I was. He was really proud that somebody he knew and who worked for him had been chosen on the team.

The next thing I knew it was the day before the game and I remember being called into the office of the company secretary, a guy called Bill Beasley. My first instinct was to think that I wasn't going to be let off work to play in

The late Derry (Starry) Crowley gets stuck in to an All Black defender with Boyle Cussen at the ready. In the distance to the right are Tom Reid and Tom Clifford.

the game the following day, so I went straight to Frank Moore to get a lead on what was going on. He said it would be ok to go into Mr Beasley's office, that there should be no problem. When I did get there, a bundle of nerves, I was congratulated. He wished me all the best and then said, 'If you would like, you can have a lie in tomorrow morning, there's no need to come in to work before the game.'

I mumbled something about being a bag of nerves and suggested that I would prefer to come in for work in the morning, before explaining that I needed to be at the Metropole Hotel for a meeting at 12 noon. He told me that wasn't a problem, it was up to me. I actually came in to work and then left about 10 minutes before 12, cycling up to the hotel to meet up with the rest of the team. I parked my bike outside the door and left it there for the day because Bill O'Brien, surprise, surprise, had a bus waiting for us. We had a bit of a meeting and then went from there straight to the ground for a short preparation before the game.

I remember it being a really tough game, a really hard battle between the forwards so that scoring chances were few and far between. They scored first but Gerry Kenny, a winger from Sunday's Well, got us back into the game *before the All Blacks scored in the last few minutes to seal the victory. The conditions had a lot to do with the low score, I reckon, because we started off in a blizzard and players were slipping all over the place. Still, I recall that there was some pretty good rugby played in patches.*

Coleman had particular praise for fellow Dolphin player, John O'Meara, who went higher up the ladder to international stardom. Like many others from that era, Coleman was awestruck by the ability of a slightly built but hugely formidable scrum half with a pass that was widely regarded as the best in the game.

It was a privilege to play on the same side as John O'Meara; he was a fantastic player with a fantastic pass that became legendary. The ironic thing is that he couldn't kick a ball out of his way – if he knows I've said that he will probably kill me – but I had to go out and help teach him kick a ball to touch. The good thing is that he was playing with Jackie Kyle for Ireland and other good out halves for Munster, so it wasn't, perhaps, necessary for him to be a good kicker. He had so much else going for him that it probably didn't matter . . .

New Zealand score a try at the Mardyke.

He was different from the scrum half of today in that he passed by diving, but that pass was like a bullet. Out halves genuinely did benefit because they got more space and I would love to have been able to measure the speed of his pass and compare it to some of the really good scrum halves out there today.

If the New Zealand 1954 vintage did not strike as much fear into opponents as previous and subsequent teams, Coleman still believes Munster deserve huge credit for pushing their opponents to the limit.

He looks back in awe at the contribution of McCarthy, and at Bertie O'Hanlon, whom he describes as a brilliant player in an era that was difficult for wingers — indeed sometimes difficult for centre three-quarters as well, given the notion that out halves should be the only playmakers, an obsession that lasted right up to the late 1980s until coaches dictated otherwise.

Yet, he had the utmost respect for the out-half that day, Dan Daly, who became known as Dan 'I am the Well' Daly.

A captivated audience at the Mardyke.

| The haka, 1954 vintage.

We all had to do our best to keep New Zealand under control and Dan did as much as anyone by kicking us into positions, putting them under pressure to get into our territory. In terms of the modern game, it was probably played with limited ambition, but that wasn't to say we didn't attack them when the opportunity arose.

In terms of performances that day, I thought Paddy Berkery was fantastic, and Robin Godfrey did pretty well too. As for John O'Meara, well, I thought he was brilliant. If there was a Lions tour that year, I'm sure that both of these guys would have made it. Unfortunately, there wasn't and circumstances changed for both of them the following season.

Coleman may have been consumed by the performance of Munster's back division, but he noted what was going on up front as well. He gives huge credit to the Munster pack for helping the province survive – and almost pull off a shock result. 'Without their resolute and powerful performance, we wouldn't have survived for as long as we did because we had to do a lot of tackling in that game. If they hadn't won so much possession, we would have had to do a lot more and I'm sure it would have been a lot more difficult to keep them at bay.'

Coleman also suffered at the hands of an amateur body. Financial reward was not a consideration; financial recompense was not even in the equation. 'The people running Munster rugby wouldn't have been generous,' he says, 'that's being polite. I have no special story to tell because it was the same for everyone, it was another world, a brutal financial regime in a sense; we bought our own socks and nicks and if you had a jersey torn in a game you didn't get a replacement. You might get a replacement from the bag in the course of a match, but that had to be returned afterwards and then you were left to repair the original.'

Still, Coleman has no regrets. He was introduced to club rugby soon after leaving school and ended up winning two Munster Senior Cup medals with Dolphin – following in the footsteps of his father, Dick, the captain of Dolphin's first cup-winning team in 1921. 'Dolphin have ever only won six Munster titles and there are three medals in the Coleman family. I'm proud of that.'

He's also delighted to relate that, in 1954, Jim McCarthy managed to get hold of a New Zealand jersey and presented it to him, without the necessity of having to return the favour. Later, Coleman passed on the jersey to a family friend who emigrated to Canada; it was framed and held pride of place there for a number of years.

The jersey was returned many years later, and Coleman bemoans the fact that his growing children took to it with such enthusiasm that it was worn away and eventually lost. But he can laugh at that; what counts is that memories can never be erased.

No prisoners here between the rival packs. John O'Meara (left) and Boyle Cussen (right) making their way to the action.

Chapter 5:
1958: REWARD AT LAST

Munster v Australia
Thomond Park – 21 January 1958

Munster 3	Australia 3
(R. Hennessy, penalty)	(Morton, try)

MUNSTER:

R. Hennessy (Cork Constitution), S. Quinlan (Highfield), J. Walsh (UCC), F. Buckley (Highfield), D. McCormack (Dolphin), M. English (Bohemians), M. Mullins (UCC), G. Wood (Garryowen) (captain), D. Geary (Bohemians), R. Dowley (Dolphin), T. Nesdale (Garryowen), M. Spillane (Old Crescent), M. O'Connell (Young Munster), T. McGrath (Garryowen), N. Murphy (Cork Constitution).

AUSTRALIA:

Curley, Morton, Potts, White, Fox, Harvey, Logan, Vaughan, Meadows, Davidson (captain), Ryan, Shehadie, Yanz, Hughes, Gunther.

1958: REWARD AT LAST

The durability of Nick Shehadie, who in 1947 had been taunted by the Munster prop forward Batt Hayes, was exemplified by his inclusion in the 1958 Wallaby squad to tour Europe, and he was included in the team that drew with Munster at a snowbound Thomond Park.

Shehadie, who went on to become internationally known in both rugby and politics, admitted years later that there was no major disappointment in being held to a draw by Munster. It was a step in the right direction following the loss to Ireland in the Test match the previous weekend.

Many believed the game would be called off following a mini-blizzard in Limerick. But the heroic efforts of hundreds of local schoolchildren in clearing the pitch over a period of several hours ensured that the contest could go ahead.

'I remember,' said Shehadie, 'being out on the streets of Limerick after we arrived, messing about in the snow, throwing snowballs; it was a pretty unique situation for a lot of guys, some of whom never saw snow in their lives.'

From Munster's point of view it was a ground-breaking result, the best ever against a touring side and the first time they avoided defeat. Inevitably, there was a feeling of self-satisfaction and little heed was paid to the fact that it was a poor game played in biting cold, punctuated by errors on a hard and slippery pitch.

But if the game had been played in the ring, Munster would have won on points over fifteen rounds; it was their game, theirs to be won and theirs not to be won. Territorially, they were on top throughout, and they produced the greatest number of scoring chances on a day when such opportunities were at a premium.

Noel Murphy was a young but richly talented flanker. The 1958 game was to be the first of four appearances for Munster against touring teams over a ten-year period; later, he was one of the heroes who finally ended years of

An Australian forward engulfed by (l–r) Martin O'Connell, Tom Nesdale and Bob Dowley at Thomond Park.

disappointment when the province beat the 1967 Australians in a pulsating and controversial game and, of course, he went on to coach Munster, Ireland and the British and Irish Lions before working as a voluntary administrator with Ireland and the International Board.

Murphy's abiding memory was of the weather rather than the game, although he recalls that Shehadie was a hugely influential figure in the Australian pack and that the wing three-quarter who scored the try, Alan Morton, was one of the quickest he had ever seen.

Many years later, at an Australian Rugby Union function to honour former international players, Morton was, along with David Campese, hailed as one of the greatest wingers in the history of the game Down Under. From Queanbeyan, then a backwater as far as Australian rugby was concerned, Morton, like Campese, made his name in the more famous surroundings of the Randwick Club in Sydney.

But if Murphy was impressed, he was still in awe of some of the players in that strong Munster team, even though he had made his international debut a few days earlier. He highlights Ray Hennessy, who was unlucky in that he was in the right place at the wrong time and did not get his full rewards from representative rugby, and Fin Buckley, whom he describes as being brilliant at soccer as well as rugby. 'Seán Quinlan, the centre who played alongside Jerry Walsh, went on to play rugby league in England. Dave McCormack was a very hard running winger and he was one of two brothers to play for Munster,' adds Murphy.

Munster has a history of producing inspirational captains, from the early days to the present time, and as Murphy recalls, 1958 was no different.

I think a huge memory of that match was the buildup, and the fantastic team talk from Gordon Wood. We were left in no doubt what was expected of us; he expressed very strongly the fact that we were following some great players and great teams; that we had a huge responsibility to uphold the tradition of Munster teams, especially Munster teams playing overseas opposition. On the day, we lived up to that expectation and we really could have won the match.

Gordon was flanked by two tough forwards, Dave Geary and Bob Dowley, two really smashing guys and very accomplished players as well. Tom Nesdale was the real hard player and he formed a pretty formidable second-row partnership with Mick Spillane, who was an underrated player, a real tough customer that never held back from confrontation. Alongside me were two equally tough guys, Martin O'Connell from Young Munster and Garryowen's Tim McGrath, who was also a smashing ball player; with these guys alongside, there was no fear of me, even though I was just a little over twenty years old.

As far as intensity was concerned, there wasn't much difference between the game and the international the few days before. It was still a daunting experience because of the tradition Munster had against touring teams. There was a level of expectation and it must be remembered that a number of that team would have seen this as an international, their international. I was lucky enough to go on to play for Ireland, but it is still a huge achievement for any player to line out against a touring side.

One should remember that Munster, and the other provinces, didn't attract a huge audience for domestic fixtures, but the games were always sold out when a touring side was in town. That made it a big occasion, and it was a huge challenge because players had to go from lining out with their clubs one week to playing for Munster the next – with the resultant huge difference in public interest. I suppose for all of us, particularly those who never encountered big crowds, it was a pretty intimidating situation to find yourself in, but an exciting one nevertheless. For me, it got easier as I gained more caps and more experience, but time swept past me in those early games; they felt as if they were over almost as soon as they began.

From that point of view, it was important to have guys like Gordon Wood in that Munster team. It reminds me, I suppose, of the day when Ronan O'Gara and Peter Stringer made their debuts for Ireland; there was that great photograph of Mick Galwey flanking them, arms draped around each of them. I'm sure it was comforting for them to know that one, or more, experienced player was going to be on the lookout for their well-being.

From my own point of view, funnily enough, being a forward didn't seem as daunting as it might have been were I playing at fullback, for instance. I'm not saying it's much easier for a forward; I wouldn't like to say a forward can hide, but any mistakes are not nearly as obvious as one made by a back way out there in open play.

Murphy enjoyed his battles with Munster against all the top southern hemisphere teams, and is disappointed that tours of that nature do not happen any more. 'It is probably the saddest happening in the professional game. I've said many times that visits from top touring teams are good for the game from every viewpoint, for the teams playing against them and for the tourists as well. The coaches, I'm sure, would love to see it happen more often, and I think that was reflected by comments after the most recent game between Munster and New Zealand.'

Back then, however, neither Murphy nor his colleagues had to worry about professionalism, and counted the time between visits from touring teams. There were no financial rewards, but the lucky ones like Murphy were able to add appearances against South Africa and New Zealand to their rugby CVs and help build a lifetime of happy memories.

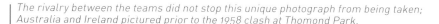

The rivalry between the teams did not stop this unique photograph from being taken; Australia and Ireland pictured prior to the 1958 clash at Thomond Park.

Chapter 6:
1960: THE LATE, LATE SHOW

Munster v South Africa
Musgrave Park – 21 December 1960

Munster 3 | South Africa 9

(N. Murphy, try) | (J. Gainsford, try; van Zyl, try; du Preez, penalty)

MUNSTER:

R. Hennessy (Cork Constitution), P. McGrath (UCC), J. Walsh (UCC), T. Kiernan (UCC),
F. Buckley (Highfield), M. English (Bohemians), T. Cleary (Bohemians) (captain),
G. Wood (Lansdowne), M. O'Callaghan (Sunday's Well), L. Murphy (Highfield),
T. Nesdale (Garryowen), M. Spillane (Old Crescent), L. Coughlan (Cork Constitution),
T. McGrath (Garryowen), N. Murphy (Garryowen).

SOUTH AFRICA:

Wilson, Antelme, Gainsford, Roux, Engelbrecht, Stewart, de Uys, Kuhn, Malan,
Myburgh, du Preez, van der Merwe, Classen (captain), van Zyl, Baard.

1960: THE LATE, LATE SHOW

Just two years after drawing with Australia, Munster turned the heat on South Africa amid the severe chill of a December afternoon in 1960. Ultimately, South Africa escaped with reputation intact thanks to two injury-time scores that denied Munster another great result against a touring team.

Noel Murphy was the try scorer that kept Munster in the game, but much of the credit for this confrontational performance went to Jerry Walsh, Mick English and flanker Liam Coughlan, all of whom were superb in denying the Springboks any semblance of superiority. That visiting pack was huge, enjoying a weight advantage the Irish public had rarely seen, even from earlier southern hemisphere visitors. In such circumstances, Gordon Wood, Mick O'Callaghan and Leo Murphy, allied to a determined second-row pairing of Tom Nesdale and Mick Spillane, did a marvellous job for an outweighed front five.

Four of this Munster team were getting a second opportunity against the South Africans: Tom Kiernan, Jerry Walsh, Gordon Wood and Noel Murphy had already featured on the Irish team beaten by the Springboks at Lansdowne Road just four days before.

It was an interesting selection by Munster, with the selectors utilising all the talent at their disposal. Kiernan, who had played for Ireland at fullback, was moved to the centre – a position he was comfortable in – to partner his school and university mate Jerry Walsh. Ray Hennessy, one of the most impressive players of his generation, featured in the number 15 position, having kicked the points to secure Munster's draw against the Wallabies two years previously.

The *Cork Examiner* report of 22 December gave due credit to Hennessy and Munster, leaving readers in no doubt that Munster should at least have earned a draw.

Cruel luck struck Magnificent Munster when, after holding the mighty South Africans for the entire match, they were beaten finally by two scores which came against the run of play.

Giving away an amount of weight which would normally prove fatal to any team and without a chance of winning even half of their own scrums, the Munster pack was a concentrated force of fire and energy which incredibly helped them match the lauded Springboks eight.

Behind the scrum, a fabulous Jerry Walsh, supported by a superb tactician in Mick English and a great wing-forward in Liam Coughlan, hit the Springboks so hard and so often that possession became more of a liability than an asset to the visitors.

These were the weapons with which Munster matched the visitors and, had they enjoyed just one or two slices of luck which often falls in favour of international opposition, they could even have made history by winning the match.

Noel Murphy playing for the British and Irish Lions gets this ball away from a line-out. Murphy was in action at Musgrave Park against the touring South Africans and scored a great try on the stroke of half time to give Munster the lead. Sadly, despite a huge second-half performance, the Springboks levelled and then grabbed a fortunate win with two late scores.

The least Munster earned from this tremendous display of determined rugby was a draw and, sadly, in the end even that was denied them.

The Munster performance was at least on a par with any of the four international teams the Springboks defeated on that Grand Slam-winning tour; the pity was they were unable to inflict what would have been a hugely popular defeat on the tourists.

Allegedly, the Springboks were still in a state of shock from the southern hemisphere series defeat in New Zealand four years earlier and were widely accused of being a reactionary side. Under captain Avril Malan they played a ruthless, forward-orientated game, the squad characterised by rigid discipline that allowed for little socialising – apparently they were the least popular rugby team to tour Europe in years.

Intimidation, it was alleged, was a key part of their game, with opponents suffering a string of controversial injuries. The tactics were successful, though, as they completed another Grand Slam when defeating Wales 3–0 on a quagmire of a pitch at the Arms Park.

But Britain and Ireland rejoiced when the Boks were ambushed in their final game against the Barbarians. The Baa-Baas' pack was described as the best ever unit to represent the club and they played an uncharacteristically pragmatic game that yielded the invitation side a narrow but totally deserved 6–0 victory.

Still, there was a huge element of respect for some members of that South African squad, among them Mof Myburgh, who went on to command a regular place in the front row of the strongest Springbok team for over a decade, and the legendary second/back-rower/goal-kicker Frik du Preez, who was at the cusp of a long and fruitful career for his country. Both played in 1960 against Munster.

In 2000, an eminent panel of South African rugby experts met to decide on the player of the century. Du Preez, to coin a phrase, won it in a breeze, because he was to South African rugby what his great rival Colin Meads was to New Zealand – a gallant, legendary and iconic figure. Du Preez epitomised, with his commitment to any team for which he played, at club, provincial or international level, all of rugby's finest values.

Frik du Preez first came to public attention in 1956 when, as a young air force officer, he out-jumped and, they say, out-punched the famous Springbok lock Salty du Randt in a match between the Defence Forces and Pretoria.

The performance won him huge respect and although it was another two years before he was chosen for Northern Transvaal, he quickly made his mark at provincial level. Indeed, he helped the Defence Forces to an unexpected 8–6 victory against the touring All Blacks in 1960, a performance that earned him a place on that 1960 tour to Britain and Ireland.

He did not take long to make a mark, scoring two tries against Southern Counties, and when selected to play in his first Test game against England at Twickenham on 7 January 1961 he wept with joy. But not for long; du Preez made his mark by converting the only try of the game to secure a 5–0 win (three points for a try in those days).

The 25-year-old du Preez continued to improve, developing into arguably the finest forward in world rugby, an assessment made by even the most partisan of observers from other countries.

He based his reputation on phenomenal workrate, uncompromising tackling and an innate ability to cope with opponents at line-out and scrum time. But it was in the loose that he set himself apart, combining lightning pace with the guile and ball-handling skills of a back. And for good measure he kicked penalties and conversions with a high average and dropped goals for fun – often just to annoy the opposition.

Du Preez also scored plenty of tries, among the most memorable of which was in the opening Test against the 1968 British and Irish Lions at Loftus Versfield, Pretoria, when he stormed around the front of a line-out and ran 40 metres to touch down near the corner.

But for a forward to do what he did in a domestic game for Northern Transvaal against Western Province in 1969 was really special. When South Africans talk about du Preez, they talk about that match more than any other. He demoralised a very competitive Western Province by knocking over a penalty from 8 metres inside his own half, then scoring a brilliant try and dropping a goal from 45 metres to round off a memorable victory.

Unusually for a player of his era, when rugby was dominated by provincial rivalry, du Preez was revered throughout South Africa; proof of this came in his last match for the Blue Bulls in Newlands in 1971, when Western Province supporters invaded the pitch and carried him off shoulder-high.

His last international, at the age of thirty-five, was on 7 August 1971 against Australia; that day he won his thirty-eighth cap, a monumental figure for a player of that era in the southern hemisphere. It was also his eighty-seventh appearance for the Springboks for whom he scored, fittingly, eighty-seven points in total.

Chapter 7:
1963: MAC THE KNIFE

Munster v New Zealand
Thomond Park – 11 December 1963

Munster 3
(H. Wall, try)

New Zealand 6
(MacRae, try; Herewini, penalty)

MUNSTER:

T. Kiernan (Cork Constitution) (captain), M. Lucey (UCC), J. Walsh (UCC), B. O'Brien (Shannon),
P. McGrath (UCC), M. English (Lansdowne), N. Kavanagh (Dolphin), M. O'Callaghan (Sunday's Well),
P. Lane (Old Crescent), M. Carey (UCD), J. Murray (Cork Constitution), M. Spillane (Old Crescent),
D. Kiely (Lansdowne), H. Wall (Dolphin), N. Murphy (Cork Constitution).

NEW ZEALAND:

Herewini, Smith, MacRae, Davis, Watt, Kirton, Laidlaw, Lochore, Barry, Stewart,
Horsley, Tremain (captain), Clarke, Major, Le Lievre.

1963: MAC THE KNIFE

To a ten-year-old schoolboy at a rugby-playing school, the arrival of the 1963 All Blacks to Munster was bound to cause a stir. The fact that Wilson Whineray's side had been heralded as one of the greatest ever to visit these shores whetted the appetite even more to see them in the flesh.

For days on end I pestered my parents to bring me to Limerick for the game. My pleas, to a father with absolutely no interest in sport, fell on deaf ears. So I had to rely on a newspaper account of the game and, I can recall, some radio coverage that gave updates as the game progressed.

Munster, again, were to be disappointed, the All Blacks winning by six points to three, but I could not have cared less the following day when my father came home from work and presented me with a New Zealand promotional magazine that featured photographs of the entire squad. Inside, to my wondrous surprise, I found that over half the All Black squad, including Whineray, Mac Herewini and Waka Nathan, the names that counted, had signed their names to the accompanying pictures. The old man – may he rest in peace – through a friend of a friend of a friend had come up trumps!

As it transpired, Herewini was the hero for New Zealand on a wet, windy day at Thomond Park. The All Black management had considered selecting one of their most famous sons, Don Clarke, at fullback but instead chose Herewini, believing he would be faster and more agile in dealing with the challenge posed by Mick English, the Munster and Irish out-half, recognised as one of the greatest tactical kickers in the game.

As usual, the famous New Zealand rugby journalist Terry McLean was there to record the game for posterity. 'Had Herewini not been there,' he said, 'the All Blacks would almost certainly have lost. Never was there such a desperate performance as this. Only three of the All Blacks, Lochore Le Lievre and Herewini, played as All Blacks should.' He continued in rather colourful prose: 'The rest trailed around like Brown's cows and were booted around like Brown's cows sometimes are when Farmer Brown gets out of bed at the wrong side at 4.30 a.m. and has to take it out on somebody.'

Fortunately for the visitors, they managed to get two crucial scores in the first half, a penalty from Herewini and a try from MacRae. But Munster dug deep to score a try from Henry Wall midway through the half before launching a continuous offensive that challenged the All Blacks defence at every turn. Time finally ran out for brave Munster, however, and, given the punishment New Zealand had to endure, the clock stopped just at the right time with the men in red pouring forward in a last-ditch attempt to secure an equalising and possibly winning score.

In the days when substitutes were not allowed, Munster were badly affected by an injury to the experienced front-row forward Mick O'Callaghan, who spent thirteen minutes off the pitch being treated, during which time the All Blacks struck for their two scores.

The *Cork Examiner* report alluded to Munster's misfortune in a report that began: 'Glorious Munster did everything but win their match against New Zealand; in rain and mud, they tore huge gaps in the great All Blacks forward machine through a second half unrivalled for its sheer ferocity. Munster rammed the tourists into desperate defence for long periods and they were held at bay only by bad luck and the genius of fullback Herewini.'

Although missing for that crucial spell in the first half, O'Callaghan was given as much credit for Munster's performance as Herewini was for the All Black victory. Indeed, the *Examiner* reporter reflected public opinion suggesting O'Callaghan deserved consideration for the upcoming Five Nations Championship. 'The Man of the Day,' according to the report, 'was Mick

Mick O'Callaghan spent thirteen minutes in the treatment room to have a head wound attended to, during which time New Zealand scored twice in the 1963 encounter. Here he is back in action contesting possession as Noel Kavanagh (to the rear and left) looks on.

O'Callaghan, who gave a display worthy of being selected on the international side. He played much of the game with a bad head wound that was heavily bandaged but he overcame that to challenge everything that moved on the opposition side; he fought for every ball, tackled like a demon and he was always ready to use his ability with a cultured "soccer boot". He must surely be selected to play against England early next year.' O'Callaghan duly won his selection and played a huge role in Ireland's 18–5 victory on 8 February 1964.

Brian O'Brien, from Shannon, as tough a centre as ever was seen, went on to win three Irish caps in 1968; Ireland were denied a Triple Crown that year when England stole a late 9–9 draw at Twickenham. That was O'Brien's debut and he participated in subsequent victories over Scotland and Wales to finish the season on a high note.

He recalls O'Callaghan's injury for Munster as crucial. 'We certainly struggled a bit during the time we were down to fourteen, but I remember that his return to the field lifted the crowd significantly.' O'Brien gave due credit to Herewini, though, agreeing with the general consensus. 'He appeared to turn up everywhere; he was very fast and agile and got the All Blacks out of trouble on a good few occasions.'

O'Brien was, however, disappointed that Munster failed to get the result he felt they deserved.

That was a very good Munster team; most of the guys were capped for Ireland at one time or the other, and the few who weren't internationals were actually high-quality representative players. It wasn't a huge Munster pack, but they would have been able to keep in step with the best of them.

We had a solid scrum and the second rows, Jerry Murray and Mick Spillane, were unrivalled in an ability to cope with the physical, although neither of them were huge men. Nobody in the forwards took a step backwards at any stage, and the game was always in the balance.

Actually, we came very close to grabbing a try that could have won the match. Tommy [Kiernan] narrowly missed a penalty and the ball bounced wide of the upright but awkwardly for the New Zealanders – Jerry Walsh and myself were up to challenge but one of the defenders just barely got the touch to make it dead and get a 25-yard drop goal.

O'Brien admits that the All Blacks at that time were held in awe around the world. 'Their arrival in Limerick was certainly hugely anticipated, but I figure they were surprised we challenged them so strongly.'

In subsequent years, as a Munster selector and team manager, O'Brien made further impact when an unplanned party piece contributed to recent folklore. Munster, as emphasised throughout, had to rely on performances against non-Irish opposition rather than domestic rivals to lay claim to fame. In 1999 they travelled to Belfast to take on Ulster and a bizarre sequence of events helped yield a result.

The 1963 Munster team before the game. Back row (l–r): P. McGrath, B. O'Brien, P. Lane, M. Carey, H. Wall, N. Murphy, M. Spillane, J. Murray; front row (l–r): M. O'Callaghan, M. Lucey, M. English, T. Kiernan, N. Kavanagh, J. Walsh, D. Kiely.

The game was moved from Ulster's bastion of Ravenhill to Queen's University grounds at Upper Malone after the Ravenhill groundsman inadvertently added weedkiller rather than fertiliser to the water system. Munster revelled in the new surroundings and emerged with a rare victory over the almost perennial Interprovincial champions of that era.

'There was a pretty raucous celebration of that victory that spilled over into the late evening at the Europa Hotel', admits O'Brien. 'Alcohol was involved and the Munster group had no hesitation in volunteering when a group [band] in the hotel asked for people to come and sing. Ultimately, I was prevailed upon and decided to sing "Stand Up and Fight", the words of which have now become known to thousands of Munster fans throughout the country. It was a spur of the moment thing, there was nothing planned, I just had to sing something.'

Munster fans will sing at the drop of a hat; they astounded the Ospreys supporters, and Tommy Bowe, at Thomond Park during the 2009 Heineken Cup quarter-final by striking up to sing Bowe's party piece 'The Black Velvet Band' as the Welsh side slid to ignominious defeat. Perhaps it was not so amusing for the unfortunate Bowe, but the wing/fullback took it in the proper spirit.

That was almost certainly a one-off; a rousing rendition of 'Stand Up and Fight' from Irish operatic icons Cara O'Sullivan or Derek Moloney has now become part of the Thomond Park match-day experience. It just would not be the same without it. Blame it all on Brian O'Brien!

Thanks a lot, I'm sure glad to be –
to be where I can see
so many friends of mine.
How am I doing,
how am I doing?

If you really want to know the truth, I'm doing fine.
Seventeen decisions on a row,
and only five on points,
the rest was all KO
Jackson and Johnson, Murphy and Bronson,
one by one they come and one by one to dream they go.
*   How's it done, you ask me how's it done.*
I've got a trainer-man,
who taught me all I know.
Sure feels good to have him in my corner,
hear his voice that's whispering low:
'Big boy, remember, you must remember:
Stand up and fight until you hear the bell,
Stand toe for toe, trade blow for blow.
Keep punting till you make your punches tell,
Show that crowd what you know,
Until you hear the bell,
Stand up and fight,
Stand up and fight like hell.
*   When you fight the ring to open air,*
In a patch of light
The ring looks small and white.
All in the darkness, all in the darkness
You can feel a hundred thousand eyes seeing the night.
Cigarettes are floating in the dark
and making pokes and darts
around the baseball park.
People are quiet. Then there's a riot.
Someone throws a punch and plants it smack in the mark.
*   Someone's hurt, you kinda think it's you*
You hang across the ropes,
it's all you want to do.
Then you look around and see your trainer's eyes
begging you to see it through.
They say, remember, big boy, remember:
Stand up and fight until you hear the bell,
Stand toe for toe, trade blow for blow.
Keep punching hard until you hear the bell,
That final bell, until you hear the bell.
Stand up and fight,
Stand up and fight like hell.

(From *Carmen Jones*, Oscar Hammerstein II)

Chapter 8:
1967: THE GLORY BOYS

Munster v Australia
Musgrave Park – 25 January 1967

Munster 11
(J. Moroney, try; T. Kiernan, two penalties, conversion)

Australia 8
(Cardy, try; Brass, penalty; Ryan, conversion)

MUNSTER:

T. Kiernan (Cork Constitution) (captain), A. Horgan (Cork Constitution),
J. Walsh (Sunday's Well), B. Bresnihan (UCD), P. McGrath (UCC),
J. Moroney (Garryowen and London Irish), L. Hall (UCC), P. O'Callaghan (Dolphin),
K. Ging (Sunday's Well), M. O'Callaghan (Young Munster), B. O'Dowd (Bohemians),
J. Murray (Cork Constitution), N. Murphy (Cork Constitution), T. Moore (Highfield), L. Coughlan (Cork Constitution).

AUSTRALIA:

Ryan, Webb, Smith, Moore, Cardy, Brass, Catchpole, Thornett (captain), Taylor, Prosser,
Heming, Purcell, O'Callaghan, Taylor, Tulloch.

CHAPTER 8

1967: THE GLORY BOYS

The year 1967 brought another opportunity for Munster against Australia. Since that first post-war clash with the Wallabies at the Mardyke two decades earlier, Munster had to dine on scraps at the masters' table. But not on this history-making occasion.

Ken Ging, a Dubliner, was a hooker with a reputation for moving clubs at regular intervals, as highlighted by the following list: Monkstown, Greystones, Lansdowne, Greystones, Sunday's Well, St Mary's and back to Greystones.

Maybe he did not stay around long enough in any one place to earn the reputation needed for stripes at Interprovincial level with Leinster, but he had to wait until his move to Cork and Sunday's Well to get on the road to fame, if not exactly fortune. Work brought him to Cork in the mid-1960s and, after briefly considering Highfield, he settled on the Tramore Road side of Musgrave Park.

He explains why: 'In my first couple of days in Cork I met [the late, great] Joe McDonnell in the city, who invited me up to Model Farm Road. I had intended doing so until I spoke to Johnny Love, who did business with my company. He said to me, "If you join any other f***ing club but the 'Well, I'll never put any business your way again." Logic prevailed and I went on to spend three very happy years with the club!'

Ging settled in enthusiastically to club life in Munster and was happy to achieve more than he had in Dublin. Fame was just around the corner. He takes up the story.

Somehow, I managed to get a Munster trial before that Australian match in 1967. I played well but didn't dare dream that I might get on the team. After the trial, we adjourned to Cruise's Hotel for something to eat and the selectors came in and named the team. I really couldn't believe it when my name was read out; for me, whose only achievement had been to get three junior trials with Leinster, this was by far and away the biggest day of my career. It was as if I had been selected for a Lions tour, it was fairytale stuff, really it was.

He approached the match with huge enthusiasm, knowing that this was his big day and fearing it could be his last. Southern hemisphere touring sides do not drop in to say hello that often, and they certainly do not come to help build local reputations. Ging recalls the nerves on the morning of the game, the pre-match lunch in a city hotel and two team talks from Tommy Kiernan (the captain), particularly the rousing speech in the dressing room before the game.

Tom was in full flight when there was a knock at the door; someone popped a head in and shouted 'photograph'. Apparently it was tradition to have the photograph taken at a certain time before kick-off before the final team talk and build-up to the game. It was tradition, but Kiernan didn't care much about tradition; he was too busy plotting the Wallabies' downfall and replied that there would be 'no f***ing photograph, f**k off with your cameras'.

I was dismayed because then, as now, I'm a photograph freak. Anyway, here I was on the biggest day I'd ever experience in my rugby career and I couldn't even think about anything but the photograph. Eventually Tommy stopped talking and there was a moment of quiet in the dressing room. I took my opportunity and said, if anyone else didn't mind, that I would like to get a photographic record of the event. I pointed out that he [Kiernan] and others might have hundreds of these photographs but that I had none, nor was I likely to ever get one that would be so important to me again.

So then Tommy responds, 'Gentlemen, Mr Ging, from Dublin, would like a photograph; should we oblige him?' We went out in the pissing rain and got the photograph taken; I suspect, in the heel of the hunt, that everyone was happy, given the way the result went. It proved to be an historic photograph after all and over the years I've been at pains to point that out to some of the other members of that team. I don't know about the others, but that picture is hanging up in pride of place in my home.

There was a hugely controversial finish to this intense struggle at Musgrave Park. With Munster leading 11–8 and time almost up, Australia forced a scrum near the home line and Ulster referee Roy Gilliland allowed the set piece to engage.

Ging was stuck in the middle of the front row ready to attempt to strike against the head when he heard someone ask the referee how much time was left. The response was that time was up and Kiernan was alleged to have shouted, 'Then blow your f***ing whistle.' Which referee Gilliland did, much to the fury of the Australians, who complained that having allowed the scrum to set he should have allowed one more play.

Years later, Ging met Noel 'Noisy' Murphy in Dublin and, recalling the game, suggested that it would not have mattered if the scrum went ahead because he was going to strike the ball against the head and give Munster an

Munster scrum half Liam Hall gets the ball away, well protected by Terry Moore and Phil O'Callaghan.

opportunity to clear the lines. 'Noisy just looked at me and said, "No, Ginger, you wouldn't, but I would have blocked down the attempted drop goal." That's Noisy for you, always had to have the last word, and always did!'

Murphy had a huge influence on that game, admits Ging. But he might not have played at all had it not been for the rallying voice of Kiernan in a pre-match team meeting earlier in the day.

These days, if a guy gets injured, he's looked after by the medical team and put into rehab straight away to ensure his well-being. Back then it was totally different; guys got knocks and half the time didn't have much of a clue what was wrong with them. A sore leg covered a multitude of injuries.

So we're there in the Met [Metropole Hotel] on the morning of the match and we go into this room for a chat about how we might play the game, basically deciding that we have to get stuck into them, upset them and do everything in our power to make them uneasy about playing the game.

In walked – hobbled – Noisy, who announced immediately, 'I'm f***ed lads, me leg is shagged, I'm flahed out, no way can I play.' There was panic and an SOS went out to get Billy O'Mahony, the UCC flanker, down to the hotel as soon as possible to act as cover. He was a smashing player, didn't get the credit he should have at that time, and I remember him come into the room, pale as a ghost and shaking with excitement, about to win a Munster cap against a touring side.

Anyway, the decision hadn't quite been made as the team meeting progressed. Tommy went into his first team talk and it was the best team talk I ever heard. He was brilliant, we were all spellbound and when he actually finished speaking, Noisy pipes up, 'Ah f**k it Tommy, I'll play.'

Poor Billy went from euphoria to the depths of despair, but Noisy played and he played a f***ing blinder. There were no subs in those days, so I suppose the only consolation was that Billy came with us to the match and got in for nothing!

Ging does not remember much about the game, apart from the dramatic finish and one particular incident. 'I recall at one stage that one of their guys pushed me out of a line-out and Mick O'Callaghan said to me, "Clobber the f***er" right in front of the guy's face. "Go on, hit him a f***ing dig, boy", as we're waiting for the ball to come out of the crowd. I didn't respond; anyway the guy heard everything and was probably waiting to get his retaliation in first. It was grand until the next line-out, when Mick stepped up and decked the guy for me!'

That front row was formidable, with Ging flanked by a prop forward who was already a household name and another who would later become one. 'God, Mick O'Callaghan didn't take any prisoners,' Ging recalls, 'and even though it was Phil O'Callaghan's first season for Munster – he was not as sure of himself then as he was later – he was still a great guy to have on your side;

better playing with him than against him, that's for sure. In later years, he used to come up with some great one-line put-down comments for opponents and referees and even then he was a bit chatty with his direct opponent, letting him know that at least he wasn't intimidated by him.'

Ging, who went on to become a highly respected administrator – indeed he was team manager for Leinster in the professional era – admits with some glee to winding up people in Dublin by constantly reminding them of Munster's achievements. 'To this day, if somebody mentions something that Leinster did in 2007, I'd respond, "Oh, yeah, that was forty years after Munster beat the Wallabies." It drives people crazy, but it's all good fun!'

Although Ging has huge respect for players such as Johnny Moroney, Barry Bresnihan, Liam Coughlan and, of course, Kiernan and Murphy, the late Jerry Walsh and Terry Moore hold a special place in his heart.

Terry Moore achieved a huge amount with Munster and Ireland, but it always appeared to be understated because he was never the type of guy who sought out attention. He was a very shy person, a difficult person to get to know, but I became very fond of him. He used to drink in a pub called The Innisfallen and a few of us adopted the pub as our regular and met there for pints and a chat from time to time.

Jerry Walsh was my hero. I suppose it's strange for a forward to idolise a back, but this guy was unbelievable; everything about him smacked of class. He was one of the bravest guys I ever saw on the pitch, and an immense tackler who was more of a creator and destroyer than the finisher. He was just a fantastic guy.

Another player Ging believed in was scrum half Liam Hall, who was only nineteen at the time of the Wallabies game. 'I roomed with him that year when we played Leinster in Dublin and got to know him. He is a smashing guy, but my abiding memory of him was the way he played that day against the Wallabies, passing brilliantly and doing everything with the confidence of a much older and more experienced guy. Apart from that, he was a hooker's dream; he was very inventive in the way he put the ball into the scrum, but it was generally rolled in crooked and that suited me down to a tee!'

Hall and Ging had something else in common – their absolute admiration for Walsh. Hall, then a young student in UCC, not long out of school in Dublin's Blackrock College, eventually moved back home to his native Limerick and played against the 1970 South Africans, representing Garryowen.

This was his first brush with the stars, and there is no doubt but that he saw the star quality in Walsh. He recalled an incident early in the game when Walsh brought off an immense tackle on one of the Australian centres. 'Jerry charged late into this guy and blew him back on his backside. The other centre went straight up and complained that the tackle was uncalled for; Jerry just looked at him straight in the eye and said, "You're f***ing next!"'

He saw it too in Johnny Moroney, scorer of Munster's only try, the decisive score in the match. His halfback partner, according to Hall, made it easy for him that day. 'He was class, no doubt. Johnny was a great athlete, into pole-vaulting and other sports at school; he played hurling and football with Tipperary at minor level. A guy with everything – great stride, fast feet, fast hands and with an eye for the line when he got within the distance.'

When Hall started in UCC there was a thriving drink culture there, particularly among the rugby-playing students, many of whom spent time – and even rent money – in their home from home, The Western Star.

Hall admits to having indulged from time to time, but feels lucky that some among the rugby fraternity attached more importance to the game than to drink. In that regard, he looked up to Dr Paddy McGrath, who played on the wing in that historic game and whom Hall describes as being hugely influential on his career. 'He was totally dedicated to the game of rugby and spent his spare time, mostly at lunch time, training up in the Mardyke. He actually rarely missed one in the week. His whole attitude and approach rubbed off on me, and I remember that if the ground at the Mardyke wasn't suitable for training, then we would drive down to Redbarn Strand and train there. I suppose his dedication was before its time.'

Over forty years on, Hall and Ging hold different views about the importance of that win and the ramifications for Munster and Irish rugby when compared to the win over New Zealand eleven years later.

Hall is happy to savour the moment he enjoyed on the day and the recognition he and the team enjoyed for a short time afterwards. But unlike 1978, the memory of that victory over the Wallabies quickly faded, probably because it was allowed to fade and because Australia, in those days, did not have the same aura about them. 'When I talk about rugby these days, that victory over the Wallabies is hardly ever brought up. In fact, I'd almost guarantee that if you asked a number of people whether Munster beat Australia forty years ago, they wouldn't know, but they would remember the All Blacks game.'

Recognising that this assessment is possibly true, Ging is, nevertheless, somewhat peeved. 'I think it's a pity that the '67 team did not get that recognition because it was a ground-breaking result and it finally put Munster on the map of world rugby. Since then, there has been one reunion of that team and, sadly, not everybody was able to turn up for one reason or another. Don't get me wrong – that '78 victory was something else and I would agree that it was a monumental achievement. But I'd like to ask those lads one question – why in f**k's name do they have to have a reunion every Wednesday?'

Munster players Liam Coughlan (third from left) and Ken Ging close in to battle for possession with an Australian player during the 1967 clash at Musgrave Park. The Munster player second from right is Jerry Murray.

Chapter 9:
1970:
MASTERCLASS

Munster v South Africa
Thomond Park – 14 January 1970

Munster 9
(J. Moroney, three penalties)

South Africa 25
(Myburgh, try; Grobler, try; van de Venter, try; Nomis, try;
D. de Villiers, two penalties, two conversions; Visagie, penalty)

MUNSTER:

A. Horgan (Cork Constitution), J. Tydings (Young Munster), G. O'Reilly (Highfield),
B. Bresnihan (London Irish), J. Moroney (Garryowen and London Irish),
B. McGann (Cork Constitution) (captain), L. Hall (Garryowen), P. O'Callaghan (Dolphin),
T. Barry (Old Crescent), O. Waldron (London Irish), S. Waldron (Cork Constitution),
E. Molloy (UCC), J. Buckley (Sunday's Well), T. Moore (Highfield), W. O'Mahony (UCC).

SOUTH AFRICA:

H. de Villiers, Grobler, Roux, Lawless, Nomis, Visagie, D. de Villiers (captain), Myburgh,
Barnard, Marais, de Wet, Carelse, Ellis, Jennings, van de Venter.

1970: MASTERCLASS

L iam Hall was perhaps better placed than anyone to speak of the public condemnation of the 1970 Springboks tour of Ireland that prompted protest marches throughout the country – one of them in Limerick prior to, during and after the match with Munster at Thomond Park.

The Munster scrum half had moved on from his student days at University College Cork and from the great triumph over the 1967 Wallabies to work with South African industrial diamond company de Beers in Shannon. De Beers took the decision to sponsor the Springboks during their stay in the mid-west, treating the entire party to a medieval dinner at Bunratty Castle and providing them with other sponsorship.

International condemnation of the apartheid system in South Africa and its manifestation in the lack of opportunity for non-white players to participate in rugby union was not yet very vocal, but there were a number of Irish people who felt they had a sense of duty to let their feelings be known.

As a result, the visiting team trained as far away from the public gaze as possible, and the post-match dinner was switched from the usual venue of Cruise's Hotel to the Shannon Arms, a hotel adjacent to Henry Street Garda station.

'That,' said Hall, 'meant that none of the protesters got near the hotel because the area was cordoned off and patrolled by a large number of Gardaí. Mind you, nobody was in any real danger; the protesters wanted to make a point but they did so in a peaceful manner. It [the public condemnation of apartheid] had not, at that stage, moved up a notch to international level.'

But it did so not long afterwards, and the final game of the tour at Twickenham some weeks later was to provide both a shock and a pleasant surprise for Hall's direct opponent, Springboks captain Dawie de Villiers.

There have been many occasions when team members have chaired their captain off the field after a great performance, but rare it is when members

On a day when South Africa were too strong, this picture features a Springbok forward in full flight with Billy O'Mahony (second from right) on his way to try to close him down. Phil O'Callaghan is in the background keeping control of the rest of the South African pack!

of the vanquished team have hoisted the victors' captain on to their shoulders and carried him off the pitch. But that was precisely what happened to de Villiers after his team had beaten the Barbarians in a thrilling game to wrap up the tour.

The shock came with the realisation that the protests had increased by the time the squad had returned to Britain from Ireland. During the Twickenham game there were a number of incursions onto the pitch. 'One guy managed to climb up on one of the crossbars,' de Villiers recalls, 'and another chained himself to an upright. It was disruptive, to say the least, and a little scary at times.'

Back in Ireland, Munster were left to lick their wounds after suffering a record defeat to a touring side in the then modern era, not counting the 1905 crash to the original All Blacks. The match itself would have been uneventful were it not for the fact that South Africa came to Ireland with one of their most talented squads ever. And it did not help that they were seriously annoyed at having been held to an 8–8 draw by Ireland on the previous Saturday at Lansdowne Road – an Irish team that included four players who would line out for Munster at Thomond Park – Tom Kiernan, Barry Bresnihan, Barry McGann and Phil O'Callaghan.

Hall held his scrum-half opponent in high regard. 'It's hard to describe what made him special, but he was; he was up to every trick in the book and got away with some. De Villiers was my main opponent and he was surely the best I've ever come up against or even seen play.'

Hall was struck by the sheer size of the South Africans.

They were absolutely huge. They had a guy called Mof Myburgh playing in the front row who had been around for some time; no lying, he had an arse on him the size of a handball alley. You wouldn't want to be an 11-stone scrum half facing up against him running at you! They beat us 25–9 and they absolutely destroyed us; they were an exceptional team of course, but it was no consolation because of the pride everyone had in the Munster jersey. All the talk at the time was that it had been the first one-sided game Munster ever encountered against a touring side, and I couldn't argue that they were just in a different league, physically and tactically.

I remember Tommy Kiernan cried off, Tony Horgan moved to fullback and Johnny Moroney came into the side that was captained by Barry McGann. There was no lack of effort and everyone got stuck in as best as possible. The trouble was that they wore us down by the necessity to keep tackling one after the other after the other.

I seem to recall that we won a decent bit of possession through Terry Moore in the line-out, but the reality is that our pack just wasn't physically strong enough to provide them with the type of opposition required to beat them, or even come close to beating them. By comparison, our pack was very light, although Billy O'Mahony and Jim Buckley were hugely brave in defence. It wasn't enough because they used that physicality to wear us down and we were really only hanging in for long periods.

Hall's view was borne out by newspaper reports of the game, including that of the *Cork Examiner*.

Munster's deep-rooted rugby pride took a rude jarring when the Springboks produced a crunching victory in a one-sided and, therefore, desperately disappointing game.

The tourists exposed a marked contrast in standards, method and even determination as they asserted superiority everywhere it mattered over a bewildered, struggling home side. No touring team had previously beaten Munster by more than six points, but this Munster side was actually flattered by the eventual margin. Indeed, had the ability and initiative of the visiting backs matched that of their forwards, they must surely have scored an utterly limitless number of points.

As it transpired, that record-breaking victory was to remain intact for a further twenty-six years, broken by another southern hemisphere opponent, Australia. South Africa have not played Munster since that 1970 January afternoon.

In his second game against an overseas touring team, Liam Hall clears with plenty of time to spare, watched by Phil O'Callaghan and Terry Moore.

Chapter 10:
1973: DENIED AT THE DEATH

Munster v New Zealand
Musgrave Park – 14 January 1973

Munster 3 | **New Zealand 3**
(B. McGann, penalty) | (Morris, penalty)

MUNSTER:
T. Kiernan (Cork Constitution) (captain), J. Barry (Dolphin), S. Dennison (Garryowen),
B. Bresnihan (London Irish), P. Parfrey (UCC), B. McGann (Cork Constitution),
D. Canniffe (Cork Constitution), P. O'Callaghan (Dolphin), J. Leahy (Cork Constitution),
K. Keyes (Sunday's Well), J. Madigan (Bohemians), M. Keane (Lansdowne),
J. Buckley (Sunday's Well), T. Moore (Highfield), S. Deering (Garryowen).

NEW ZEALAND:
Morris, Williams, Hales, Skudder, Stevens, Parkinson, Colling, Lambert, Ulrich,
McNichol, Holmes, Eliason, Haden, Wyllie (captain), Sutherland.

1973: DENIED AT THE DEATH

At last Munster were to get some reward for all the effort over the years against the All Blacks; yet most of those that witnessed this thrilling draw at Musgrave Park would feel hard done by because the game ended in stalemate rather than victory for the men in red.

My former colleague Dermot Russell captured the mood in the *Cork Examiner* the following day as he described an epic struggle between two very determined teams.

The largest crowd ever to watch a rugby game in the south of Ireland roared with exultation as mighty Munster tamed the All Blacks – and then sank to dumb frustration when the tourists got out of hell with an equalising penalty goal only ninety seconds from the finish.

Anti-climax sank to the vitals of the 15,000 spectators, and it was such daylight robbery that only in retrospect did the magnificence of Munster's achievement take on clarity again. Only then was absorbed the knowledge that this draw was the finest result ever achieved by an Irish team against the All Blacks, only then did the body of an epic struggle take its memory form again.

The hero for the All Blacks was fullback Trevor Morris, but it was captain Alex (Grizz) Wyllie who did the real damage when he charged for the Munster line and, by all accounts, passed illegally off the ground when tackled. Munster somehow managed to clear upfield but a ruck formed and they were penalised, with Morris stepping up to get his side out of jail.

The New Zealanders were clearly relieved. 'On balance, Munster probably deserved to win,' tour manager Ernie Todd commented. 'We played our worst rugby of the tour, but then again we weren't allowed to play as we wanted.'

The All Blacks' performance was reflected in the fact that only four of the team were chosen for the Test game with Ireland the following weekend when at least seven were expected to have made the cut. In the event, Ireland had to settle for a similar outcome – a 10–10 draw.

*Terry Moore charges down an attempted New Zealand
clearance as Jim Buckley moves in as support.*

Wyllie was one of the lucky few, but that was no surprise given his status as one of New Zealand's top wing-forwards of the time, a man who went on to coach at the highest levels both in his own country and in Argentina.

Wyllie began his career with Canterbury in 1964, playing 210 times for the province until 1979 and serving as captain on over a hundred occasions. He helped Canterbury wrestle the Ranfurly Shield from Hawke's Bay in 1969 and from Auckland in 1972; he also captained the province to wins over a number of international touring sides, including England in 1973, Scotland in 1975 and Ireland in 1976.

Wyllie finally became an All Black in 1970 when selected to tour South Africa, where he played in the second and third Tests. In the next three years, he played forty matches for New Zealand, including eleven Tests, and was captain on three occasions. Although his international career ended after 1973, Wyllie remained a prominent player for Canterbury until 1979.

In 1982, Wyllie became coach of Canterbury and immediately enjoyed success by wrestling the Ranfurly Shield from Wellington and holding on to the trophy for a record-equalling three years. Under Wyllie's coaching, Canterbury won the National Provincial Championship (NPC) in 1983, and also recorded victories against international sides, including the Lions in 1983 and the Wallabies in 1986.

Alex Wyllie became a national selector in 1986 and, along with his Auckland rival John Hart, served as assistant coach to Brian Lochore when the All Blacks won the 1987 World Cup. In 1988 Wyllie succeeded Lochore as coach, much to the annoyance of many, especially in Auckland, who favoured Hart.

Despite initial success, a decline in the 1991 season led to the New Zealand Rugby Union (NZRU) appointing Hart as joint coach for that year's World Cup, but following the unsuccessful campaign, both men were overlooked when Laurie Mains took over the stewardship of the national side.

Wyllie went on to take various coaching roles in England, Ireland, South Africa and Argentina and from 1996 to 1999 was in charge of the Argentine national side, taking the Pumas to the quarter-finals of the 1999 World Cup.

In charge of Munster for that 1973 game against the All Blacks was Noel Murphy, who had made the move from player to coach a couple of years before. He recalls the disappointment of not winning.

The team was only two minutes away from glory, from creating history and it would have been some achievement because we only had the benefit of a few training sessions together before the match. We did get together the day before the match and the biggest problem I had as coach was that Pat Whelan, who was such an integral part of the team, had to be withdrawn. He wanted to play but I think it turned out that he had developed a bout of pneumonia, and Jerry Leahy came in as replacement.

Jerry played well, as did all the players, and really they deserved better. Still, I think it was a big achievement and it wouldn't be right if the fact that Munster got a draw, the best ever at that stage against New Zealand, were to be forgotten. Tommy [Kiernan] often refers to the fact that it was a huge

New Zealand scrum half Lyn Colling gets the ball away as Jim Buckley begins the chase. Barry McGann, the Munster out-half who kicked his side's only points, is on the far left.

achievement at the time and, indeed, it may have played some part in the inspiring win over the All Blacks five years later.

Murphy was well pleased with the way the Munster pack stood up to a very accomplished New Zealand eight, but he did admit that the visitors had the upper hand in the rucking battle, despite Munster's pre-planned but only relatively successful programme of disruption.

The one thing about New Zealand is that they were absolutely ruthless in that aspect of play, and not too many teams, at any level, were able to combat them. Some people mistook it as brutality, but they rucked the ball with the player, and I always felt that I would rather be rucked by a New Zealander than kicked by somebody from a different rugby environment and culture. They did it so clinically and clean; they rucked you and you came out just about in front of the ball.

The thing was, as an opposition forward, you knew the risk by confronting them with collapsed mauls and the like. In that particular game, our plan was to attempt to frustrate them at every turn; to counteract their rucking, we threw bodies on the ground to make it difficult for them to isolate any one of our players. It was to make sure that whatever possession they got came out slowly. We frustrated them only in part.

Munster's brave effort was not enough, and Murphy recalls the mood in the dressing room afterwards. 'The mood in that room was one I'd like to forget; they were absolutely devastated. On another day they might have gloried in the result, but not on that occasion. It took a while for them to accept that a 3–3 draw against what was recognised as the best and strongest rugby-playing nation in the world was actually no shame.'

Thirty-five years on, Murphy recalls some of the fine players who lined out that day, and reflects with sadness that all three of Munster's back row – Jim Buckley, Terry Moore and Shay Deering – have since died.

These guys were great players and really nice people; it's such a pity that their lives were cut short. Each of them will be remembered in their own way for helping to push New Zealand to the limit and for nearly bringing home the result that Munster's efforts would have deserved.

It was one of Moss Keane's first major representative games, and I remember that he was a rather shy but very proud young player that day. The pack yielded nothing in the set pieces that day; we had two brilliant and very aggressive prop forwards in Kevin Keyes and Phil [O'Callaghan], so there was little danger of being overrun. Philo was able to turn on a very special type of smile for the opposition, the smile that said, "C'mon, I've taken what ye have thrown at me, now I want a little bit more."

We had some quality backs available as well, with Barry McGann, who kicked our penalty, Donal Canniffe, who effectively was an extra forward at halfback and of course Séamus Dennison and Barry Bresnihan in the centre, two fine footballers who never took a backward step.

Of course, Tommy [Kiernan] was also an influential figure. It was his last season after a hugely successful career. One thing was that he had the full respect of the players; even when he was coming towards the end of his career, he had this great ability to be in the right place at the right time.

His positional sense was second to none; I played a lot of games in the same team, and I could nearly bet on the exact position he was going to land the ball in when he kicked. He could read a game so well, and he was someone you would always have confidence in because he wasn't the type ever to drop a ball or do something silly.

He was absolutely reliable; the type of guy who inspired others and as a captain he was brilliant in delegating responsibility throughout the team and around the pitch. That helped make him a really top-class captain; pity was that this could have been his finest, rather than a most significant, hour in a Munster jersey.

Donal Canniffe, in the first of four appearances for Munster against overseas touring teams – he also played against New Zealand in 1974 and 1978 and Australia in 1976 – makes a fine clearance from a scrum in the 1973 encounter. Terry Moore is on the left.

Chapter 11:
1974: THE JOEY KARAM SHOW

Munster v New Zealand
Thomond Park – 9 November 1974

Munster 4	**New Zealand 14**
(T. Moore, try)	(Batty, try; Williams, try; Karam, two penalties)

MUNSTER:

D. Spring (Cork Constitution), P. Parfrey (UCC), L. Moloney (Garryowen), J. Coleman (Highfield), P. Lavery (London Irish), B. McGann (Cork Constitution) (captain), D. Canniffe (Lansdowne), O. Waldron (Clontarf), P. Whelan (Garryowen), P. O'Callaghan (Dolphin), J. Madigan (Bohemians), M. Keane (Lansdowne), C. Tucker (Shannon), T. Moore (Highfield), S. Deering (Garryowen)

NEW ZEALAND:

Karam, Williams, B. Robertson, Morgan, Batty, D. Robertson, Going, Tanner, Norton, Gardiner, Macdonald, Whiting, Kirkpatrick, Leslie (captain), Stewart.
Replacement: Stevens for Going.

1974: THE JOEY KARAM SHOW

A year on from the match known in parts of New Zealand as 'The Great Escape', the All Blacks returned to Ireland to help the IRFU celebrate Centenary Year. But they did not come to Ireland to make friends by losing and, even though Munster had opportunities to hurt the visitors, there was really only one team in this Thomond Park battle.

Although the Munster challenge was relentless, they lacked the ability to turn possession into adequate scoring chances as the All Blacks showed too much finishing power. Brian Williams and Grant Batty showed clean heels throughout and each was rewarded with a try, while Joey Karam, the fullback, kicked two penalties.

Karam was a most interesting character in that, the season after the Munster game, at just twenty-five years of age, he turned his back on the All Blacks to play rugby league with a part-time professional team in Auckland.

The fullback had come successfully through what was described as the All Blacks' most difficult season in 1973 when the Springbok tour was cancelled and there were losses to the NZ Juniors, a Colin Meads XV and a pretty ordinary English side.

Of that year's squad, Karam was one of only ten to survive and he excelled against Australia the following season. In the Test against Ireland he scored all fifteen of the All Blacks points, including a first-half try from fullback when he punched into the line. He was the first of the modern New Zealand running fullbacks.

The next season, 1975, was a quiet one for New Zealand, playing just one Test against Scotland at Eden Park, Auckland. It became known as the 'water polo' match, such was the amount of water on the pitch for the duration of a game that should really never have been played. Karam brilliantly kicked four penalty goals, two of them from distance.

Terry Moore (hidden) crashes over for Munster's only try in the 14–4 defeat by the All Blacks at Thomond Park in 1974.

The much anticipated tour to South Africa was due the following year; Karam would have been the first player picked, but he stunned the rugby fraternity by switching to rugby league at a time when nobody ever did – at least not in New Zealand. He joined the Glenora Club in Auckland, a semi-professional side, and it is said that he turned down a contract worth five times what he eventually agreed. Glenora became famous for one thing only – signing Joe Karam!

How Ireland and Munster wished Karam had brought forward that decision a couple of years. Former Irish and Munster flanker Colm Tucker recalls the Thomond Park defeat.

We had a bloody good side out that day, we had a formidable enough pack; the only thing was that they weren't taking any chances after the scare of 1973. They put out a Test side against us; the side was captained by Andy Leslie and included a host of internationally known names.

Clearly, they were the better side until we finally got our game together in the last twenty minutes, but again there was a little bit of controversy. I recall we were called back for a forward pass when we were about to score at a crucial stage earlier in the match. That score would have kept us in the game and it might have been a different outcome. Still, the better side won on the day, and that guy Karam was amazing.

Up to then, I had never seen a guy kick a ball farther than Johnny Moroney, but Karam beat him. He actually had a funny way of kicking; he seemed to throw it down to meet his foot, but it had some effect – the ball just flew through the air and always seemed to go exactly where he wanted it to go.

Every time things seemed to be going our way, we found ourselves back down our end of the pitch, and there was nothing much we could do about it.

The last twenty minutes, however, proved some consolation, as Tucker explains. 'I suppose the fact that the All Blacks were so far ahead on the scoreline led to the rather muted response from the crowd. I suppose they had nothing much to shout about. At least we got a score before the end and it was no more than we deserved. It wasn't as if we played badly; it was just that they didn't allow us to play well. They knew what to expect after the previous year and they obviously came prepared.'

Tucker highlights a number of exceptional individual performances for Munster, including those of Barry McGann and Shay Deering.

Other out-halves have had a higher public profile than McGann, but for me he was really the best. He always had a battle to keep his weight down and that was a problem, but he was a fantastic rugby player; I would rate him as the best I've seen, honestly.

Syd Going, the famous All Black scrum half, gets the ball away from a scrum during that 1974 encounter, as Donal Canniffe and Colm Tucker (far right) challenge him from different angles.

Deering was very special too; he had all the ingredients required for a wing-forward and the determination to go with it. He played so many good games that it's hard to recall one in particular, but I seem to remember he was in special form that day.

Moss Keane from Kerry and John Madigan from Charleville formed the second-row partnership, and for Tucker there was not a more combative unit to take on the might of the All Blacks.

Keane of the flowing words and Madigan of the flowing locks (Madigan was nicknamed Cochise due to the similarity of hair style with the great Apache chief) tended to take no prisoners. 'Neither,' said Tucker, 'would take a backward step.'

That, apparently, was a feature of their partnership off the pitch as well. Tucker won his first Munster cap in a game to officially open Waterpark's new grounds in Ballinakill. 'We ended up at a party in a Waterford hotel that evening and I never in my life saw anyone like Keane and Madigan to wade their way through so many pint bottles – as if they were drinking milk; I was almost getting sick looking at them!'

The experienced Phil O'Callaghan was one of the front row against the All Blacks and Tucker always felt protected in the presence of the Dolphin man. 'He was one tough player, a guy who knew how to rise the opposition. Philo would probably start a row in a telephone booth with himself! It was just his way, to let the opposition know he was around; he was quick-witted and liked to mark out his territory from the start, which he invariably did.'

Tucker may have enjoyed a decent meal and a few drinks courtesy of Waterpark following his first cap, but he was soon to learn that amateur representative rugby might bring him fame but certainly not fortune. Senior officials charged with running the game were often blamed for keeping a tight hold on purse strings, but Tucker argues that the mean streak ran right through the committee ranks. Nobody, he suggests, was prepared to stand up and make a case for the players to be given better treatment. 'I remember going to Wales to win my second cap, sitting down to eat and looking forward to nothing but a decent steak. I was hungry, I needed a good meal, but my request led to consternation and I was told I had to have what was on the menu, chicken or something. The IRFU secretary was called to the table and a big issue made of my request. To cut a long story short, I didn't get a steak.'

With Munster he remembers the long nights of training in cold, damp conditions in Fermoy, and afterwards retiring to the Grand Hotel for tea and sandwiches. 'My abiding memory of Fermoy on a Wednesday night was that there would be a bigger rush after training than during it. The aim of that was to get the hell down to the hotel as quickly as possible and get up the stairs fast to get a bit to eat. If you didn't get there before Moss Keane and Gerry McLoughlin, well, there wouldn't be a sliver of meat left between the bread.

It really was that bad, the way the players were treated.'

Tucker learned quickly that physical survival cost money – if he wanted decent food, he often had to get it somewhere else. Also, there was little support for players who got injured. 'Back in the 1970s and 1980s the international players often had to play a club game on Saturday, go to Dublin for an Irish training session on Sunday and then come back and go to work on Monday. We sometimes would be carrying injuries from Saturday to Sunday and it didn't help by training the following day. We had hardly heard of the word physiotherapist. If we had an injury, it was generally put down as a sore muscle!'

Not many international players can boast of victories over all three southern hemisphere giants. Tucker can. In 1978 he played in that famous Munster win over New Zealand. Two years later, after being chosen as a wildcard selection, he helped the British and Irish Lions to victory in the final Test over South Africa, while the following year he was back with Munster to participate in a Musgrave Park victory over the Wallabies.

He never got the recognition in the Irish national set-up, however, that shrewd rugby observers believe he deserved, but his contribution to Munster rugby – both as player and then senior selector when the province took its first, tentative, steps into European rugby – has been exceptional. Like so many before him, Tucker, rather than walk away, stayed to give something tangible back to the game he adorned as a player so magnificently and for so long, particularly with Shannon, Munster, Ireland and the Lions.

Moss Keane is all arms as he attempts to prevent a New Zealand forward offensive in the 1974 encounter at Thomond Park. Terry Moore (far right) and Phil O'Callaghan (third from right) are on the way to support.

Chapter 12:
1976: LOST OPPORTUNITY

Munster v Australia
Musgrave Park – 13 January 1976

Munster 13
(S. Deering, try, conversion; T. Ward, two penalties, drop goal)

Australia 15
(Ryan, try; McLean, 3 penalties, conversion)

MUNSTER:
L. Moloney (Garryowen), P. Parfrey (UCC), P. Lavery (London Irish), S. Dennison (Garryowen), B. Smith (Cork Constitution), T. Ward (Garryowen), D. Canniffe (Lansdowne), G. McLoughlin (Shannon), P. Whelan (Garryowen), P. O'Callaghan (Dolphin), M. Keane (Lansdowne), E. Molloy (Garryowen), N. Elliott (Dolphin), B. Foley (Shannon), S. Deering (Garryowen, captain).

AUSTRALIA:
McLean (captain), Monaghan, Berne, Shaw, Ryan, Weatherstone, Hauser, Graham, Carberry, Meadows, Fay, Smith, Shaw, Loane, Cornelson.

1976: LOST OPPORTUNITY

Yet again, lady luck smiled on the touring side when Australia escaped by the skin of their teeth with victory over Munster at Musgrave Park.

The key moment of this action-packed game came in the seventy-fourth minute when Australia launched a counter-attack that yielded a try, despite vigorous protestations from the bulk of the 10,000 supporters that the scoring pass was blatantly forward. No matter; the Wallabies turned a delicately balanced 9–9 draw into a 15–9 advantage, and they just about held out to the end, despite an injury-time score from Munster.

Shay Deering played a captain's role by grabbing that late score wide out; unfortunately, the impressive Tony Ward, called into the team for the injured Barry McGann on the morning of the match, was unable to convert from the right-hand touchline. Nobody was in the mood for criticising Ward, however, for he marked out his territory with a tremendous display and a scoring contribution of two penalties and a drop goal to help Munster into a 9–6 lead at the interval.

The missed conversion was never a subsequent talking point, with all the focus on that forward pass from winger John Ryan to Paul McLean, who sent John Weatherstone in for the controversial try that McLean converted.

English referee Peter Hughes came in for heavy criticism in the *Cork Examiner* the following day.

Referee Peter Hughes of Burnley, so technically proficient that he awarded 31 penalties in all (24 of them against Munster), incredibly missed the forward pass. The score even obscured memory of the background to the halfway-line penalty which McLean had kicked four minutes into the second half to level the game. That is one the referee should want to forget too.

The packs went down for a scrum, Australian scrum half Rob Hauser was slow to put the ball in as rival props Phil O'Callaghan and Ron Graham

Séamus Deering takes centre stage as captain of this Munster team in 1976 who marginally failed to hold the Australians to a draw. Deering scored a late try far out and Tony Ward's attempted conversion drifted narrowly wide. The Wallabies held on for a 15–13 win. Back row (l–r): G. McLoughlin, B. Smith, E. Molloy, M. Keane, B. Foley, P. Whelan, P. Lavery, D. Canniffe; front row (l–r): L. Moloney, N. Elliott, P. Parfrey, S. Deering, T. Ward, S. Dennison, P. O'Callaghan.

struggled; Hauser turned and literally asked for a penalty. He was given it, and McLean kicked it; really, Mr Hughes was quite incredible.

Actually, O'Callaghan did not remember much about the incident given that he was in the midst of the battle against his opposite number, but he was disappointed at the outcome in what was to be his last appearance for Munster against a touring team.

Between Munster and Ireland, O'Callaghan actually played against the Wallabies on four occasions and finished on the winning side three times. That game at Musgrave Park was to be the only blight on his record.

In 1967, O'Callaghan helped Ireland, twice, and Munster to success, and he recalled how Terry Moore, on a tour to Australia, spearheaded the Irish challenge that ended in an 11–5 win in Sydney. That win, the first by a northern hemisphere side in a Test down under, was marked, recalls O'Callaghan proudly, by the appearance of five players from Cork, each of them from the senior city clubs.

That was surely unique – Tom Kiernan from Constitution, Jerry Walsh of Sunday's Well, Paddy McGrath from UCC, myself from Dolphin and Terry from Highfield.

Munster have every reason to thank Terry Moore for some great displays over the years, but his best by far was reserved for Australia. Ireland actually built the whole tour around Terry, he was phenomenal down there, outfield and in the line-outs, running, passing; the whole gamut. He was absolutely outstanding. I've never seen an individual display like it. He had some great games for Munster back home as well, but the form he showed in Australia was superb.

O'Callaghan had his own admirers, although the ex-Dolphin man does not subscribe to the notion that he had many between 1970 and 1976, at least among the Irish selectors, when he had to be content with a career that embraced just club and provincial rugby.

He might have claim to being clairvoyant; while in 'exile', he predicted he would come back triumphantly to win his twenty-first international cap – and that it would happen on the planned 1976 tour to New Zealand. And that is how it transpired, his optimism having borne fruit. He was happy to be back, although Ireland lost that game in Wellington by eleven points to three.

Pat Parfrey does not get the ball in mid-air but he did get his man and his tackle helped set up a Munster counter-attack.

But Munster's loss to Australia is something that still annoys him.

It was a match we should have won; there were a few incidents that went against us. Whatever, I am convinced to this day that we deserved at least a draw.

It was a good Australian side, but we certainly weren't pushed around; we were able to hold our ground without too much trouble and I suppose that was to be expected given the personnel in the team, strong characters like Pa Whelan, Gerry McLoughlin, Brendan Foley, Moss Keane and Shay Deering, who had the heart of a lion; absolutely a great player.

I don't think I can speak highly enough of Shay; he was just a spectacular player. All you have to do is look at the team, at guys like Larry Moloney, Séamus Dennison, Tony Ward and Canniffe as well as some of the forwards; you had the basis of the team that went on to beat the All Blacks a couple of years later. There were some great players in that side, so it wasn't any wonder we ran the Wallabies to the wire.

All eyes on the ball as Australia win this line-out. Munster's Brendan Foley (father of Anthony) is in the middle with captain Shay Deering to the left and Noel Elliott to the right.

O'Callaghan didn't come through the traditional route, walking in one day in his late teens to Dolphin and announcing that he wanted to play rugby. Sport played a major part in his young life; he was such a keen soccer and GAA player that he often, in his youth, played a couple of matches a day at weekends.

He explains how he eventually veered towards rugby. 'Rugby was to make a difference. Ultimately, I gave it my full attention, and I was delighted to have taken that decision. There was more discipline in rugby than in any other game, I felt, and it suited me. There was a structure and a discipline there that wasn't evident in, say, soccer.'

O'Callaghan, whose verbal spats with referees and opponents were well documented over the years, remarks how, in rugby, physical intimidation of officials was never an issue. 'In other sports at that time, sometimes referees were assaulted, but that never happened in rugby, at least not physically anyway.'

He also recalls how Ireland's most famous referee of the era, John West, gave him a ticking off the first time they crossed paths. 'I was giving him a good examination, letting him know how I felt about certain decisions and, basically, chancing my arm. He was about to send me off, but for whatever reason he changed his mind; he might have caught the glint in my eye, and he let me off the hook. Years later, he used to thank me, tongue in cheek, for imparting all the advice that day because, he said, he would never have got the opportunity to referee so many internationals without me telling him where exactly he was going wrong!'

Stories, particularly rugby stories, tend to grow legs as the months and years pass, but O'Callaghan did confirm that one comment attributed to him was absolutely true. It happened during an Ireland–Scotland game when the referee told O'Callaghan, as he penalised him for scrummaging illegally, 'You're boring', to which the bold Philo responded, 'And you're not so bloody amusing yourself!'

O'Callaghan admits that at times he pushed his luck to the limit, with both referees and opponents.

God, there would be no point in getting on with the game unless you had tested the waters. If it happened that your nose was going to be cut off quickly, then you didn't cast out too far, you just reeled in and kept your mouth shut.

People talk about me, but what about Noisy [Noel Murphy]? Goodness, he was always at it, testing, testing and testing right up to the limit. He would try to rise everyone, giving guys s**t, and trying to gauge the reaction; it was symptomatic of the times we were in.

The thing about opponents was that you had to give as good as you got; yes, from time to time, there was a punch thrown here and there, you couldn't let a guy get on top of you because you could be taken to pieces. Still, it wasn't a dirty game, it couldn't have been when you'd be getting together with your opponent after the game and drinking pints with him; the next time you'd see him, the rivalry would start all over again.

It went on like that; they were different times and different rules, I suppose. Things didn't always go according to my plan, but I have no regrets because we all got great enjoyment out of playing the game, out of meeting people and making friends – and a lot of those friendships endure to this day. The unfortunate thing is that good guys like Shay [Deering], Terry [Moore] and, more recently, Jim Buckley are no longer with us. That would be my only regret.

Pat Lavery (foreground) unleashing a Munster attack against
Australia at Musgrave Park in 1976.

Chapter 13:
1978: SEVENTH HEAVEN

Munster v New Zealand
Thomond Park – 31 October 1978

Munster 12   New Zealand 0

(C. Cantillon, try; T. Ward, two drop goals, penalty)

MUNSTER:

L. Moloney (Garryowen), M. Finn (UCC), S. Dennison (Garryowen), G. Barrett (Cork Constitution), J. Bowen (Cork Constitution), T. Ward (St Mary's College), D. Canniffe (Lansdowne) (captain), G. McLoughlin (Shannon), P. Whelan (Garryowen), L. White (London Irish), M. Keane (Lansdowne), B. Foley (Shannon), C. Tucker (Shannon), D. Spring (Dublin University), C. Cantillon (Cork Constitution).

NEW ZEALAND:

McKechnie, Williams, Robertson, Jaffray, Wilson, Dunn, Donaldson, Johnstone, Black, Knight, Haden, Oliver, Mourie (captain), McGregor, Graham.
Replacements: Osborne for Robertson.

CHAPTER 13

1978: SEVENTH HEAVEN

From the northern to the southern hemisphere, rugby fans will never be allowed forget the date 31 October 1978, the day Munster beat the New Zealand All Blacks for the first and only time. It is a result famed in song and story, one regularly recalled on stage or by those with access to library bookshelves around the world.

Not so well documented, however, is Munster's low-key tour to London earlier the same year; indeed, it might best be forgotten given the outcome of matches against Middlesex and London Irish in a four-day period in early September. Neither is it widely known that coach Tom Kiernan got the job of plotting the famous victory over New Zealand more by accident than design. Kiernan had already served as Munster coach for three years before being elected Munster Branch president. He finished that term of office in April 1978 and was only called upon for a return to coaching following the resignation, for personal reasons, of the late Des Barry.

Any year that includes a fixture against a touring side is a big year. Kiernan, a veteran of Munster teams that had come close against New Zealand, saw the bigger picture; if his side were to beat the All Blacks, they would have to be better prepared than any other team that had gone before.

Five years earlier at Musgrave Park, Kiernan and his Munster colleagues were on the threshold of victory when New Zealand's Trevor Morris kicked a late equalising penalty. Munster had come that close despite the fact that they had virtually no training time together before the game.

The Munster Branch in those days did not have a lot of money to spare and they tended to hold on to what little they had. But Kiernan was obviously a skilful negotiator, because after gentle persuasion, two of the most influential people in the branch, Hon. Secretary Bill O'Brien and Hon. Treasurer Tom Collery, agreed to release the funds needed to send Munster to London.

Pat Parfrey, a great servant of Munster and Irish rugby, was based in London at the time and acted as the unofficial ground handling agent, negotiating with Middlesex and London Irish for the matches and St Paul's School for the provision of training facilities. If the results against Middlesex – a heavy defeat – and London Irish – a fortuitous draw – were hardly inspirational, Kiernan was happy enough. 'We really didn't mind how strong or weak the opposition were, the key was to have games to prepare us for the All Blacks, our first official game of the season.'

Key to that preparation was the arrival by special delivery from London of a video containing action from matches involving the All Blacks. In an age when such technology was only beginning to assume importance, the delivery of the tape by Brian Busteed, a friend of Kiernan's from his student days in UCC, was extremely valuable. The arrival of a London Irish forward by the name of Les White to fill a troublesome loose-head prop vacancy, allied to the introduction of training sessions in Fermoy, added to the intrigue during the build-up to the game.

In those days, Munster training sessions were few and far between, but Kiernan saw the necessity to bring the squad together more often than usual, and so players travelled from Limerick, Cork and Dublin at least once a week for six weeks prior to the big day. This dedication, Kiernan suggests, undoubtedly helped in the quest for victory, but he also highlights the importance of Munster's great tradition against previous touring teams. 'The tradition went a long way back; my first time watching a touring side was Australia in 1947 at the Mardyke and they scored in the last minute to beat Munster. In 1963 and 1973, Munster had marvellous games against the All Blacks, losing the first one 6–3 in Limerick and then conceding a late penalty goal to allow them draw 3–3 at Musgrave Park. Munster beat Australia in 1967 but had been short of luck against the All Blacks, so I suppose you could say the 1978 win was coming.'

A coach with pride in his work can never forget achievement. If the 1978 win at Thomond Park was the highlight of that season and beyond, Kiernan likes to think that Munster will also be remembered for the subsequent Inter-provincial Championship title win.

He ranks that almost as highly as the win over New Zealand. 'That was a huge feat because Munster didn't always do so well in the championship in those days; when they did they tended to do so from the role of underdogs. The difference in 1978 was that they went into the championship from the pedestal they had been put on after beating New Zealand. To win the title in such circumstances was, I felt, a magnificent feat.'

Despite their first defeat at the hands of Munster, despite the fact that it was the only loss on a long tour for a remarkable team led so brilliantly by Graham Mourie, history will reflect kindly on the 1978 All Blacks.

The Munster team that famously beat the All Blacks at Thomond Park on 31
October 1978. Back row (l–r): Munster Branch President S. Gavin, touch judge
J. Cole, G. McLoughlin, L. White, M. Keane, D. Spring, C. Tucker, P. Whelan,
B. Foley, referee C. Thomas, touch judge M. Walsh; front row (l–r): T. Ward,
C. Cantillon, M. Finn, S. Dennison, D. Canniffe, G. Barrett, J. Bowen, L. Moloney.

Having absorbed the shock of a 12–0 defeat, New Zealand, apart from a
post-match rant from team manager Jack Gleeson, accepted defeat graciously;
indeed, their arrival at the post-match dinner in Limerick drew some smiles as
the team arrived singing the song made famous in *Snow White and the Seven
Dwarfs*, 'Hi ho, hi ho, it's off to work we go . . .'

For an insight into the reaction of the ordinary New Zealander, *Mourie's All
Blacks: The Team That Found Itself* (Auckland, 1979), a book by New Zealand's
top rugby writer of the era, Terry McLean, is worth a read. Although much of
the book heaps praise on Mourie's team, the section dealing with the Munster
match is revealing. Veteran of several overseas tours and author of dozens of
rugby books over a forty-year career in journalism, McLean admits candidly
that the defeat was not wholly unexpected.

*There was no doubt that New Zealand had it coming against Munster; our
forebears of 1954 had defeated Munster by just six points to three; it was a
scoreline repeated in 1963, while the All Blacks barely managed a draw in 1973
when Trevor Morris placed a penalty goal to make it three points to three.*

Pat Whelan turns, clenching his fist, and heads back for the celebration after Munster flanker Christy Cantillon scored the crucial try against the All Blacks at Thomond Park in 1978.

These events proclaimed that the men of Munster, whether projected on to the field at Cork or on to the cute little beauty, Thomond Park of Limerick, where Mourie's men took their tumble, were actuated by patriotism fiercer than a burning oil-well.

Not ever will Mourie's men get out of their minds the chants of MUN-STER, MUN-STER which, beginning as timid choruses, progressed, as no-side neared, to stentorian shouts that might have carried halfway across the neighbouring Atlantic.

Fermented and spirituous liquors were consumed in substantial quantities at the park after the match. All Limerick was given over to libation that evening. It was thought, for a time, that it might be a good idea to reprint the programme of the match so that gentlemen of Ireland who had not been there could, by gazing at the names of the heroes, dimly grasp the feel of the match and the holy ground on which Munster had performed its mighty deed.

Heroes! In only the fifth minute, Séamus Dennison, him the fellow that wore the jersey number 13 in the centre, was knocked down in a tackle. He came from the Garryowen Club, which might explain his subsequent actions – to join that club, so it has been said, one must walk barefoot over broken glass, charge naked through searing fires, run the severest gauntlets and, as a final test of manhood, prepare with unfaltering gaze to make a catch of the highest ball ever kicked while aware that at least eight thundering members of your own team are about to knock you down, trample you all over and into the bargain hiss nasty words at you because you forgot to cry out, while going down for the one and only time, 'Mark!'

Whatever exaggeration the virtues needed to join a rugby club, there was none in the writer's praise of a brilliant Dennison on that memorable day.

Dennis was pretty badly hurt apparently. Later, he was hurt again, more seriously. 'I think, Séamus,' said the attending doctor, 'that you would do well to rest by the touchline for two minutes. You will feel much better when you go back.'

'Push off,' said Séamus – they know that naughty word in Limerick too. 'Séamus,' said the doctor more earnestly, 'that shoulder is quite damaged. It will be better if you rest it. No more, just two minutes.'

Munster coach Tom Kiernan has plenty of advisors on the touchline during the match in 1978. Different days!

'Push off,' said Dennison, flatly, finally, forever. He was in pain, no question. But was he going to leave the field? Not bloody likely.

New Zealand were, said McLean, treated royally in Limerick right up until kick-off and again after the match. For eighty minutes, however, they suffered the type of torture one might have expected centuries earlier in Bunratty Castle, which the team visited on the night of their arrival in Ireland. McLean identifies some ominous signs for the tourists.

There were, perhaps, two portents to the defeat. After flying from Heathrow to Shannon on the Sunday prior to the game, the All Blacks were festively dined at Bunratty. This ancient pile had been restored for the tourist trade which had poured into Ireland for twenty years after the end of the Second World War and which only tailed off after the bombers of Belfast had threatened, with an execution here and an assassination or firebombing there, to set all of Ireland alight.

Bunratty's banqueting rules were cute. The chief guest, in this instance Russell Thomas [All Blacks manager], was installed as the Earl of Thomond and in office was invested with enormous powers. Earl Thomas exercised one of these by bidding that Barry Ashworth be cast into the dungeon. To Irish songs sung by beguilingly beautiful colleens and with much pomp and ceremony, the All Blacks drank mulled mead, tossed the bones of their meat over their shoulders and were more medieval than they might even be in Patea on a wild Saturday night.

Yet the Earl was not entirely serene. Ashworth's shrieks and groans and cries of mercy, mercy from the dungeon were a little too lifelike to make an appetite as keen as it ought to have been. They anticipated by about forty-eight hours the innermost reactions of the All Blacks as they faced a nil–9 deficit going into the second half of a match against a team massively well organised in defence and boundlessly energetic in chasing anything and everything.

The other portent was offered about midday of the Monday, a little more than twenty-four hours before kick-off, in a training run of the Munster team. Training runs may come and training runs may go, and the faster and farther most of them go, the better. They are tedious and boring gallops-about in which unenthusiastic men commit errors without cause and silently bear the criticisms of their coach.

Munster's run was another matter. It lasted no more than twenty minutes. After the inevitable and essential preliminaries of warming-up, the players were directed by their coach, Tom Kiernan, into an unusual exercise. Tossing the ball out in front of the forwards, he would command one or more of them to go down upon it. The others were then to move on to man and ball to practise the heel to the scrum half, Donal Canniffe, and the setting up of a fast passing more to the wing three-quarters, as often as not with the fullback, Larry Moloney, joining in.

Now this had been done before, times without number by teams without number. Tellingly, however, the bite in the rucking and heeling was genuine. The man who had gone down on the ball was not treated as a friend. Tellingly, too, the passes from Canniffe were not only crisp, but also were not dropped. Most tellingly of all, the wing-forwards of the team, especially a nuggety man from Cork Constitution, Christy Cantillon, moved so fast in support of the backs that the wings, Moss Finn and Jimmy Bowen, were aware of their comrades, fewer than 5 metres distant, as they galloped into their passes. The merits of the training were threefold: vigour, as to the forward effort; accuracy, as to the handling of the backs; and most of all, speed, as to the support play of the forwards.

Donal Spring moves up from the back to secure possession from this line-out. Other Munster players visible (from left), Colm Tucker, Moss Keane, Gerry McLoughlin and (far right) Donal Canniffe.

McLean gives due credit to the role played by Kiernan in the downfall of his beloved national side.

Tommy Kiernan is a lean, grizzled man with a face almost cadaverously thin. He played fullback for Ireland more than fifty times. He captained the British and Irish Lions who set South Africa by the ears in 1968 by exhibiting the wild, juvenile behaviour of a military mess on the wampo.

It is his natural disposition to look on the darker side of things. The attitude expresses the Irish genius for conning outsiders into believing what they, the Irish, want them to believe. Kiernan's is a sharp, subtle and penetrating mind. His memory bank of rugby knowledge has the depth of the Mindanao Deep. Having played against the All Blacks led by Whinerary, Lochore and Kirkpatrick, he knew much, if not all, about New Zealand rugby; and he had taken very good care indeed to be provided with video tapes of the first four matches of Mourie's tour.

At the end of a training run, a New Zealander who in the practices of his profession had watched about a million training runs by about a thousand teams said, sincerely, 'Tommy, you've a damned good team here.' 'Ah, bejaysus,' said Tommy in a flat, sorrowful voice, 'they are no more than a good bunch of lads. They don't stand a chance against the All Blacks.'

So much for the brush-off, suggested McLean, who went on to describe the opening period of the game.

Pow! In the first minute, the first time he received the ball, Canniffe uncoiled his right leg, which appeared to take up two-thirds of his body of more than six feet, and booted a Garryowen high into the air. The ball rose as from a howitzer and descended vertically. As it came down, those Munster forwards, who now did not have to worry about heeling the ball from the arms of one of their men, arrived in concert, snorting like St George's dragon. They did not, then or later, merely charge. They hurtled. Wilson was shocked into a knock-on, Donaldson into a wild pass. In their own quarter, Munster won the ball and Canniffe smartly passed it to Ward. This dark, chunky, powerful man who in the previous international season had equalled the Irish scoring record by tallying thirty-eight points from various means, mostly penalty goals and drop kicks, immediately revealed why he could have, if he had wanted, made a career in professional soccer.

His kick across the field to Bowen on the left wing was, in effect, a square pass. The ball bounced kindly and Bowen, sprinting at his fastest, was clear of the first line of defenders as he grasped it. Far upfield, in the great vacant area which theoretically was the All Blacks defensive zone, McKechnie awaited his man.

No Horatius, this McKechnie. Not this time, anyway. Bowen faintly conveyed, with a feint, that he intended to veer left towards the touchline. McKechnie obligingly covered. Instantaneously, Bowen propped infield, still at speed and untouched by human hand. But now his speed was slightly faltering. Carrying the ball was a hindrance. So was the excitement – the match was only five minutes old. Bowen could hear the All Black cover moving at him, Jaffray with a dive almost clipping his heels; Wilson and others running helter-skelter in hurried defence. It was now that the fine moves of the training run paid a dividend.

Not 5 metres from Bowen, Cantillon appeared, fresh, fit and fast. As securely as in the training run, he held the pass. As he ran in to score beside the left upright, the entire audience of 10,000 and more Irish leaped madly in the air. They leaped madly, moments later, when Ward, without the least concern, placed the conversion.

Yet again, in the sixteenth minute, with the game not yet into its second quarter, the Munsterians leaped in utter joy. McKechnie conceded a scrum in the sixteenth minute and another chance fell to Munster. Canniffe put in, Pat Whelan heeled cleanly, Canniffe passed to Ward and the out half dropped a goal. Nine points to nil for Munster and, to coin a famous old remark, the way the All Blacks were playing, they were damned lucky to have the nil.

The Kiwi is critical of the All Blacks for the way they failed to react positively to that Munster dominance on the scoreboard.

Even Kiernan admitted that New Zealand could still have won the match but for shortcomings they failed to address during the course of the game. Soon after Cantillon's try, Robertson retired hurt and was replaced by Osborne. In the development of play, especially for a long period after half time when the All Blacks forwards were decisively in command, it became apparent that [substitute Bill] Osborne and Wilson could be match-winners if they were given the ball. Regrettably, this was not done.

Dunn stifled some attacks by failing to bring Wilson into the running. Jaffray stifled more – more and more as the play developed frenetic touches in the second half – by aiming to break the line himself before letting the three-quarters have the ball. Nor were the backs solely at fault. Haden, perhaps the best of the team, won plenty of possession but the persistence of the pack in driving play became more wearisome and when the backs did eventually get ball, they were frustrated by the magnificent tackling of the Munster men.

It was the first time in five matches that the tourists were stumped for ideas, suggests McLean – and it was to be the last time, as New Zealand went on to record seventeen wins from eighteen games.

Certainly, Graham Mourie was not totally in command, as he proved himself capable throughout the tour and in some very difficult games. New Zealand failed to close down great holes in the front of the line-out through which Pat Whelan, Gerry McLoughlin and Brendan Foley poured. Nor was he able to devise counters to the ball-winning of the tall number 8, Donal Spring, up against relatively small men at the tail of the line-out.

New Zealand's Mark Donaldson is wrapped up by Pat Whelan as Les White (third from right) and Gerry McLoughlin move in. Support is coming from the left in the form of Donal Spring (far left) and Moss Keane.

No doubt, the blind side attacking ploy was worth pursuing against the well poised and incredibly brave Munster defence on the open side of the field, but insufficient gain was made because Munster appeared to have numbers to check there too.

As the game went on, frustration crept in and the cry of MUN-STER, MUN-STER gradually became a religious chant. A kick, very long, set Wilson to the chase twelve minutes from the end. As the ball bounced, having been touched, in the All Blacks in-goal, he moved too rapidly to gather it for a punt back to touch, or an attempt to counter-attack.

His feet went from under him and involuntarily, as he hit the ground, he touched down to concede a scrum. It was ABC stuff for Munster's forwards to heel the ball and for Canniffe to pass at such speed that Ward was able to drop the goal in total comfort.

It was total comfort for Munster, but total subjection for the All Blacks. Except on a very, very few occasions, notably in internationals, New Zealand teams have always been able to score, even in defeat. This time, despite Kiernan's kindly appreciation, they were out of their class.

As an immediate reaction, some of them blamed the Welsh referee, Corrie Thomas, for allowing Munster men, particularly wing-forwards and inside backs, excessive latitude in staging their offensive-defensive tackles from offside positions.

The real gripe came from Gleeson next day. The All Blacks were waiting to board their bus for the tip to Dublin and all of the touring reporters were anxious to get follow-up copy to the sensational defeat. Gleeson, not at all a jovial Jack, gave it to them. The Munster men, he charged, had been kamikaze types. Operating outside the law, they had tackled, unquestionably with extraordinary efficiency and bravery, but from illegal positions, so Jack said, as far as 10 yards ahead of the ball.

Warming up and speaking sternly, Gleeson said the All Blacks had set out on their tour with the intention of playing fifteen-man rugby. It was vital to the good of the game as a whole that they should do this – rugby had suffered too much from obsessive and excessive defence. But if teams were to adopt the Munster pattern and do all they could do to stultify the All Blacks' aims in attack, then the tour would suffer, So, too, would the game.

It was a stern, severe criticism which wanted in fairness on two grounds. It did not sufficiently praise the spirit of Munster or the presence, within the one team, of fifteen men who each emerged from the match much lager than life-sized. Secondly, it was ingenuous or, more accurately, naïve. Gleeson thought it sinful Ward had not once passed the ball. It was worse, he said, that Munster had made aggressive defence the only arm of their attack. Now what on earth, it could be asked, was Kiernan to do with his team? Urge them to be as gormless as London Counties [whom the All Blacks beat 37–12]?

The very thought was ridiculous. Kiernan held a fine hand with top trumps in Spring, Cantillon, Foley and Whelan in the forwards, and Canniffe, Ward, Dennison, Bowen and Moloney in the backs – and even the very best man, who might I reckon have been Cantillon, was only a wisp ahead of the very worst of the team. What was Kiernan to do – play as New Zealand wanted the match to be played, all open and free, with fine running from first to last? Or play to his strength, which, principally, was the absolute bravery of his men?

Tommy Kiernan wasn't born yesterday. He knew what he wanted, and got it. He played to the strength of his team and upon the suspected *weaknesses of the All Blacks. If you listen carefully, you may still hear, wafting o'er the Atlantic, the mad, glad cry of MUN-STER! MUN-STER! They call part of Limerick the Golden Vale. Why not? The tears of the All Blacks may still be running in the broad River Shannon nearby. No wonder Barry Ashworth cried for mercy; bedad, the fellow must have been clairvoyant.*

The referee that day was Corris Thomas, who certainly was not clairvoyant. In fact, Thomas had not a clue what to expect on his first trip to Limerick. Many years on, the memories are all happy ones, and he still has the piece of paper on which he recorded the timings and scores of the game: 'Goal, DG, DG, full time 4.33 p.m.'

Those are the vital statistics that made up one of the greatest occasions in Irish sporting history and which earned Welshman Thomas his most prized memento of an illustrious seventeen-year career as a referee. A month later he was back in Munster to referee a game between Dolphin and Shannon.

'I was with my "minder" in the clubhouse bar after the game when the room was called to order. I was thanked for my part in the game that day and then everyone was reminded that I had been in charge of the game against the All Blacks. Then I was handed a Munster jersey used in the game as a permanent reminder of the win over New Zealand. However, the number was ripped off the back so that nobody could tell who it belonged to. I've had it framed and it now hangs in my local club, Cardiff HSOB.'

Thomas' refereeing career included five internationals and four New Zealand tour games, yet he never experienced anything quite like the occasion of 31 October 1978. From the moment he arrived at Thomond Park he felt 'there was something in the air'.

Donal Spring made the point years later that the fact there was no film of the whole game was the best thing that ever happened. The great deeds of that Munster team have been handed down from one generation to the next and there is nothing to challenge the way the stories have been embellished.

The first thing I said after the game was that this is a story I will be able to tell my grandchildren. It was a result that had significance from the moment it happened. Everyone in rugby has heard about the day Munster beat the All Blacks. Other great games and results have been forgotten, but this one has been immortalised in print and on the stage. I've been to see the play Alone it Stands a number of times and it is a remarkable piece of work that certainly captures the spirit and enormity of what was a very special occasion.

The whole tone of the game was set by the tackle from Séamus Dennison on Stu Wilson. We rarely saw the big hits of today in the game in 1978 because the players were much smaller and tended to go low into the tackle. Dennison's tackle was perfect and it was as though Wilson had run into a brick wall – he crumpled into a heap. In that moment every Munster player grew a foot and started to believe they could achieve the ultimate goal. I felt the temperature of the whole occasion change after that tackle and the crowd roared their approval.

Thomas was on the Welsh international panel at the time of his appointment, along with Clive Norling and Ken Rowlands, and was delighted when given 'the pick of the crop of Wales' three All Blacks tour fixtures'.

'I'd never refereed Munster before, nor had the honour of controlling a game at Thomond Park, and I was really looking forward to the occasion. I'd been used to refereeing big club matches in Wales with crowds of 10,000 and being told in no uncertain terms what they thought about me and my decisions. What I found at Thomond Park was that the crowd ignored me and didn't give me any abuse. And then, of course, there was the perfect, eerie silence every time there was a kick at goal.'

Not that there were many of those. Thomas was renowned for his open style, and games in which he was in charge invariably had low penalty counts. That is exactly how it was when the man who was to become the most senior and respected rugby analyst in the world – he became head of game analysis for the International Rugby Board (IRB) in 2002 – refereed the game over thirty years ago.

I felt very happy with my performance at the end of the game. There were very few penalties – around ten I think – and only one kick at goal. But the game in 2008 bears no relationship to the game thirty years earlier. The heaviest All Black back in the 1970s was around twelve and a half stone. Five yeas ago the average weight of international backs was fifteen stone.

In 1978 the average number of rucks and mauls in a game was thirty-five, whereas you can expect about 160 in a modern game. There were probably 100 line-outs and scrums in the game in 1978, but you expect less than fifty these days. And the ball-in-play time has risen over the past thirty years from around 30 per cent to anything up to 45 per cent.

The physical demands on the modern players, and referees [in 1978], had increased dramatically. The line-out was a jungle and a nightmare to referee and the game was much dirtier. Now referees have to be much quicker in thought and deed. They have to make so many instant decisions at the breakdown and the game really is more demanding both mentally and physically.

Thomas can still recall the 'mayhem' at the end of the game at Thomond Park. 'The moment I blew the whistle the field was flooded with fans. The All Blacks were very gracious in defeat, but while the Munster fans were ecstatic, many were dumbstruck. There was a group of nine of us who went around the pubs after the post-match dinner at the Limerick Inn and it was incredible to see people in the pubs shaking their heads in disbelief at what they had witnessed earlier in the day. It was an incredible end to an unbelievable day; one I do often tell my grandchildren about!'

Chapter 14:
1981: STUDENT PRINCES

Munster v Australia
Musgrave Park – 17 November 1981

Munster 15
(P. Derham, try; T. Ward, three penalties,
drop goal, conversion)

Australia 6
(P. Grigg, try; M. O'Connor, conversion)

MUNSTER:

J. Barry UCC), E. Griffin (Garryowen), M. Kiernan (Dolphin), P. Cross (Young Munster),
J. Crotty (UCC), T. Ward (Garryowen), A. O'Regan (UCC), T. Hennessy (London Irish), P. Derham (UCC),
G. McLoughlin (Shannon), B. Foley (Shannon), D. Lenihan (UCC), C. Tucker (Shannon),
A. O'Leary (Wanderers) (captain), C. Cantillon (Cork Constitution).

AUSTRALIA:

G. Ella, Grigg, Cox, O'Connor, Moon, M. Ella, Parker, Meadows, Carberry,
Curran, Mathers (captain), McLean, Poidevin, Hall, Lucas.

CHAPTER 14

1981: STUDENT PRINCES

Paul 'Pakie' Derham has every reason to remember his first appearance in a Munster jersey. His was the most daunting of tasks – a debut for his province against one of the top sides in the world – yet he need not have worried about his ability to fill the shoes of one of Ireland's greatest hookers, Pat Whelan, when he scored an early try that helped propel Munster to an unlikely but fully deserved triumph over the touring team.

Whelan, the Garryowen veteran, had come to the end of the road, but the trainee solicitor was just one of a number of candidates to take over the hooking duties for the men in red. 'Pa was just about finished and the selectors were looking for someone to take over,' Derham recalls. 'It probably came down to myself and Noel Glynn from Shannon – we played against one another in the previous season's Munster Cup final, although Eugene Carley from Highfield would also have been in the shake up.'

Derham was thrilled when told of his selection. He was still a member of UCC but by then was studying for his final law exams in Dublin and had little or no involvement with the team. 'It was a huge honour, it was my first real introduction to the Munster squad although I had participated in a couple of training sessions in Cashel, having travelled from Dublin with Tony Ward, Moss Keane and Donal Spring.'

Proud though he was at being selected for his biggest game to date, Derham remembers the old days as did many others before and after him; his abiding memory is of trying to extricate a few bob from the tight-fisted Munster Branch.

I remember, for instance, being presented with a commemorative tie to mark the occasion of the Australian game. That, and a tacky plastic kit bag produced by an erstwhile sponsor, was just about all we got for our troubles in those days.

If we had to spend money, and I did to get from Dublin to either Cashel or Cork, I would have to go to Lawson's in MacCurtain Street to reclaim expenses from the honorary secretary Bill O'Brien. Being a student, I needed the money but there was always some excuse to reduce the expenses claim and there was no arguing.

I remember being told by an older player that we were lucky to be given a pair of socks as well as a jersey before matches. The thing was that we had to give the socks back – imagine that – and there was a hunt in the dressing room afterwards when officials would check all the bags if there was so much as one sock missing. The socks were recycled for the next game!

Notwithstanding that, he was both proud and relatively calm as he prepared for the big match. Derham had soldiered successfully with a significant number of players involved in that Australian game.

He was part of the team that brought off a shock but thoroughly deserved Munster Senior Cup triumph over Shannon at Musgrave Park in April of that year

Anthony O'Leary captained the Munster team to victory over Australia in 1981. Five of the team came from a high-quality UCC team. Back row (l–r): A. O'Regan, G. McLoughlin, B. Foley, D. Lenihan, T. Hennessy, C. Tucker; middle row (l–r): P. Cross, C. Cantillon, P. Derham, A. O'Leary, J. Crotty, M. Kiernan, E. Griffin; front: (l–r) T. Ward, J. Barry.

under the captaincy of Finbarr Dennehy; UCC provided a significant number of players to that Munster team, although Dennehy was not one of them.

Derham points out that there were no fewer than eleven current or former UCC players on the Munster panel that day – John Barry, Pat Cross, Jim Crotty, Alex O'Regan, Donal Lenihan, Anthony O'Leary, Christy Cantillon, Donal Daly, Peter Rolls, Paul Collins and himself.

I would say I felt comfortable going in for my first cap in such a situation; these guys were all quality players with whom I had gone to battle and there was a feel-good factor in the camp without being in the least bit overconfident.

Add in the Shannon contingent to the mix – Colm Tucker, Ginger [Gerry McLoughlin] and Brendan Foley – and we would have had a fair idea of who we were playing with and what we were capable of. Around that time, we had gone through a few right tough battles against Shannon and there would have been a degree of mutual respect there between us, so going to war with a touring side would never have been a problem.

And there was not much difficulty on the day. In fact, Derham recalls that it was much easier than expected. After eight minutes, Munster were on the way, with Derham a scoring hero when he charged through on a sloppy tap down from a line-out and beat the cover for a try, which Tony Ward converted.

His positioning was no accident; indeed he believes that Donal Lenihan, rather than an Australian, might even have been the man to tap the ball down into his path.

I'm not sure, but I think it was. It happened very quickly, but it would have been something that he [Lenihan] and I would had practised many times with College; you must remember that there was no lifting allowed in those days, so you really had to engineer many different ways to win possession from the line-outs. That was one of them and, whatever happened, it worked. It was close at the end, with me battling against their scrum half [Tony Parker] to get the touch. I did just about make it before him and it was a huge boost so early on.

Ward went on to kick two penalties and a drop goal to push Munster into an amazing fifteen points to nil lead, an advantage only cut late in the game when Peter Grigg got in for a try and Michael O'Connor converted. That try came at the end of the only decent Australian move all day, as Derham explains.

The fact is that we gave them nothing. We took four balls against the head against the Australian Test hooker [Chris Carberry]. Considering that neither myself nor Tom Hennessy [the tight-head prop] were unknowns, that was a good achievement against formidable opposition.

As would have been the way in those days, there was a great slag among the Australians levelled at Carberry at the dinner that night; guys shouting at him all night long asking whether he had lost one, two or three or four. The guy was destroyed by his own colleagues, but he took it on the chin; we had a few drinks together and a good chat in between the slagging.

I suppose a sign of how much the game has changed is that you will never see a ball struck against the head now unless it's a major mistake. That art or skill of hooking is gone, primarily because it was dangerous; you swung out and you had to swing in and your body was in a bad position were there to be a collapsed scrum. Unless your two props knew very well what they were doing and had the physique to hold firm, the hooker could have been in big trouble.

But Derham was never remotely troubled on that occasion, giving huge credit to the men alongside and behind him for keeping the scrum upright and subjecting Australia to a troubled afternoon.

With a guy like Brendan Foley packing down behind, scrums never tended to move anywhere unless forward. He was a great man, a powerful figure, to have in any team and I reckon the pack in its entirety produced a marvellous display that day.

I suppose one shouldn't have been too surprised. If Foley was the father figure of the pack, we had as good a back row as you would get anywhere. Anthony O'Leary, Christy Cantillon and Colm Tucker had all given incredible service to the game and didn't always get the rewards they deserved.

It was a back row short on international caps but it should have been a thirty-plus cap back row. I could never figure how 'Wog' [O'Leary] or Cantillon failed to get capped, and Tucker never got the credit he deserved. In another time, five years younger or older, Tucker would have been a fixture on the Ireland team – he was that good.

There were others on that team who deserved more at international level. Johnny Barry, for instance, came very close to being capped. He was picked as a sub against England and the match was called off; by the time the match came around again he had done his ankle in a club game against Waterpark and he never again got the opportunity.

Alex O'Regan sat on the bench for the Triple Crown side in 1982 but never got to come on, and there weren't too many better wingers around anywhere than Jim Crotty, another guy who didn't get the full credit or recognition he deserved.

Others fared better; Donal Lenihan was at the start of a remarkable career and so too was Michael Kiernan, both going on to great heights both for Ireland and the Lions. All things being equal, it wasn't a shock that Australia were beaten, although I honestly don't believe the team has been given the credit that was due to it for both the achievement and the way the victory was achieved.

In the days before video analysis, Munster knew little about Australia other than that they would be keen to play a running game – and Munster would steer as far away as possible from that. Derham recounts the story of the game.

Fergus Walsh, the coach, gave us as much information as he could on the strengths and weaknesses of the Australian team. We knew they had a back

Donal Lenihan appears to be hampered as he contests possession in this line-out, but Gerry McLoughlin and Brendan Foley (wearing number 4) are there to make sure Australia get no advantage.

division that would be keen to run the ball, particularly because it included Glen and Mark Ella, two of the three famous brothers.

I'm not sure whether Fergus had the team he wanted or not – back then, the coach very often didn't get the side he wanted. He was given a team rather that selecting a team; even after the match was over, he might not have had a great say in what changes were to be made. Nevertheless, he appeared to have confidence in us being able to carry out a fairly straightforward game plan devised to frustrate Australia; it was to be a low-risk game plan in a sense, but one designed to beat them.

The plan was simple – have go at them up front, attack their scrums, keep the pressure on them, get the ball out to Wardy, kick for the corners, get into drop goal positions and territory where they might give away penalties under pressure. I suppose, from talking to players on previous teams, it was no different from any game plan for any Munster team that played a touring side.

We were to take them on at everything and never allow them to get in the comfort zone or to allow the game break up and get loose; we were to contest until we dropped and make sure the Ella brothers got absolutely no room. If I can recall correctly they really only got one chance to attack in space; it involved a lovely switch in the centre and Peter Grigg got in for a try. Otherwise, we made it very uncomfortable for them and kept them under pressure, so the game plan worked a treat.

Part of it was down to the fact that we started well and stayed going well. They never bothered us, their pack never beat us up, we were in no bother dealing with their scrums, we were comfortable in the line-outs; they never applied pressure aside from Grigg's try. A lot of people said afterwards that it was a poor Australian performance; it was – but that was because we forced them into playing a type of game they weren't comfortable with.

We got up their noses, and I don't really think they expected to have to contend with what we threw at them, even if they should have known better and taken into account the Munster victory over the All Blacks a few years earlier.

Derham could afford a celebration that evening and found his Australian counterparts more than willing to engage.

It was a different era. We would have been out the night before the game for a couple, or maybe a few, pints to calm the nerves; everyone did it at the time and it wasn't disadvantageous.

The night of the match was different. Once you got to the dinner, you would check out your direct opponent and see who could drink who to death. I normally lost that one badly, but we had good craic. Because it was my first cap, there was drink coming at me from all angles, and being a student, I obliged for as long as I could; the big thing was making sure we could stitch up the Munster Branch by ordering brandy and ports for the toasts – all crazy stuff and, to be honest, I can't recall much about that night!

On his Munster debut Paul Derham grounds the ball for a crucial Munster try in the opening minutes of the clash with the Wallabies.

The coach would have been more measured in his celebrations. Given the background to Munster's triumph – defeats by Cardiff and Ulster – Fergus Walsh was relieved to have been part of one of the province's greatest results of all time. Yet, speaking at that time, he diverted attention back towards the players.

Most of all, I am delighted for the guys – they were the ones that had to produce the goods on the pitch. We came into this game after losing two games, but I was still confident they would deliver; it was just a gut feeling that there was a lot more to come from them. I am really proud; they did everything required of them to beat a top-class international team, they stuck to the game plan and they took the scoring chances when they arose. I don't think there was a time during the match when I was seriously worried about the outcome. They were that accomplished on the day.

He had no argument from Australian manager Sir Nick Shehadie, a veteran of previous overseas tours with the Wallabies. 'We will just have to move on from here. Defeats happen on tour but we have time to rectify the problems that became apparent in this game. We give due credit to Munster, but now we must get the show back on the road and put this one to bed.'

Chapter 15:
1984: THE GREAT FOG

Munster v Australia
Thomond Park – 17 November 1984

Munster 19

(E. O'Sullivan, try; J. Barry, try; T. Ward,
three penalties, conversion)

Australia 31

(Farr-Jones, try; Poidevin, try; Williams, try;
Gould, five penalties, two conversions)

MUNSTER:

J. Barry (UCC), E. O'Sullivan (Garryowen), M. Kiernan (Lansdowne), J. O'Neill (Waterpark),
D. Aherne (St Mary's College), T. Ward (St Mary's College), M. Bradley (Cork Constitution),
T. Hennessy (London Irish), P. Derham (Cork Constitution), T. Mulcahy (Bohemians),
D. Lenihan (Cork Constitution) (captain), M. Moylett (Shannon), P. O'Hara (Sunday's Well),
P. Collins (Highfield), W. Sexton (Garryowen).

AUSTRALIA:

Gould, Williams, Hawker, Slack (captain), Hanley, Ella, Farr-Jones, Rodriguez,
Lawton, Burrow, Williams, Cutler, Codey, Tuynman, Poidevin.

1984: THE GREAT FOG

It was the day of the big fog, a day when a rugby game should never have been played. Those who paid their money at Thomond Park saw only half a game, because the conditions were such that only one side or end of the pitch could be seen at any given time.

The try-scoring hero of 1981, Paul Derham, was back for a second bite at the Wallabies but ended up, as he recalls, bitten by a team forewarned and forearmed.

We had a good side out, but Australia were hugely formidable; they had a huge pack, a classy backline and a huge fullback in Roger Gould, who was simply immense.

Physically, Australia were much stronger than 1981; they went for us all day, attack, attack and attack. We just never really got into the game and the crowd certainly didn't because they couldn't see the hell what was going on, so the atmosphere wasn't what you would expect, not what we expected anyway.

On that tour, Australia proved that they had come a long way in a short few years, although I suppose they were building towards it in 1981. Whereas we got in front of them a few years earlier, they never gave us a chance from the word go. Physically, they dominated us and we ended up just having to make too many tackles on the back foot. That certainly wasn't part of the plan.

It didn't help that the referee, Roger Quittenton, was a bit generous in awarding them one try, if not two of them, because there was a big doubt. I definitely got under their man who was awarded one of the tries; he didn't get the touchdown, but the score was given. Still, they ran some lovely lines, and I don't know whether there would have been a huge difference anyway because they had put us under so much pressure for much of the game.

Nick Farr-Jones attempting to evade the attention of Munster hooker Paul Derham in the fog of Thomond Park in 1984, with Donal Lenihan (left and rear) looking on.

One reason for Australia's dominance was the performance of their captain, Andrew Slack, a vital part of that successful Grand Slam Wallaby team. Derham singles him out for special mention.

You could see the important role he played in the win that day; he was well on top of things, orchestrating the assault from the middle of the field, but he also had a say in what was going on in the forwards.

I don't know how much he had to do with the difference in conditioning, but I could see, three years down the line, that this was an altogether improved Australian side from the physical point of view. It was as if they came on in leaps and bounds, while we really hadn't progressed that much. Their bodies were stronger and more toned because of the work they had obviously done in the gymnasium over a period of time. We were fit, but not really in the same category.

Slack will forever be remembered for his leadership qualities in helping the Wallabies to victory in all four Tests when they amassed a hundred points and conceded just thirty-three. His side had several ace cards, among them out-half Mark Ella – who scored a try in each of the four Tests – and David Campese. Slack, who for a time played club rugby in Dublin, captained Australia nineteen times in thirty-nine appearances between 1978 and 1987, scoring ten Test tries. He also played 133 times for Queensland.

Another admirer of Slack's was Munster captain that day, Donal Lenihan, who went on to provide immense leadership for Ireland and the Lions in the following years.

Lenihan studied Slack's technique before the game, and also had great time for the Ella brothers, especially Mark. Slack, however, was a particular favourite. 'Slack was a great captain, he was the brains behind the team and an extension of management if you like. Australia had superstars in the making, and Slack let all of them, guys like Campese who scored tries for fun, for instance, do the flashy stuff while he organised everything. He was a superb passer of the ball, a master tactician and even if he wasn't blessed with the pace of some of the rest, he was the chief organiser alongside their coach Alan Jones. Slack was ahead of his time in that he was almost like a coach on the pitch.'

Fullback Roger Gould, who was also in top form for Australia that day, was persuaded by Alan Jones to come out of exile in Argentina to help set new standards in modern attacking rugby. Jones once said of him: 'He was flawless, a freak, he just did wonderful things in this game of rugby.'

Lenihan is inclined to agree, referring back to Gould's display on that foggy Thomond Park day. 'If it wasn't so serious at the time, it would have been funny. In my capacity as captain, I had to make a speech at the dinner that night and I noted that Gould had coped with everything – all the high balls included – admirably and punished us in response. I reckoned that he was actually so good, had we kicked the ball out over the wall, Gould would have been out on the road waiting to collect it! If that wasn't bad enough, he also kicked penalties even when it must have been almost impossible to see the target; he was simply amazing.'

But Gould was not the only reason Munster lost. Lenihan attributes some of the blame to English referee Roger Quittenton, who warned him before the match: 'I'm going to referee the line-outs today.'

That, admitted Lenihan, was bad news for Munster, because a week before, at Lansdowne Road, the Cork Constitution man had helped deny Australia the prolific possession they expected to gain through their huge second-row combination of 6 foot 8 inch Steve Williams and 6 foot 10 inch giant Steve Cutler.

Lenihan was a fairly imposing figure by any stretch of the imagination, but against these two, with different rules and regulations pertaining in the line-outs, he was short.

In the Test match, we [he and Willie Anderson] did what we had to do to secure possession, and we were relatively successful. Australia won the game but it was close enough and they certainly didn't have things their own way.

In the build-up to the Munster game, they [Australia] spent a lot of time complaining, and there is no doubt that it had an effect on the referee. Remember, back then, touring teams had a say in the appointment of match officials, and Quittenton let me know in no uncertain terms that we would have to watch our step. He was as good as his word; in fact he blew us off the park at every opportunity.

But Lenihan admits there were other, more important, factors in Munster's demise.

On a day when communication was near impossible – remember, the fog was so thick that we couldn't see where our fullback or far wings were standing when we set up line-outs or scrums – Australia would have had an advantage of sorts given that they were together for a long number of weeks.

We only got together the day before the match, played a bit of pitch and putt in Ennis and then went out to take on a touring side that had been training together day after day. It was what it was in those days, but it didn't make it easy, particularly when you didn't have a clue where half your team was positioned at any given time.

It was the weirdest game I ever played in. I played in three inches of mud, lashing rain on pitches like an aqua park, in the freezing cold and rock-hard surfaces, but I never played in a game when I couldn't see half the guys I was playing with, not to mind the guys I was playing against!

Another contributory factor, believes Lenihan, was the lack of influence of the Munster supporters.

We had a good young side that was really up for the challenge, but met with a very highly motivated Australian side on top of their form. Added to that was the fact that, because of the fog, the crowd couldn't get into the game as they normally would at Thomond Park.

The 1981 game in Cork wasn't the greatest of matches, but we managed to put Australia under pressure from the start and the supporters went ballistic.

| *Mick Moylett (wearing number 4) contests a line-out during the foggy game at Thomond Park.*

CHAPTER 16

1989: BUCK'S BLACKS ON SONG

Terry Kingston would have his day in the sun, but when New Zealand came to Munster for the first time in eleven years there was only going to be one outcome – and that was not, unfortunately, a home victory.

The All Blacks insisted, for instance, that the game take place on a Saturday, one week before the Test game with Ireland at Lansdowne Road; that gave them the opportunity to field the bulk of what they regarded as their top team.

The household names slip easily off the tongue: John Gallagher, Joe Stanley, Terry Wright, Grant Fox, Sean Fitzpatrick, Richard Loe, Murray Pierce, Mike Brewer, Zinzan Brooke and, of course, Wayne Shelford, the captain.

Shelford was a traditionalist but also a rebel; he is credited with bringing the new style of the traditional All Blacks 'Ka Mate' haka into prominence, yet he was one of the twenty-eight players who held up two fingers to the New Zealand rugby authorities when he joined the infamous Cavaliers tour to South Africa in 1986.

Despite threats of sanction, the NZRU was forced to bury the hatchet because so many of the top players actually participated in that tour; Shelford, like many others, survived and went on to make his Test debut against France in a 19–7 victory in Toulouse later that year.

He was a notable victim of the infamous 'Battle of Nantes' in the second Test. Roughly twenty minutes into the match, he was caught at the bottom of what observers described as a rather aggressive ruck, and an errant French boot found its way into Shelford's groin, somehow ripping his scrotum and leaving one testicle hanging free. He also lost four teeth in a secondary but simultaneous incident. Incredibly, after discovering the injury to his scrotum, he calmly asked the physiotherapist to stitch up the tear and returned to the field before a blow to his head left him concussed. He was substituted and watched the remainder of the game from the stand where he witnessed the All Blacks lose 16–3. Shelford has no memory of the game, which is probably just as well.

The 'down-under' injury alone would leave most men screaming in agony and heading for the nearest hospital. But not Shelford. The French public were aghast as an overeager pitchside cameraman filmed the stomach-turning surgery, and even more so when Shelford returned to the field and carried on playing.

'I was knocked out cold,' the number 8 recalled, 'lost a few teeth and had a few stitches down below. It's a game I still can't remember – I have no memory of it whatsoever. I had to watch a video to realise what the game was actually like. I don't even remember what the score was, I don't really want to either.'

It was the only time Shelford was on the losing side during his distinguished international career, a result which he appropriately describes as a 'faux pas'.

In 1987, the first Rugby World Cup was held in New Zealand. Shelford played in five of the six All Blacks games and was a member of the team that won the final against France 29–9. He took over as captain after the World Cup, first leading the side during the 1987 tour of Japan and, during that

John Fitzgerald scores for Ireland against Scotland. Fitzgerald was loose-head prop in the 1989 encounter with the All Blacks.

Graeme Bachop of New Zealand gets the ball away for the All Blacks with (l–r) Ken O'Connell, Peter Clohessy, Mick Galwey and Donal Lenihan about to challenge.

captaincy from 1987 to 1990, the All Blacks did not lose a game, only drawing once against Australia – in 1988.

In 1990, Shelford was controversially dropped after the Test series against Scotland, prompting furious protests among the general public, especially after the All Blacks lost the third Test of their next series against Australia to end a seventeen-Test winning streak and forty-nine matches in total. For a long time, fans appeared at games with signs saying 'Bring Back Buck'; even today, it is not unusual to see such signs appear from time to time at rugby matches in New Zealand, lest anyone forgets the name of Buck Shelford.

Given his charismatic leadership and the rich quality that was evident right throughout the New Zealand team, it was little wonder that Munster were on a hiding to nothing.

Add Munster's enthusiastic flank forward Ken O'Connell to that mix. The Sunday's Well man thrived on the physical side of rugby, from the time he lined out with Presentation Brothers College Cork through to a memorable Irish Schools tour of Australia and then on to Munster and beyond.

The passionate O'Connell went on to win two caps for Ireland, the first against France in Paris and the second as international rugby's first blood replacement against England at Twickenham, in 1993. Like so many Irish back row forwards before him, O'Connell was cursed to have to earn his first cap

Zinzan Brooke, the New Zealand back row forward, trains in Cork prior to the 1989 game with Munster. Brooke was a keen fan of Gaelic games and played football for Auckland in a Pacific tournament on two occasions after being introduced to it by All Black Irish passport holder Bernie McCahill.

Michael Bradley gets the ball away safely despite the attentions of All Black skipper Wayne Shelford in the 1989 encounter. Shelford and Ken O'Connell (on his left) had a big struggle for supremacy that day, with World Cup winner Shelford winning by a 'knock-out'. In the background are (l–r): John Fitzgerald, Donal Lenihan and Terry Kingston.

in Paris. Like so many Irish teams in that particular era, the result was not favourable as France cut loose to record a 30–15 victory. He was one of just two players (along with Vinny Cunningham) to pay for that loss.

The high point of O'Connell's short career was his brief participation in Ireland's sensational 13–12 victory at Twickenham five weeks later; otherwise, he had to satisfy himself with a longer spell in the red of Munster and then, in the professional era, a few seasons with both London Irish and Castres alongside one of his best friends, Irish and Lions second row, Jeremy Davidson.

The pinnacle of his Munster career at a time when visiting overseas tours had become a rarity was that 1989 game. O'Connell decided to throw down the gauntlet by squaring up in his own inimitable fashion to the haka. He also spent much of the game doing his level best – with a degree of success – to upset the New Zealanders, and in particular Shelford. Years on, he has no regrets, but does concede it probably was a mistake from a health and safety point of view!

While the All Blacks were doing the haka, we linked arms and moved slowly forward but for some reason I became detached and ended up three or four feet away from Shelford. I was glaring at him and he was glaring back, but when I looked left, and looked right, there was nobody to support me until somebody dragged me out of the zone that I found myself in. I think something like that happened in the Test game a week later when Willie Anderson faced them down, but wasn't on his own like me.

I think as far as I was concerned, that set the tone for the day. We were fairly confident we could win the match, and we knew we would have to get physical with them if we were to have any chance of doing that. That was my style of play, and I really was hyped up. There was a huge crowd, some of them housed in a temporary stand that probably would be condemned by the health and safety people nowadays, and the buzz was electric.

I remember that our team secretary Ralph Murphy also presented us with Munster blazers before the match, and for me that set the adrenalin racing because we never really got anything decent from the branch before that, except maybe the loan of tracksuits; yes, the tracksuits had to be returned after use. Can you believe that? But the fact that they went to the trouble of giving us blazers did highlight how important the occasion was in Munster rugby history, and it certainly had a beneficial effect on me. Funny, isn't it, how you remember small gestures like that?

In the heat of battle, there were no goodwill gestures from Shelford, who had his fill of O'Connell long before the end. In the last quarter, having ignored warnings from the All Blacks captain, O'Connell was put out of the match with an elbow to the back of the head.

Looking back, O'Connell can laugh. 'I was giving it everything all day, going at him, in his face and, in fairness, he warned me twice that he was getting rightly pissed off. In a sense, he paid me the finest compliment by taking me out of the game – and he did take me out, no doubt.'

But O'Connell did have some happier memories of the match, insisting that Munster were not as outplayed as the 31–9 scoreline suggests. 'I thought we faced up to them pretty well, but it should be remembered that they put out a full top-class international side against us. They were world champions at the time, and it showed in the way they played; they were just so composed, so skilled.'

Among that group was an English-born Irish-qualified fullback by the name of John Gallagher, a young man who had, two years earlier, helped New Zealand to victory in the first Rugby World Cup with a series of spectacular displays.

The title of Gallagher's autobiography is *The World's Best Rugby Player*? (Harrogate, 1991), but that might be fanciful given the brevity of his career. Yet, during the late 1980s, Gallagher was rated as the most talented, certainly the most effective, fullback in world rugby. He could have played for England or Ireland, and during his visit to Ireland he took great delight in visiting his grandmother in Limerick and in highlighting his strong Irish ancestry.

Munster centre Charlie Murphy safely gets the touch over his own line to give his side a 22 dropout, with Pat O'Hara (second from right) and captain Paul Collins in the defensive zone just to be sure.

Jim Galvin dips to try to get past New Zealand's Terry Wright. It was not a good day for Munster, but Galvin would return to Musgrave Park three years later and boot his side to victory over the Wallabies.

Within a short time of moving to New Zealand, where he joined the police, he had been picked up by Wellington and quickly worked his way into the All Blacks camp. He was absolutely brilliant in the 1987 World Cup and scored four tries in the 71–15 rout of Fiji in the pool stages of the competition.

Gallagher ended the decade with a remarkable march through Wales and Ireland, but shortly after New Zealand were beaten in the final of the Hong Kong Sevens by Fiji, he decided to move on. He signed for English rugby league side Leeds, who were looking for a world-class star to revive their fortunes. It was a move that did not work for either party and it was not helpful either to the All Blacks, who struggled to find an adequate successor. Matthew Ridge, regarded as Gallagher's heir apparent, also moved to rugby league and New Zealand experimented with three fullbacks during that 1991 World Cup campaign – which ended in an ignominious defeat to eventual winners Australia in the semi-final.

In 1989, however, Gallagher was still on top of the rugby union world, and New Zealand had no doubt that, were it a Grand Slam tour, they would have emerged with a 100 per cent record. Eventually in that Musgrave Park encounter, not even the best efforts of Donal Lenihan, Mick Galwey, Paul Collins, Ken O'Connell, Ralph Keyes, Mick Bradley, Peter Clohessy et al. was enough, as the All Blacks did what the All Blacks do best – turn pressure into chances and turn chances into scores to pull away from a dogged, competitive Munster.

Chapter 17:
1992: CHAMPIONS BITE THE DUST

Munster v Australia

Musgrave Park – 21 October 1992

Munster 22

(Penalty try; C. Haly, conversion,
four penalties; J. Galvin, drop goal)

Australia 19

(T. Kelaher, try, conversion, four penalties)

MUNSTER:

C. Haly (Cork Constitution), R. Wallace (Garryowen), P. Danaher (Garryowen),
B. Walsh (Cork Constitution), J. Clarke (Dolphin), D. Larkin (Garryowen), D. Tobin (Young Munster),
P. McCarthy (Cork Constitution), T. Kingston (Dolphin) (captain), P. Clohessy (Young Munster),
R. Costello (Garryowen), M. Galwey (Shannon), G. Clohessy (Young Munster),
B. Cronin (Garryowen), G. Earls (Young Munster).
Replacements: J. Galvin (Shannon) for Larkin, E. O'Sullivan (Old Crescent) for Costello.

AUSTRALIA:

Kelaher, Smith, Herbert, Tombs, Junee, Kahl, Ekert, Lilicrap, Nucifora (captain),
Crowley, Waugh, Morgan, Brial, Scott-Young, Coker.
Replacement: McKenzie for Crowley.

1992: CHAMPIONS BITE THE DUST

For Terry Kingston, there was a lot more riding on this match than just helping Munster to win. It was to be a personal challenge such as he had never experienced in his career, and an opportunity to repay the faith shown in him by the provincial selectors.

Kingston was pleasantly surprised to be named as captain, just a few days after being excluded from the Irish panel. Greystones and Leinster hooker John Murphy was given the international number 2 shirt to play Australia, while Keith Wood, reserve to Kingston with Munster, was chosen as backup. 'I'm sure the [Munster] selectors must have felt under pressure when they sat down to choose the team; they might have gone along the lines of the national selectors and maybe even dropped me for Woodie, but thankfully they decided to place their faith in me.'

Kingston does not mind being described by some of his colleagues as a 'boot, bullock and bite' type motivator, but if he was inclined to get somewhat excited in the build-up, he fully realised that matches were not won on emotion alone.

I was always proud to wear the Munster jersey and well aware of some of the great names that had gone before us. We all recognised that success at domestic level didn't come easy, but the whole history of Munster playing against touring sides is something that cannot be understated.

Sure, I would have used details of that proud history as a big motivating factor; I would have stressed to the players that the heroes of the 1978 win over New Zealand were, before that match, pretty much like us, not very well known and certainly not famous. Here we were, ordinary guys, pitting ourselves against one of the top teams in the world, giving ourselves a chance to achieve something huge. I was going to use any motivating tool I could to whip them up.

On a calmer level, Kingston believed in the team's ability.

There was a really good blend of experience and youthful talent. I could never quite put my finger on why I believed that we would beat Australia, but I was convinced it was possible. Of course, I was realistic enough to know that it would be very difficult, but as the match unfolded I became more and more certain that we would win.

We went out with a relatively simple game plan; we played to our strengths and we kept mistakes down to a minimum. We didn't have a great first quarter and they appeared to pick off scores at will. Then, for some reason, they seemed to get nervous; we sensed that they were taking a lot more time than was necessary at line-outs, that their scrum was creaking a bit and that the body language between the players just wasn't quite right.

We sensed it and we did something about it by attacking them with everything we had. We attacked their line-out, we attacked their scrum and we struck a killer blow when they were forced to collapse a scrum to concede a penalty try. We knew we were in with a right chance then.

In relation to the scrum, Munster had a pre-match plan not to allow any engagement unless the body positions were perfect. If any of the Munster pack found themselves in an uncomfortable position, the plan, says Kingston, was to go to ground shouting *'síos'* or *'ar an talamh'*. 'Basically it was an attempt to keep them guessing and, by saying it in Irish, they shouldn't have had a clue what the hell we were talking about!'

The Munster team that defeated Australia at Musgrave Park in 1992. Back row (l–r): G. Clohessy, B. Cronin, R. Costelloe, M. Galwey, G. Earls, R. Wallace, P. McCarthy, P. Clohessy; front row (l–r): J. Clarke, B. Walsh, C. Haly, C. Downes (Munster Branch President), T. Kingston (captain), D. Larkin, D. Tobin, P. Danaher.

Dismay on the faces of Australian players after Munster were awarded a penalty try in the 1992 Musgrave Park clash. Munster captain Terry Kingston (clenched fist) leads the celebrations along with Mick Galwey (third from left), Peter Clohessy (kneeling), Paul McCarthy (third from right) and Richard Costello (second from right).

Kingston explained that it worked like a dream on two or three occasions during the match. 'We just didn't want to be caught in a position where they could push us back or turn us. On one occasion, however, Peter Clohessy shouted *'ag sugrath'* and there was no reaction as Australia got the shove on and disrupted our scrum. We asked him afterwards what he had been on about and he said, "Ah, for f**k sake lads, I forgot the Irish for going to ground" and berated us accordingly for not picking up on his new couple of Irish words!'

Clohessy was about to embark on a memorable, albeit at times controversial, career, and Kingston describes him as one of the most durable prop forwards he has ever packed down with.

Let's put it this way, I'd prefer to be on his side than opposite him, but I think Paul McCarthy also deserves huge credit for his display that day. In much the same way as the selectors made a big call in naming me as captain, they showed bottle by picking Paul above John Fitzgerald, who had been a fixture on the Munster team for so long at that stage. It was rough justice on Paco [Fitzgerald], of course, but Macker [McCarthy] had a great game.

It was a very strong Munster pack, with Mick Galwey and Richard Costello combining very well in the second row. They gave as good, if not better, than they got from the Wallabies. It was an unheralded back-row combination in a sense; but the trio did brilliantly. Ben Cronin was the classy footballer of the trio, but Ger Clohessy was the guy you would want to have going forward with ball in hand and ready to die for the team, while Ger Earls was totally underestimated. He had pace, aggression and really did a huge job for us in securing possession when the ball went to ground.

The old saying about rugby that forwards decide which team wins the match and the backs decide by how much is pretty true even to this day. It was close, but on this occasion the backs did make a huge contribution to a pretty tight match. One of them even got the winner!

Stand Up (or fall down) and Fight: confrontation between Munster and Australia. Garrick Morgan (Australia) and Michael Galwey were both sent off, but received a mere five days' suspension.

Derek Tobin gets possession to the backline, watched by Munster players Ben Cronin (third from left), Ger Earls (sixth from left) and Richard Costello (seventh from left), both on the ground, and Mick Galwey (far right).

Kingston pays huge tribute to the centre partnership of Brian Walsh and Philip Danaher, the latter of whom captained Ireland on a near productive (they lost the first Test in controversial circumstances 21–24), but ultimately ill-fated Irish trip to New Zealand that summer. 'God, they were two fine players, Danaher so strong in attack and defence. Brian had a different style; he was surely underrated, maybe he underrated himself, because he ran like a guy that was never going to get into top speed. But he had that gliding, relaxed, motion of running that was frustrating and difficult for opponents to deal with. Then, at fullback, it didn't harm us that Charlie Haly kicked every chance he got, if my memory serves me correctly.'

In the absence of another recognised goal-kicker, Haly was entrusted with the duties by coach Garrett Fitzgerald. On the day, it proved an inspired decision. Haly had successfully kicked for Oxford University in the English varsity match some time before that, and he was not in the least bit fazed by the request from the coach. There was just one occasion near the end of the game, he explains, when he felt the full weight of that duty.

We were trailing by three points late in the game and we got a penalty to bring it back to 19–19. Suddenly I was engulfed by Ger Clohessy, who started shaking me furiously as if to celebrate a score before it even came. I didn't know what he was at; then all of a sudden, Terry Kingston lunged at Ger, clattered him on the shoulder and told him to f**k off away from me.

To be honest, at the time I was a bit confused as to whether Ger was encouraging or threatening me. Either way, I knew I couldn't miss the opportunity and I was relieved to see it sail over for the equalising points.

A short time later, Haly was being chaired off the pitch by strangers; seconds before, Jim Galvin had taken the game by the scruff of the neck with a magnificent drop goal from a difficult position to send Munster supporters into orbit.

Galvin, says Haly, was a fantastic player who was grossly underestimated.

I suppose he was fortunate to be in the team, as it transpired. If memory serves me correctly, George O'Sullivan would likely have been on the bench but for an injury and Jim was called in. Still, he wasn't entering the unknown – he played for Munster [on the wing] against the All Blacks in 1989 and was a hugely experienced and influential player at club level over a number of seasons. He was a great guy to get the backline going and could fire out long, accurate passes. On top of that, he was always looking to engineer a drop goal opportunity and was pretty successful at scoring them.

He came on when Dan Larkin got injured. Dan was a very talented player too, but more of a fullback or centre than out-half, and the arrival of Jim gave the back division a more threatening look about it; certainly, Brian Walsh and Philip Danaher made a lot of ground up the middle of the pitch after Jim came on. It was a small thing in that they didn't score any tries, but it was an important

Derek Tobin finds a long distance touch with Mick Galwey (third from left) looking on approvingly.

aspect because it gave us a bit more go-forward ball and momentum to keep piling the pressure on Australia.

Haly remembers the drop goal well. 'I've replayed it over and over again in my mind. Ben Cronin won a great line-out, knocked it down to Derek Tobin and his long, flat pass found Jim in space. The rest is history, a perfect drop goal, a perfect execution. It was unbelievable; they didn't even get time to kick off and they couldn't believe it was all over. Some of us threw ourselves on the ground; others ran around mindlessly screaming like excited children. It was amazing.'

Professionalism might have been just around the corner, but that 1992 team got little or nothing out of this game other than the brief adulation they enjoyed from the public. 'It was a different time, for sure, and I think we did get a commemorative tie but that was about it,' said Haly. But he adds that the players were quite happy to make do with the excitement of the day, a few drinks (a good few) and a meal afterwards.

It was a case of enjoying a job well done. Terry [Kingston] was immense in that game; he was a brilliant captain that pushed all the right buttons. Terry was basically a captain that motivated through his voice; he was always quick to let you know what was required, how you had to live up to the tradition of the Munster jersey.

Garrett Fitzgerald [coach] was calmer but got his views across in a very sound, calculated way. We all had great time for Garrett and we got the feeling that he was one of the few coaches of his time who was able to get the team he actually wanted to have on the pitch. He was very firm in his dealings with Munster officials, arguing that the team had to be put first at all times. He got his point across on a trip to London before that game when some officials wanted to go straight to the hotel from the airport. Garrett insisted, with darkness closing in, that the team would train first, and that the alickadoos would have to wait to partake of the hotel facilities until he was good and ready.

I'm sure he had a big input into selection at a time when there really was a lack of trust in some of the selectors, in what their motivation was. In those days you just never knew what agenda they were working off, but Garrett talked to the players and took their views on board. You knew where you stood with him, and that was great because it was so rare back then.

Haly was incensed that Australian coach Bob Dwyer attempted to demean the Munster achievement by blaming the home side for the violent incidents that threatened to ruin the game.

Let's put it this way, we didn't go out to start trouble but we met it when it happened. I make no secret of the fact that we went for their flanker, Sam Scott-Young, but that was after he clothes-lined Dan Larkin and was involved in other incidents. A couple of others had been well out of order in the early stages of the match and it was only natural that there would be a reaction from us.

Ironically, Michael Galwey and Garrick Morgan, the respective second rows, were sent off for their role in a brawl, but that was really only handbag stuff and didn't merit the action taken by the referee. I suppose he had to show a firm hand and they were the two unlucky guys to get sent. Afterwards, I think they got a suspension of just four days, which tells its own story. Still, there were one or two of the Australian team that were lucky to escape more serious attention.

Haly could understand Dwyer's motives, but was not in the least bit sympathetic.

Look, he was a top coach at the time, his team lost the match and we were the first team to beat Australia after the World Cup win of 1991; we were the first team to sink his battleship, so it was no wonder he wasn't pleased. It was obvious that he would try to lay the blame on someone else and deflect criticism away from himself and his team. Given all the circumstances of the game, the way the scores arrived, the way they played and the way we played, I have no doubt that we were well worth the win; it wasn't luck, bad luck or good luck, it was just one team being beaten by a better team.

Although Munster may have had reason for giving one or two Australians a frosty reception at the after-match dinner, Haly recalls a pleasant evening during which the touring players appeared to accept defeat more graciously than their coach. 'It was still an amateur game in 1992 and I suppose things were tolerated then that wouldn't be tolerated now. I remember being caught in rucks early on in the game and I got kicked in the back and punched in the head even when I wasn't remotely near the ball. But, hey, I survived, and like everyone back then we sought out players from the opposing side and sat down to drink pints with them. It was the done thing; most of the on-field stuff was completely forgotten afterwards. I suppose it's easier to forget things when you win!'

Following an already drama-filled afternoon, Haly was to experience another incident in the early hours of the morning when leaving a nightclub with his then girlfriend – now wife – Eileen. He admits to having experienced a 'speed wobble' before stumbling out through a door and landing on the ground near a Garda car. One of the guards instantly recognised him, engaged him in conversion about the game and offered to transport the couple home, courtesy of the state. 'We were just sat in the car when most of the remainder of the guys emerged and figured I was being taken away for some wrong-doing. The car took off and, as a joke, the driver put on the flashing lights as he made his way up the street, much to the amusement of some and the horror of some other players. It wasn't a bad way to finish a great day.'

The final words on that great day go, fittingly, to Kingston, who refutes the serious allegations of foul and dirty play made by Wallaby coach Dwyer.

We could discuss this forever. No doubt there were incidents, I'm sure, of which neither side will be proud, but Dwyer got it wrong; he got it wrong in blaming Peter Clohessy for the cut sustained by Dan Crowley, and he got it wrong in his allegations of illegal scrummaging against Peter because we had the Australian front row in all sorts of trouble for most of the afternoon.

It wasn't the nicest of games to be involved in because things did happen off the ball, but they started it for sure. I remember being warned by Tom Kiernan that I would be asked some awkward questions after the game and I kind of thought, what's going on here? I didn't know anything about the Bob Dwyer rant until then. Nobody, from our side at any rate, went out to hurt any member of the opposition; there were some incidents, but they were responsorial maybe. So, OK, I went to meet the press, said that the referee had been there, had made his decisions based on what he saw and that was the end of the matter from my point of view.

Maybe it was all about Australia being beaten by a better side on the day. Maybe it was about Australia, or some of the party, not accepting that such was the case. As far as I'm concerned, we won the game and we won it fair and square, and we won it by playing some pretty tidy football.

Charlie Haly accepts the acclaim of the crowd as he tries to make his way off the pitch. Behind him, and directly in front of the partially shielded Ger Clohessy, is former Munster fullback Ray Hennessy who played in the 3–3 draw with Australia in 1958 and on the same ground in 1960 when South Africa beat Munster 9–3 with two late tries. Hennessy was regarded as, arguably, the best player never to be capped for Ireland.

PART 2

Chapter 18:
THE TURNING

THE TURNING

G arrett Fitzgerald had the distinction of being the last Munster coach to mastermind victory over a touring side in the amateur or professional era; the fact that it was Australia, the reigning world champions, made it extra special.

A quality front-row forward in his day, Fitzgerald was a pragmatic coach who only asked that his players do their best. He worked in the financial sector most of his life; back in 1992 he had no notion of giving it up for a full-time role in rugby, but after Terry Kingston led Munster to yet another triumph over a touring side, things were to change.

The face of rugby union changed forever after the 1995 World Cup, and Fitzgerald's relationship with the game would also change a few years later. Ireland embraced professionalism more out of necessity than desire and the IRFU moved slowly; while players were being paid, the game was, for all intents and purposes, still run by amateurs.

It was 1999 when Munster finally advertised for a chief executive. Fitzgerald applied for the position even though he was not quite sure what was involved. In fact, he hoped it would not be too demanding. While he knew it would be different from anything he had experienced in the workplace up to then, he figured he would have plenty of spare time to reduce his golf handicap out of the rugby season!

On that front he was disappointed, and he readily admits today that his golf clubs remained locked in a cupboard for two years afterwards as he found himself immersed in what he terms as 'fire brigade action'. 'It was all quite hectic; I didn't know the difference between the staff in the IRFU, the ERC [European Rugby Cup], Heineken, et al., as everything started taking off at 100 miles an hour. I was appointed in December of that year and Munster got to the final of the Heineken Cup in May. There was only one other full-time staff, John Coleman, who was branch administrator, and there was a part-time receptionist. We had to look at everything from sponsorship, to the size of jerseys, to lining the pitch.'

That first season was chaotic as the Munster machine gathered momentum; Fitzgerald suggests that Northampton, whom Munster met in the Heineken Cup final of 2000, were the ultimate beneficiaries of the Irish province trying to come to grips with new circumstances. 'I think it's fair to say we were – everyone – all over the shop that particular weekend; the sheer size of the event and everything that was going on around was something we had never experienced before. I think that even the players had exhausted themselves before they ever got to play in the final. I was on the outside, but I could see it happening; it was taking a lot out of people, management, players, everyone was trying to do the right thing and consider the right thing that would have to be done if Munster won the title.'

If that was a learning process, Munster certainly took note and the last decade has been hugely exciting for Fitzgerald and his ever growing team of employees. Munster is now much more than a cottage industry – it is big business. But the chief executive has feet firmly on the ground, explaining it is a business that must be worked at 24/7.

We have focused exceptionally well on the whole commercial and sponsorship thing; our success to date has been assisted by the fact that we have been successful on the field.

When people talk about marketing and strategies, the basic template is all-important; the best marketing strategy for Munster is how the team performs on the weekend between the four white lines on the pitch. You can spend a fortune, but if your team isn't performing then people won't support you. We are living in a society where people want to see winners if at all possible, but at least they want the people playing to the maximum of their ability.

We have been lucky enough to have a group of players that, 99 per cent of the time, whether they win or lose, will give the full 100 per cent; that's what the people respect, the players have worked hard at it and we have worked hard to develop facilities for the comfort of our supporters with the provision of facilities that make them proud of what has been achieved on the pitch.

The development of Thomond Park would not have been possible were it not for the success of the team; that has given us the ability to attract bigger crowds and take advantage of more commercial opportunities. The development of Musgrave Park will follow.

The future, he believes, is bright, even though competition will come from both within and outside. It is, admitted, Fitzgerald, getting tougher. But many things have improved, with overseas agents, for example, now recognising that Ireland is a place for the top players to be. But Munster will never go in search of riches from abroad, insists Fitzgerald, emphasising that the province remains firmly of the view that homegrown talent is best. Still, he accepts that at times the team needs to be strengthened, in which case the plan is always to choose players who buy into the Munster concept of how rugby should be lived. Munster, he says, have benefited from the signatures over the years of players such as John Langford, Jim Williams, Christian Cullen and Doug Howlett.

Munster CEO Garrett Fitzgerald.

Garrett Fitzgerald endorsed the Munster policy to buy quality rather than quantity when looking at overseas players. An example is former New Zealand legend Doug Howlett, seen here driving for the line in a Heineken Cup clash with Clermont Auvergne in 2009.

We signed good-quality players, and that is the way we want to continue. You would only have to go back six or seven years to notice the difference; players from the southern hemisphere certainly weren't looking at the option of joining Munster, but now they are. We're recognised as being one of the top three clubs this side of the world for a variety of reasons, including the work ethic, a success rate and the fact that the system allows for a very good support mechanism for the players.

Overseas players coming to Munster get paid a top-market rate; the level of coaching and conditioning is as good as you will get anywhere in the world, medical facilities are probably better than anywhere in Europe and the players don't have to play as many matches as they would, for instance, in France. Everything, apart maybe from the weather, is a bonus.

Fitzgerald and Munster know a lot about that word, having started out well over a decade ago on a wing and a prayer. Defeats were hard to take – some particularly hard – but that made victory all the more special. Along the way, Munster built up a solid fan base of which every club in Europe is now in awe. The hard days have made Munster more humble; those occasions have made it easier for them to accept the bad and enjoy the good.

The story of the modern Munster will unfold in the following pages.

Munster make no secret of aspiring to greatness on a continuous basis. Paul O'Connell is a prime example of the hard work ethic employed by the players. He is seen here reaching for the stars in another way, in Des Barry's marvellous study of line-out play.

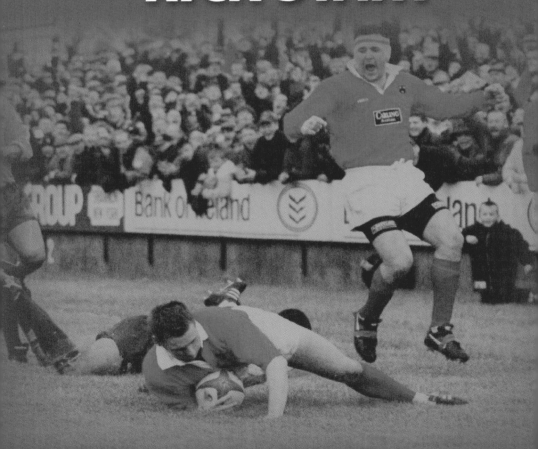

Chapter 19:
1995/6: THE KICK-START

1995/6: THE KICK-START

Munster's opening European Cup game, on 1 November 1995, ended in triumph against Swansea at Thomond Park, but they needed a late try from captain Pat Murray to secure a 17–13 victory.

Munster were coming off an eight-match unbeaten run, including two victories on a short tour of Italy, but displayed little of the form that had contributed to that sparkling record. Swansea led 13–10 when Murray struck in the seventy-ninth minute and Kenny Smith's conversion gave them the insurance points as Swansea launched a furious late assault.

A crowd of more than 6,000 were disappointed by the low-quality rugby on view, in a game marked by an equally poor display from English referee Ed Morrison. Complaints were plentiful; Swansea argued that Munster's opening try should not have been awarded after Mr Morrison had been flattened in the lead-up following a collision with Munster prop John Fitzgerald. Munster argued vociferously throughout that Swansea had taken great liberty with the offside laws.

Munster, had they lost, would only have had themselves to blame; although leading 7–6 at the break, they failed to make the most of the wind advantage in the second half. Instead, Swansea jumped into that 13–10 lead and defended it comfortably through most of the last quarter, until Munster finally pieced together a move of some quality.

Anthony Foley, Peter Clohessy and Paul Burke were all involved in the build-up that led to Pat Murray slipping in for the match-winning try, thundering into the line as he broke a tackle to get through at the posts.

Murray recalls that it was Munster's only real opportunity in the game. 'Their defensive line was very hard to break down; they spread right across the pitch, so we decided to try to attack them in a more direct manner. I don't think they expected it. I happened to be in the right place at the right time,

It was a great relief to score because we found, I think, the pace a lot faster than anything we had been used to in the past. It was certainly a step above the Interprovincial Championship, no doubt.'

Murray's views were echoed by coach Jerry Holland. 'We looked tired in the second half; Swansea's fitness was superior and nearly told. We didn't win enough primary possession and didn't adapt to the referee. The experience will do us no harm, though; we will have to learn to be more patient,'

Swansea led through an Aled Williams penalty before Richard Wallace got an opening try that Smith converted. Williams narrowed the gap with a penalty in first-half injury time before Smith kicked a penalty ahead of Alan Harris grabbing a Swansea try, converted by Williams. But it was last draw to Munster, to Murray and to Smith, who combined to produce the seven points needed to start a first ever European campaign with the requisite victory.

One week later, Munster left Ireland for a trip into the unknown. The team based themselves in Toulouse – whose home team in those days were the aristocrats of French rugby – as they prepared to meet Castres, located some sixty miles away.

They had a two-hour coach trip for the midweek evening match. The game had to be moved from Castres' own stadium to a soccer stadium in a nearby town called Mazamet because the club's home ground did not have floodlights.

Myself, Edmund van Esbeck of *The Irish Times* and Len Dinneen of Limerick radio fame, accompanied by a handful of supporters, made the journey with the official party from Ireland. Those supporters were joined by maybe a dozen more who turned up from various parts of France to experience the most hostile reception one could have imagined.

It certainly was a new experience to have local supporters hammering on the glass window of an indoor press facility, spitting fire and brimstone when anything went wrong for the local team and right for Munster. The players had to endure similar conditions on the pitch, and ultimately they were horribly unlucky to controversially lose the match deep into injury time, thereby making an early exit from the tournament.

Having had to cope with some poor refereeing decisions in Thomond Park the week before, a bad call by Welsh referee David Davies provided Castres with the opportunity to seal victory eight minutes into injury time. A draw would have been enough for Munster to march on to the semi-finals, but all they could do was hang their heads in disbelief at the end of an energy-sapping battle.

Munster looked to have survived a late Castres offensive when the home side knocked on. However, Mr Davies allowed Munster flanker David Corkery to come away with the ball. Corkery's break out of defence brought him just a few yards before losing possession; Castres launched another offensive after

Pat Murray, who captained Munster into the inaugural European campaign in the 1995/6 season.

which centre Nicolas Combes scored a try that Laurent Labit converted to secure the win.

However, Munster proved themselves worthy participants against the second-best club side in France at the time. Gabriel Fulcher and Paul O'Connor, then with Lansdowne, were in the second row that evening, and provided the visitors with a steady stream of possession, ably assisted by Mick Galwey, who lined out alongside Anthony Foley and David Corkery in the back row.

Killian Keane, one of the unsung heroes of the Munster team for a number of seasons in the early part of the professional era right up to the European Cup final in 2002, scores against Australia in 1996, the try celebrated by Anthony Foley and David Corkery (far right).

Munster shocked Castres with the intensity of an early challenge and Kenny Smith kicked three penalties before Labit did likewise to leave the teams level at the break. The goal kickers had one apiece in the second half and the game was heading for an honourable draw when disaster struck.

Pat Murray had been a stalwart of Munster rugby for a few seasons up to that point. In the amateur era, he was a bank official with TSB, and still holds a senior position with Permanent TSB today. In the aftermath of the 1995 World Cup, and in the race to establish a professional rugby structure, Irish rugby had reacted slowly. A number of players were signed as professionals but, Murray points out, they were still amateur in everything but name.

The only difference was, he said, the fact that they had to train on a regular basis rather than holding down a day job. He was one of the day-job brigade, and for his trouble was paid IR£400 appearance money for domestic competitive games and £600 for each of the two European Cup games. That year, Munster also took on the Exiles as part of the Interprovincial Championship, so Murray earned the sum total of £2,800. The money was welcome, but being allowed to keep the Munster jersey at the end of the season was more important.

He recalls playing against Transvaal in a friendly at Musgrave Park on 2 December 1995, and was seated next to visiting captain Kobus Wiese at the top table. The discussion eventually moved on to money and Wiese revealed that he was earning something in the region of €25,000 with Transvaal and a similar amount when playing for the Springboks. Wiese asked Murray how much he was being paid and nearly choked on his food when the Munster captain responded, 'For this game, I'll be lucky to be allowed keep the jersey.' 'In a sense,' says Murray, 'that's how far behind the South Africans we were, even though some of our team on either national or provincial contracts were earning a wage. He couldn't believe that there could have been a part-timer chosen as captain.'

It was not the only eye-opening experience for Murray that season. After Munster had set down an all-important marker at Thomond Park by beating Swansea, the atmosphere at the subsequent Castres game was a first.

After beating Swansea, we knew we were really in a knockout situation even though the round-robin series of games was played on a league basis. We knew there would be a place in the semi-finals if we won, that even a draw might be enough.

In those days, Castres wouldn't have been well known to us, in fact most of us didn't have a clue where it was, so it was really a venture into the unknown. That was both good and bad, good in the sense that we weren't shaking with fear going out there, as some teams might if they had to play Toulouse in France around that time, bad because we didn't know what hit us when we stepped onto the pitch.

In fact the pitch was probably the safest place to be, given the level of noise and intimidation coming from around the ground! I remember we came out on the pitch first to a chorus of boos, we went through our pre-match drills to a chorus of boos, and when our names were announced before the match, when we were introduced to the local mayor before the match, the crowd continued to hiss and boo.

At some stage of the pre-match warm-up, Kenny Smith [goal kicker] decided to go down to the other [quieter] end of the pitch to kick a few goals, because there was such noise being directed at us where we were. He wouldn't have been used to that given the silence you would get at Thomond Park when someone is kicking for goal.

He wished afterwards that he had endured the abuse. We were awarded a penalty early on and Kenny ran up confidently to aim for goal; just as he began his run, there was a chorus of boos and a band struck up. Poor Kenny nearly hit the corner flag with his attempt, the ball dropped into the winger's hands and he ran the ball back 60 yards at us before myself and Axel [Foley] managed to knock him into touch.

The noise continued, the bands struck up at key moments and we really had a hard time coping with the whole scenario. In the circumstances I thought we played very well, and it really was disappointing to lose the game the way we did. Even though Munster had to endure difficult assignments abroad after that, I doubt if any of them could compare to that first match; I've never come across anything like it.

Mick Galwey and Peter Clohessy had developed a unique friendship from across the club divide (Shannon and Young Munster) and it was well known that when the two played in the same team, opponents took both of them on if they took one on.

Galwey was first capped against France in 1991, toured Namibia and was in the Irish World Cup squad that year; he went on to play in 1992, 1993, toured with the Lions the same year, went to Australia in 1994 but was passed over following the 1995 encounter with England. Clohessy was also capped against France (1993) for the first time, played through the 1994 season and was then dropped for Gary Halpin after the Welsh game in 1995, and was also passed over for selection in Ireland's World Cup games in South Africa.

After the physically exhausting contest against Castres, the Munster dressing room was eerily silent, heads bowed in reflection. Pat Murray, however, recalls one light moment, when Irish coach Murray Kidd walked in. 'I was sitting in between the two lads [Galwey and Clohessy]. Kidd came in from the right and approached Peter, who was on my right, inviting him back into the Irish squad before moving on past me and Mick and heading out the door. Suddenly Gaillimh [Galwey] turned to the Claw [Clohessy] and said, 'Thanks for asking him about me', to which Peter replied, 'Gaillimh – you're on your f***ing own, kid!'

Munster (v Swansea):

P. Murray (captain), R. Wallace, S. McCahill, D. Larkin, K. Smith, P. Burke, D. O'Mahony, J. Fitzgerald, T. Kingston, P. Clohessy, M. Galwey, G. Fulcher, E. Halvey, A. Foley, D. Corkery. Replacements: B. Toland for Halvey, M. Fitzgerald for J. Fitzgerald.

Munster (v Castres):

P. Murray (captain), R. Wallace, S. McCahill, D. Larkin, K. Smith, P. Burke, D. O'Mahony, J. Fitzgerald, T. Kingston, P. Clohessy, P. O'Connor, G. Fulcher, M. Galwey, A. Foley, D. Corkery. Replacements: B. Walsh for Burke, B. Toland for Corkery (temporary).

Chapter 20:
1996/7: A SEASON OF CONTRASTS

CHAPTER 20

1996/7: A SEASON OF CONTRASTS

M unster may have enjoyed a relatively painless introduction to European rugby with a win and a respectable defeat; certainly the 1995/6 season was not bad in the overall scheme of things. Munster played ten times; they won six, drew one and lost three, although defeats to Ulster and Leinster would not have gone down well in the province, even if the margin in each was just four points.

Things started brightly the following season. Munster beat Manchester and Orrell on a pre-season tour, lost by just a point to an Ireland XV at Thomond Park before going on to beat a St Munchin's Presidents XV, Connacht, Leinster, Ulster and Milan, rattling up an impressive points total.

But in the European Cup Munster were drawn away to Cardiff and Toulouse, the two finalists in the inaugural European Cup final the year before. They were paired against London Wasps at home, however, and produced a stunning performance to record a 49–22 victory at Thomond Park. But on either side of that win there was only embarrassment, and after a heavy defeat to Toulouse at the Stade les Sept Deniers on 2 November, worse was to follow, with defeats against Western Samoa and Australia – the latter proving a particularly humiliating experience.

If Munster inflicted a brutal battering on Wasps, they received such punishment in equal measure from Cardiff, Toulouse and Australia. Nobody tried to hide the pain – nor could they – when conceding nine tries in a 19–60 defeat to the French side. Munster did their best to put on a brave face; indeed, at times in Toulouse they looked capable of mounting a challenge to the champions. But those were the days when Irish teams shuddered at the prospect of playing serious rugby games in France; nine tries to one did not tell the full story of the game but it did show the gulf in class. When Toulouse got scoring opportunities, they took them.

Butter wouldn't melt: old buddies Mick Galwey (left) and Peter Clohessy assess the match prospects from a place on the bench. The 1995 captain Pat Murray would not agree that they were innocents abroad, however. They look as if they are planning the next prank!

For David Corkery, Anthony Foley and Killian Keane, Munster's three best players that day, it was a chastening experience as Toulouse stormed into a 17–3 lead after just twelve minutes. Following this disastrous start, however, Munster clawed their way back to 17–9 and might have scored tries on either side of the interval. But once Toulouse regrouped, there was only going to be one winner.

Colm Tucker, chairman of the Munster selectors at the time, believes Munster might have come much closer had they capitalised on territorial advantage before and after the break; but following a Munster mistake close to the Toulouse line, the home side streaked away to score a clinching try and never looked back.

Coach Jerry Holland, who just a fortnight previously had watched his side destroy Wasps, says Munster made it hard for themselves against Toulouse. 'You cannot afford to hand a French team, playing at home, the initiative early in the game. We spent too long playing catch-up rugby.'

Mick Galwey, then writing for the *Irish Examiner*, said it was all too much for his team (he had taken over the captaincy from Pat Murray) but bemoaned the fact that English referee Tony Spreadbury had made what he described as two very bad decisions. 'I'm not blaming him for the defeat; they were mistakes, but they just about summed up our day for us. You don't dare blink against a team of that quality. I don't quite know where we go from here; the only consolation is that we won both our home matches and home advantage, based on other results, seemed to be crucial this year.'

The responsibility of the captaincy did not stop Galwey – or indeed his official prankster running-mate Clohessy – from playing an outrageous practical joke on the way to Toulouse via Shannon and London. The two international colleagues called to pick up Pat Murray around 6 a.m. en route for Shannon. Murray had left his passport on the kitchen table as he finished packing his bags, but it was missing when he went to pick it up. He confronted his two colleagues who, of course, denied all knowledge and, assuming they had stuffed it into one of their own bags, Murray left the house.

He asked for the passport back on several occasions but to no avail. The team stopped off in London for a training run and there was no requirement to produce the document there, so it only became an issue on their arrival back at the airport. But the passport was not in any bag; it had been hidden under a pot plant back in Murray's house in Limerick! After several telephone calls and proxy dealings with immigration in both Shannon and London, Murray was issued with a piece of paper that the French authorities had agreed would suffice to gain entry to the country, and so it all looked like ending well.

That was not the end of the saga, however. On the way home, Murray was required to produce the same document to gain entry to London; he put his hand in a back pocket to retrieve the piece of paper, only to find that it was

John Lacey, now a referee of note, scores a fine try for Munster against Ulster. Lacey was a fixture in Munster's early Heineken Cup matches and a regular try scorer as well.

also missing. The boys had been at work again, and it took another period of time to persuade the authorities in London to allow him through to catch his connecting flight to Shannon, as Clohessy and Galwey loudly drew attention to the fact that Murray had no travel documents.

'These were the kinds of things we had to put up with in those days when guys like Claw and Gaillimh were in full flight,' Murray recalls with a grin. 'Looking back, it was funny, but we were lucky that we encountered so many people willing to help out and find a solution.'

The high points of that season were the victory over Wasps and the Inter-provincial Championship Grand Slam, with Munster amassing a record points total of 117. Wasps came to Thomond Park with a big reputation and a hugely physical side that included a winger who was larger than some of the Munster forwards. Va'aiga Tuigamala, the All Black, who had terrorised defences throughout the world, was described by Munster centre, the Kiwi Sean McCahill, as 'a frightening opponent to have in front of you'.

Tuigamala got little argument from Munster scrum half Steve McIvor who encountered him in straight up confrontation in the early moments of the game. 'I thought he had knocked my head off my shoulders,' says McIvor. 'I was pleasantly surprised to find my head still attached.'

There was quality throughout the Wasps side, with high-profile names such as Canadian out-half Gareth Rees, England scrum half Andy Gomarsall, Mike Griffiths of Wales, Damian Cronin of Scotland, Chris Sheasby of England and, of course, the legendary Lawrence Dallaglio. They expected to win easily, and Dallaglio was moved to admit: 'We're disappointed, we were humiliated. We contributed to our own downfall by giving away two intercept tries, but we were forced into making basic errors and I can't take away anything from Munster; they scored a lot of tries [seven] and put us to the sword.'

Tuigamala had a quiet game, but only after Munster stymied all attempts to put him away in space. Wasps coach Nigel Melville, the former England and Lions scrum half, acknowledged Munster's performance. 'We didn't come here to get beaten like that, we were outclassed and we will have to get back to the drawing board very quickly.'

It was a different story in the last game of the season, however, when Munster ended up on the wrong side of a 55–19 scoreline against Australia. It was Munster's heaviest ever defeat by a touring side and a thoroughly dismal performance to boot.

Coach Jerry Holland summed up the mood. 'There is a proud tradition in Munster when playing against touring teams, but we let that tradition down.'

All but a few came out with diminished reputations. Killian Keane escaped criticism for a wholeheartedly brave performance, while Richard Wallace, Steve McIvor, Pat Murray, Anthony Foley and David Corkery were also awarded some credit for their efforts.

The Wallabies were in full flight in a win that yielded them a staggering nine tries. The presence of Stephen Larkham, Jason Little, David Campese and Owen Finegan – all of whom went on to become household names in world rugby – in that Australian team would, in the passage of time, provide the only consolation to the men in red.

For Pat Murray, it was the end of the road, although his decision to withdraw from representative rugby had nothing to do with the Australia defeat. After a second season of semi-professional rugby, Murray concluded that there was no place for part-time players in a game that had become increasingly physical. He was never one to shirk a tackle or a challenge, but he did not even have to look beyond the Munster camp to realise that it would be impossible to keep up with the full-time professionals.

Murray's decision was prompted by the physical development of a young Shannon player who went on to become an Irish rugby legend. 'We were expected to train at the same intense level as the full-time players, who spent increasing amounts of time working out in the gym. Quite honestly, we would go out there and have to train as we hoped to play; it got more and more difficult. People like Anthony [Foley] got hugely physical and it became somewhat of a real punishment for guys like me to cope with the physicality of those sessions. Quite simply, the professional guys had gone to a different level.'

Munster (v Wasps):

P. Murray, R. Wallace, B. Walsh, S.McCahill, D. Crotty, K. Keane, S. McIvor, J. Fitzgerald, T. Kingston, N. Healy, M. Galwey (captain), G. Fulcher, A. Foley, B. Cronin, D. Corkery.

Munster (v Toulouse):

P. Murray, R. Wallace, B. Walsh, S. McCahill, D. Crotty, K. Keane, S. McIvor, J. Fitzgerald, T. Kingston, N. Healy, M. Galwey (captain), G. Fulcher, A. Foley, B. Cronin, D. Crokery.
Replacements: P. McCarthy for Healy, L. Dinneen for Cronin, I. Murray for McCarthy.

Munster (v Australia):

P. Murray, R. Wallace, B. Walsh, S.McCahill, D. Crotty, K. Keane, S. McIvor, J. Fitzgerald, T. Kingston, N. Healy, M. Galwey (captain), G. Fulcher, A. Foley, B. Cronin, D. Corkery.

Australia: S. Larkham, B. Tune, J. Little, R. Tombs, D. Campese, P. Howard, S. Payne, C. Blades, M. Caputo, A. Heath, T. Gavin, D. Giffin, T. Kefu, O. Finegan, B. Robinson (captain).
Replacements: A. Murdoch for Little, T. Wallace for Larkham.

Chapter 21:
1997/8: THE MAORI INFLUENCE

1997/8: THE MAORI INFLUENCE

The demands of the European Cup continued to grow in the 1997/8 season, with participants required to play six games, and home and away fixtures were introduced for the first time. The pool games were packed into the months of September and October, therefore requiring the Irish Interprovincial Championship to be completed beforehand.

Munster went on a short pre-season tour to Scotland where they emerged with wins over Edinburgh and District and Caledonia Reds under a new coaching team comprised of Declan Kidney and Niall O'Donovan. It got better when they swept past Connacht and then beat Leinster in the opening games of the domestic championship before coming back down to reality with a 12–22 loss to Ulster at Ravenhill, a result that did not surprise many given Munster's appalling record at the venue. As events transpired, that defeat cost Munster the championship because Connacht went on to beat Ulster, and Leinster did likewise to secure two victories and take the title on points difference (plus fifteen against plus thirteen).

Given that Munster had yet to win a European game on the road, there would have been a degree of trepidation about the visit to the Stoop, the London home of Harlequins. The English club would have fancied themselves, having decided quickly that the best way to European Cup success was to buy in top players from around Britain and Europe. A side that included Will Carling, Thierry Lacroix, Jason Leonard, Gareth Llewellyn and Laurent Cabannes was captained by none other than Ireland's Munster-born-and-bred hooker, Keith Wood.

Munster had moved on a bit, introducing Shannon's New Zealand centre Rhys Ellison and a young, raw, but hugely talented out-half by the name of Ronan O'Gara.

Ronan O'Gara kicks another goal for Munster. He has come a long way since his 1997/8 Heineken Cup debut away to Harlequins. The English side anticipated winning well, but Munster stretched them in an eighty-eight point thriller, with O'Gara contributing three penalties and three conversions.

Galwey was in his second year of what would be a long residency as captain, having taken over from Murray the season before, and Alan Quinlan hit the European stage for the first time, too.

It was to be another fruitless mission, but Munster managed to send shockwaves through English rugby in their opening game with a performance that forced the hotly fancied Harlequins to fight for every scrap before emerging 48–40 winners in a classic game of rugby. Indeed, had Munster not subjected themselves to such a disastrous opening-quarter performance, after which they trailed by seventeen points, it was a game they could have won.

They battled back magnificently to draw level at thirty points apiece seven minutes into the second half and had an opportunity to take control with two gilt-edged, try-scoring opportunities immediately afterwards. Ironically, it was two of the Munster heroes, O'Gara and Quinlan, who were unable to take advantage of impressive build-ups, and in the end the greater fitness of Harlequins told as they led 48–33 two minutes into stoppage time. Even then, though, Munster found a little more and created a fine try for newcomer Conor Burke that confirmed their hearts were very much in the right place.

Niall O'Donovan admitted that the concession of twenty points early on was crucial. 'Bad enough to do that anywhere, but it was an impossible situation from which to recover away from home. Our defence was a bit flaky, as the concession of forty-eight points would suggest, but at least we proved we're capable of scoring tries,' he said, referring to the five garnered by Munster.

The positives stretched further than that, with Ellison making a hugely impressive debut. He would go on to make a significant contribution to the later success of Munster, and the development of young home-grown backs, over a period of two seasons.

That game at the Stoop had a significant element of confrontation, with Wood and Galwey embroiled in on-field controversy when the Munster captain allegedly punched his counterpart so hard that Wood was left with a black eye, swollen nose and blurred vision – and out of the game after thirty-eight minutes. Galwey denied there was anything untoward, but he was sent to the sin bin – much to the dissatisfaction of the home crowd, who viewed it as a sending-off offence.

He explained: 'I was trying to drive Woody out of a maul with a kind of straight-arm tackle which obviously went in high and caught him on the face. I wasn't trying to put him out of the match; I'm not that kind of a player and it was a complete accident.'

Wood was inclined not to agree. 'I was trying to get at the ball, battling for possession with Mark McDermott (I think) when I got a box in the eye. I realised then it was Gaillimh; he is one of my best friends for years with Ireland and Munster and I'm not going to make an issue of it. Still, punching is a sending-off offence.'

Dominic Crotty had a taste of European rugby in the first half of Munster's 1996/7 campaign before Pat Murray returned from injury. When Murray retired, Crotty established himself as the number one fullback the following season and went on to play a huge role in the development of the team over six eventful campaigns. He is seen here scoring a try against Bath at Thomond Park in a 2002 friendly.

Munster went on to play Cardiff the following week and were not quite as good, with the Welsh side easing to a comfortable win (43–23) to leave Munster without a point after two matches. French side Bourgoin provided stern opposition in the third game at Thomond Park but Munster held their nerve to secure a 17–15 win before, disappointingly, losing the fourth game at Musgrave Park to Cardiff, a late try proving decisive in a 37–32 victory. That was Munster 's first European Cup defeat on Irish soil and they subsequently maintained an unbeaten record for a staggering nine seasons, until Leicester Tigers secured a 13–6 win on 20 January 2007.

But if the fifth game against Bourgoin brought with it another defeat, Munster wrapped up the campaign with a sensational victory over Harlequins in the return fixture at Thomond Park on 12 October 1997. It was a costly defeat for the English side because, even though still finishing top of the group ahead of Cardiff, they missed the cut for a home draw and had to travel to Toulouse for a quarter-final that they lost heavily, 51–10.

Munster won the game 23–16 – deservedly so – and the defeat was greeted with horror by the Harlequins' management team on behalf of the owners. Shocked into silence, Harlequins retreated to the dressing room for an inordinate period of time before coaching director Andy Keast emerged to launch a verbal assault on his players, whom he accused of reneging on their responsibilities. 'The players have a commercial responsibility to the club. They can't expect to hold out one hand and take and not hold out the other to give. This is a massive financial blow,' he said, bemoaning the loss of a money-spinning home draw.

Comparisons were inevitable: Harlequins, an old established club with a 'bought and paid for' attitude towards the players, and Munster, with home-grown boys and a solitary 'blow-in' from the southern hemisphere – Rhys Ellison. The outcome of this game, allied to ever-improving performances and the ability to cope with cash-rich opposition, was enough to convince Munster that the path they were taking was the right one.

To this day, the philosophy remains the same – buy only when it is absolutely necessary, and buy well. Ellison was the first overseas signing and he was a good one. Right up to the present time, Munster can boast a huge success rate with the importation of players, many of whom have given as much to the cause off the pitch (coaching and assisting with development and academy players) as on it.

This victory over Harlequins marked an occasion when Munster, without the big names boasted by their opponents, gave the Irish game a huge boost, a powerful effort from the pack proving crucial. Defensively, there were shades of the Munster performance against the All Blacks in 1978, albeit not quite against the same quality of opposition. Galwey, on a warning from Wood that retribution might be on the cards for the alleged punch in London some weeks earlier, was at his dynamic best and the entire pack, even an injury-hit Shane Leahy, rallied to the cause.

The match provided an opportunity for a back-row combination of Eddie Halvey, Alan Quinlan and Anthony Foley to provide inspiration, after slowly but surely gelling together into a unit that ultimately served Munster superbly over a longer period of time. Equally, John Lacey was starting to make a name for himself on the right wing, and John Kelly had begun to ease his way gently into his new career, one that proved to be long and distinguished as he participated in some of the great Munster days in the years ahead.

This was not Munster at their spectacular best, but it was a Munster that had started to flex some muscle in the heavyweight arena; it was a Munster that would become one of the principal giants of European rugby. They turned a corner on that October day, and Ellison helped them do it.

O'Donovan admitted there had been some soul-searching before it was decided to look to the outside market for players. He insisted it was done with a huge measure of consideration for the implications but now, looking back, he is convinced that it was absolutely the way forward, particularly given the set of demands that Munster imposed on anyone who signed for them.

At the time, the Munster team was probably made up of players from four clubs who were winning the AIL [All Ireland League]; Rhys brought something extra to the table. He had played a high level of rugby in New Zealand with Otago and Waikato, got a few trials for the All Blacks and played for the Maori on many occasions [once against Mick Galwey and the Lions in 1993], so he was pretty battle-hardened.

He added a huge amount for us from a playing point of view, and his presence certainly proved beneficial for the Irish players because he prepared for matches in a different way; they were able to take something from him and add to what they already had. It was a time for learning; we were all learning at the time and he certainly brought us on a step, just as John Langford did when he joined Munster from the Brumbies a couple of years later.

Ellison's easy personality set even higher standards for future signings, as O'Donovan explains.

The Munster scene was possibly a difficult one for outsiders to break into, not because the guys weren't welcoming but because the newcomers would have had to be thick-skinned enough. The Munster lads, from Cork, Limerick or wherever, didn't suffer fools gladly and everyone had to be able to take the slagging; we had to be very careful who we were bringing in as a result of that – anyone, including locals – but Rhys slipped easily into the environment.

Most of the guys we signed subsequently were guys who gave a lot more than they got out of the scene, although I'm sure they would all say they got a lot from it. When you sign somebody from any different environment you're certainly taking a risk; Rhys was fantastic and he stayed here in Ireland for a number of years after his contract ended. He stayed to finish off his law studies, married a Limerick girl and one of his children was born here. He would have a special bond with Munster, even to this day.

Munster (v Harlequins):

D. Crotty, J. Lacey, M. Lynch, R. Ellison, J. Kelly, K. Keane, B. O'Meara, I. Murray, M. McDermott, P. Clohessy, M. Galwey (captain), S. Leahy, E. Halvey, A. Quinlan, A. Foley.
Replacement: S. McIvor for O'Meara.

Jerry Holland coached and managed Munster through those difficult but exciting early seasons of professionalism, right through to the days of wine and roses.

Chapter 22:
1998/9: ANOTHER BRICK IN THE WALL

1998/9: ANOTHER BRICK IN THE WALL

Another season dawned and the experience Munster gained over the previous three years was put to good use in the 1998/9 European campaign.

The season was, yet again, broken into two distinct sections, with club/provincial games to be played in the first half, leaving post-Christmas activity to the clubs and international teams in the various participating countries.

Unusually then, the season started for Munster at the back end of July when they played Rumney and Llanelli as part of a short tour. The signs were good after securing two big victories, followed by wins over Connacht and Morocco (yes Morocco!) before Leinster broke the winning sequence with a 24–18 win at Dooradoyle – in front, incidentally, of no more than 400, an attendance that reflected the lack of public interest in watching 'summer' rugby.

Briefly, Munster found themselves at the bottom of the Interprovincial table on points difference from Connacht, an unthinkable position when considering it was now a professional set-up, albeit one in the very early stages. I was less than generous in my appraisal of Munster's performance that day, and the position at the bottom of the table was unacceptable considering the 'highly paid' players and coach.

Weeks later, Munster were en route to their first Heineken Cup quarter-final and won the domestic championship after losing only once – to Ulster in Ravenhill. It was Munster's first in a run of three Interprovincial titles and, I suppose, the comments made in August deserved a cynical response from dry-witted coach Declan Kidney following the 25–10 win over Leinster two months later.

Kidney's post-match interviews with the press included words of praise for the way his team had battled back to win the title. He moved off down the hall, and just before stepping into the dressing room called back, 'Barry, just one other thing . . . I'm not that highly paid!' As the door slammed shut I uttered one quiet word, out of earshot: 'Touché!'

That was a side of Kidney we were to experience in the years that followed; although not quite auditioning for the comedy club, he was able to deliver some wonderful one-liners to fit the occasion. The day before Munster's first Heineken Cup final against Northampton in 2000, for instance, he was hosting the largest press conference he had ever experienced, with worldwide interest in what he had to say. He was understandably nervous but immediately disarmed the 150 or so press people present when replying to the opening question from an English journalist: 'Declan, how did the boys sleep last night?' Quick as a flash, Kidney responded, 'Don't know, I'm afraid; I coach them, don't sleep with them!'

Just one season before (1997/8), Munster's progress was not confined to the domestic market. In the European Cup they were drawn against Padova, Neath and Perpignan, and Munster proved up to the task. They began with a less-than-classic victory over Padova at Musgrave Park on 19 September, winning 20–13 but drawing negative comments from Padova coach Vittorio Munari, who suggested the Irish team would struggle to get out of the group.

But Munster improved as the campaign went on and followed that win with a much more accomplished 34–10 victory over Neath. They fell at the third hurdle away to Perpignan, not surprising given their previous lack of success on French soil. Perpignan won 41–24 and Munster were left with no option but to pick up points on the road if they were to survive. They went to Neath the following week and managed to secure an 18–18 draw – the team's best result away from home and one that ultimately proved crucial to their qualifying for the knockout stages for the first time.

Much was made of Munster's return fixture against Perpignan fixed for Musgrave Park on 31 October 1998, twenty years to the day that the province beat the All Blacks. The venue was different, however, as was the opposition, and the weather was appalling. Neither side was able to play any type of decent rugby but Munster went for the jugular and got their revenge with a hard-fought but highly important 13–5 win; Peter Clohessy scored a try that was converted by Killian Keane, who also kicked two penalties.

So it was on to Padova to play a team that took much pride from their performances that season. Apart from a 67–8 defeat away to Perpignan, the Italians had more than justified their inclusion in the competition, beating Neath at home and running Perpignan, the group winners, to just eight points on Italian soil.

After losing narrowly to both Munster and Neath in the away legs, Padova had high hopes of finishing the group stages with a flourish, perhaps in third position above the Welsh team. But Munster reserved their best until last, and the display that yielded a 35–21 (it should have been more) victory had Munari

Mike Lynch (right) gets to grips with Padova fullback Kelly Rolleston during the 1998/9 clash at Musgrave Park, while Ronan O'Gara (centre) closes in.

drooling. 'It certainly was a different Munster team from the one that played in Cork; they were sensational, they left us for dead. We didn't think they would be *that* good and we couldn't cope. It was the most complete performance from any of our opponents this season, better ever than Perpignan because we played so badly there. We played OK against Munster, but they exposed us badly.'

The same day, Ulster defeated Edinburgh Reivers to secure a home quarter-final, while Munster were drawn away to Colomiers. Coach Kidney could have complained, but did not. 'It's a great day for Irish rugby,' he declared as he hailed Munster's first away win in the Heineken Cup and also Ulster's achievement. 'Two teams from Ireland in the quarter-final, great.' And having to play away from home did not worry him unduly. 'There are no easy matches in the competition, and Colomiers are obviously a very strong side. Still, it's my view that we could have had a more difficult draw.' As it happened, Munster would have qualified for the knockout stages even if they had lost in Padova, the difference being that their quarter-final opponents would have been Ulster, the eventual winners of the competition.

Acknowledging at that time the stern opposition that Padova had provided for all the teams in the group, Kidney insisted that it was a highly important psychological boost for Munster. 'The guys had to be mentally tough to come through this one against a very good team away from home. Some of them will have grown up out there today.'

Captain Mick Galwey had to leave ahead of the rest to link up with the Irish squad who were gathering in Belfast that night. He would like to have been around to help the team celebrate but quipped, 'Tomorrow, I'll be glad I missed the party.' Like Kidney, Galwey also recognised the importance of the win in Italy.

Not winning away from home was, I suppose, a millstone; that's gone now and we can build from here. There is now a feeling within the squad that we can take on anyone and beat them if we reach our potential on the day. Professionalism has been brilliant; things have been building slowly but surely, and the benefits are showing. It's great to see two Irish teams involved after having to listen to all we have had to listen to over the years. For us, this could be the start of a new era; we have proved we're able to compete with and beat teams away from home, and we're all looking forward to taking it a step further next month.

Sadly, they were unable to take it that stage further; they would have to wait another twelve months for that. At that time, Colomiers, so often in the shadow of more illustrious big city neighbours Toulouse, were competing at a high level in France. Munster, bit by bit, had been knocking the bricks from a well-built wall, but it was a task too far when they took on Colomiers at Stade Selery on 13 December. Colomiers won 23–9, having established that irreversible lead in the opening forty minutes.

There was a festive atmosphere that day, with the usual French bands and the pom-pom girls providing pre-match, mid-match and post-match entertainment. But there was no champagne rugby, neither from Colomiers nor from Munster. From the outset the French gave a fiercely competitive display from a heavyweight pack in the scrums and line-outs. Munster struggled in all aspects of forward play and both backs and forwards were under pressure for much of this one-sided contest.

Munster deserved full credit for their resilient second-half performance, however, as they held the home team scoreless; indeed they might well have put themselves in a more challenging position as Colomiers ruthlessly protected the lead by persistent obstruction and by slowing up all Munster's ruck ball by foul or fair means. The French side had two players sent to the sin bin by referee Nigel Whitehouse of Wales, but as he came under fierce pressure from the home fans the penalties stopped going Munster's way and possession, good possession at any rate, quickly dried up. Munster's players were as frustrated as they were annoyed at the tactics employed by the French, although Galwey recognised that it had, essentially, been a one-horse race because of the physical pressure the pack had to endure.

Ulster met Colomiers at Lansdowne Road in that season's Heineken Cup decider. There would have been no love lost between Munster and Ulster, between Galwey and some of his Ulster opponents either, but the Munster captain had come to dislike Colomiers for the way his side was dumped out of the competition. Therefore, he had little or no sympathy for them when they came badly unstuck at Lansdowne Road.

A huge Ulster crowd was augmented by thousands of rugby fans from the South, and Lansdowne Road was packed to capacity. All joined in to ensure that Ulster had a marked superiority in the stands and terraces, just as they enjoyed a marked superiority on the pitch. Ulster secured a 21–6 win, with Simon Mason kicking six penalty goals and David Humphreys adding a drop goal in a one-sided contest that brought a smile to Galwey's face. Ironically, there was a Munster link to that great Irish success – former provincial, Irish and Lions flanker Noel Murphy was president of the IRFU on that momentous day.

Galwey would have longed for immediate revenge on the French side, but Munster's day against Colomiers would come. For now, some retribution had been exacted on his behalf by Mason, Humphreys et al.

Munster (v Colomiers):

B. Roche, J. O'Neill, K. Keane, R. Ellison, M. Lynch, B Everitt, P. Stringer, P. Clohessy, M. McDermott, J. Hayes, M. Galwey (captain), M. O'Driscoll, D. Corkery, A. Foley, E. Halvey.
Replacements: D. Clohessy for Hayes, T. Tierney for Stringer, D. Wallace for Corkery, S. Leahy for O'Driscoll.

Eddie Halvey scores a crucial try in the hard-fought win over Padova., while Brian O'Meara leaps over his fallen opponent.

Chapter 23:
1999/2000: THE NEARLY MEN

1999/2000: THE NEARLY MEN

Munster's incredible European journey continued beyond their wildest dreams, thanks to a process of reorganisation and the unearthing of some remarkable new players. Wallaby international John Langford was one, arriving in Ireland boasting Super 12 final appearances with Australian side the Brumbies. He proved to be ready and able for the challenge of a Heineken Cup campaign – and some more.

Munster will hardly boast of the narrow victory over lowly Welsh club Dunvant in a pre-season friendly, but they went on to beat Leinster, Connacht and Ulster home and away to create a new Interprovincial Championship record and secure the title for the second successive year. Beating Ulster in Belfast for the first time in two decades was hugely satisfying, especially as the Northerners were the reigning European champions, but the men in red were also delighted with the comprehensive double over Leinster and a record-breaking sequence against Connacht.

This was World Cup year – 1999 – and Munster did not fare too well in terms of selection. Several players had an opportunity to prove a point when Munster took on an Irish XV in a warm-up game that was supposed to benefit the national side. However, the match at Musgrave Park on 9 September was not of much benefit to Ireland as Munster, roared on by several thousand supporters irate at the treatment of some of their heroes, won a thoroughly enjoyable match by 26 points to 19. It was seen as a triumph for Munster; if nothing else it spurred the team on to an unprecedented run of thirteen victories.

They had already secured eight wins by the time they opened their Heineken Cup campaign, a year in which they drew Colomiers in the pool stages. It was a tough group; Colomiers were still ranked highly in France, and it did not help that Saracens and Pontypridd completed the picture. But by now Munster feared very few sides, and the players saw the inclusion of Colomiers as an opportunity to exact revenge, noting that the French team could be broken down like any other, as Ulster had shown en route to Heineken Cup glory in the previous season's decider.

Pontypridd were still among the Welsh elite, while Saracens had signed a number of top-class players, including South Africa's 1995 World Cup-winning captain, Francois Pienaar. The English side, whose squad also featured Thierry Lacroix, Mark Mapletoft, George Chute, Scott Murray, Danny Grewcock, Richard Hill and Tony Diprose, had a showbusiness-style approach to home matches at Vicarage Road.

Rhys Ellison was gone, and so Conor Mahony was back in the frame for the opening game against the Welsh, but there were other changes behind the scrum as well.

Mike Mullins was a new signing, joining the squad just a few weeks after Langford, while Ronan O'Gara was about to become a permanent fixture on the team, establishing a long-term and highly fruitful halfback partnership with Peter Stringer.

Munster duly disposed of Pontypridd at Thomond Park in the opening game on 20 November 1999, with two tries from Killian Keane and Alan Quinlan, and O'Gara making an immediate impact by kicking both the conversions, five penalties and a drop goal. That was the shape of things to come for the young out-half, and for Munster.

Nothing was left to chance for the match against Saracens the following week, with the squad travelling to London on the Friday, two days before the game. Munster went to see Watford play Sunderland in the Premiership at Vicarage Road on the Saturday and even got to meet Niall Quinn before the game, but that was not the purpose of the exercise. Although not their first time playing in a football stadium, Munster were keen to sample the atmosphere and try to judge the parameters of the pitch.

Sunday was to be a red-letter day for Munster, who battled back brilliantly after falling 21–9 behind. And despite falling away again, their never-say-die attitude was epitomised in the closing stages when Jeremy Staunton scored a marvellous try, which O'Gara converted. It was not over yet, however. When Saracens won a scrum near the Munster line, Lacroix was shaping up for the inevitable drop goal attempt; but Munster stunned their illustrious opponents when the pack surged forward to turn possession over, and an unlikely and unexpected victory was secured.

The audacity of the Munster pack, and the final result, sent a strong message to the English and French clubs in particular; Munster had arrived at the table and struck a blow for all clubs lacking the financial clout of others. Munster eventually came undone in the last match away to Pontypridd at Sardis Road by two points in a high-scoring game, but the highs continued unabated in between, and Munster's long road to success was only beginning.

Declan Kidney called up Jason Holland, who was playing club rugby with Midleton, for the second game of the campaign against Colomiers, with Marcus Horan replacing the injured Peter Clohessy. Remarkably, Munster won the match with a measure of control they had not enjoyed in London. Holland scored two tries, Horan and Keith Wood one apiece, and O'Gara rounded off a polished performance by kicking three penalties and a conversion in a thoroughly deserved 31–15 win.

A week later at Musgrave Park, Colomiers' interest in the tournament ended when Munster secured a comfortable 23–5 win to set the scene for what proved to be a winner-takes-all clash with Saracens in the return fixture at Thomond Park on 8 January 2000. It was another classic, with an almost identical finish.

Munster had to sweat over the fitness of their captain, who was becoming increasingly influential, and Galwey's appearance was met by a sigh of relief. He had sustained a badly cut knee in an AIB League match and was restricted to little or no training in the days leading up to the game. But the injury was well managed, said Galwey in his autobiography, and he revealed that Phyllis Dolan, the team physiotherapist, came up with the idea of putting a layer of bubble wrap inside the outer bandaging prior to the match. 'I never even thought about the injury throughout the game.'

The game was close from start to finish. Galwey scored an early try to settle the nerves, but Munster were never allowed to pull away; just as they had inflicted pain on the home team at Vicarage Road, Saracens attempted to do likewise to Munster – and they very nearly succeeded. With less than two minutes to go, they grabbed a converted try to lead 30–24; things looked grim for Munster.

But Galwey, Wood, Langford and company were in no mood to throw away all the hard work. The skipper takes up the story.

We were awarded a penalty; kicked it to touch, Woody threw it in, Langford caught it, we drove it and Woody got over the line. It all sounds simple but it was a very hard thing to achieve against such tough opposition. Then there was the matter of a conversion to come, and it was a fantastic kick under severe pressure by Ronan [O'Gara]. It was a famous kick and you have to give him huge credit; he was in the same position in the same circumstances just a few weeks before.

After all that happened on the pitch, we had to face another battle – to get from one side of the pitch to the dressing room. The crowd just went mad, out of their head. We were in the quarter-finals, we had a home draw, and we went over to Pontypridd knowing that the result didn't matter. We went there to win but we probably didn't put in the same effort and they caught us by two points with a late converted try, a dose of our own medicine if you like.

Key to Munster's pool success was the contribution of Langford, whose strange love affair with Ireland began in 1996 when John Eales was injured on the Wallabies tour of Britain and Ireland. Langford was summoned as a replacement; he was due to appear against Munster in Thomond Park but never got his boots on. 'After a twenty-six-hour journey, I arrived just before the kick-off. I sat in the stand, and nearly froze to death.'

Australia beat Munster easily and Langford was at least able to enjoy the after-match hospitality.

Arriving at Shannon three years later, the weather conditions, he recalls, were similar. 'On our way down, the plane was tossed about a bit; it was scary at times, but worse was to follow. We hit the ground with a loud thud and the plane seemed to lift off again before landing with another big bump. This time we managed to stay down, and eventually we came to a halt. It was pretty scary, but then the captain announced, "Ladies and gentlemen, welcome to Shannon, where, sometimes, you get two landings for the price of one." At that stage you could only laugh, but it was, to say the least, a rather unusual welcome greeting to Ireland.'

If that was not enough, Langford was quickly thrown into a bonding session for the squad. In Munster terms, that meant a piss-up. 'We went to Kilkee, had a bit of fun and a good few drinks. I remember wondering to myself whether I was mad to have made the move.'

Galwey gives a more detailed account.

John's arrival in Ireland coincided with a group session we had planned for Kilkee that week. We trained in Coonagh [Shannon's ground] that morning and then headed to Clare; there were pints involved, for sure. Being honest, it was a piss-up; I don't know what John was thinking, nor what Declan [Kidney] was thinking, but he gave it the go-ahead. On those occasions, which at that stage were few and far between, Deccie used to suggest to us that we have beer shandies instead of pints. We said we would, of course – yeah, right! Anyway, we would have to explain to him that we would, be sick after the sugar that a shandy contains, so it was never an option!

Galwey insists that, whatever Langford thought of his welcome, it was not long before the big Aussie was immersed in the tradition of Munster rugby. He was, says the former captain, a thorough professional who was to become an important role model for the younger players.

Anyone joining Munster, of course, has to endure the good-natured banter that has been part and parcel of the set-up since the amateur days. Langford used to harp on about his experience with the Brumbies whenever he tried to make a point. It was a mistake he was to make over and over, says Galwey.

We used to give him a fierce time. One of his things when making a point was to tell us how, when he was back with the Brumbies, they used to do *things a certain way. We would listen to so much of that, then turn around and tell him to go f**k off back to the Brumbies if they were so much better . . . we made it into one big joke, but he kept on telling us, we kept on listening and we kept on telling him to f**k off back home to learn some more!*

The thing was that we accepted he had come from a very professional background and from a very successful club; some of that rubbed off on us through him, but the most important thing was that he turned out to be a high-quality player; he earned his stripes with us and he commanded our total respect because of it. Rhys Ellison was the first overseas player in and he was a great bit of stuff; he brought a huge intensity and hardness to our defence, our backs learned a huge amount from him. Langford achieved the same with the forwards.

The arrival of Langford was not the only development that year, with Galwey pointing to a number of initiatives in the early stages of the season. 'For instance, Brian O'Meara and Tom Tierney went to the World Cup, but Peter Stringer established himself in the side during their absence, and neither could find a way back.'

Though disappointed at losing to Pontypridd and a friendly away to Leicester at Welford Road, Galwey insists that self-belief ran through the squad as they prepared for a quarter-final clash with Stade Français at Thomond Park. Munster had an enviable home record to protect and they wanted to send a message to all cash-rich clubs that money was not necessary for success. They got the message across, emphatically.

Stade had a number of top-quality players in a multinational squad, including Christophe Dominici, the French winger with a habit of skinning opponents, Brian Lima, Sylvian Marconnet, David Auradou, Marc Lièvremont and, of course, goal-kicking machine Diego Dominguez.

Dominguez was used to contending with raucous fans the length and breadth of France, of supporters howling disapproval as he stepped up to take a penalty; nothing, he was to admit after Munster romped to a 27–10 win, prepared him for the silence afforded goal kickers at Thomond Park. 'It was bizarre, I never experienced anything like it. You could feel the silence; when I ran up to kick, I was waiting for an eruption, but it never came. It troubled me, I have to admit, it put me off; imagine, good manners putting an experienced goal-kicker off, but it happened.'

Dominguez described Munster's performance as 'magnificent'. 'They stopped us from playing, they didn't allow us to get our game together and they put us under pressure from the start. It was one of those days, a difficult one from the very beginning to the very end.'

Next up for Munster was their most difficult match to date in Europe – an away tie to high-flyers Toulouse, who were, at that stage, red-hot favourites to take their second title. Had Munster seen the odds offered against them

Happy days: former Munster and Irish flanker Ken O'Connell makes light work of Peter Stringer after the sensational Heineken cup semi-final victory (31–25) over Toulouse at Stade Lescure, Bordeaux, on 6 May 2000.

winning, they might not even have travelled. But in the blistering heat of a glorious summer's day in Bordeaux, the neutral venue selected by ERC to host the game, Munster came of age.

For Galwey, it was a particularly triumphant afternoon as he led the team to a stirring 31–25 triumph, on a day when Munster challenged the Toulouse fans by warming up on their patch and putting up with the resultant abuse. Munster's team manager at the time was Brian O'Brien, who was about to take on a similar role with Ireland. Full of passion, O'Brien was delighted with Munster's win. 'This has to be the greatest Munster team of all time.' High praise indeed from the man who had put his body on the line on many occasions for the province, once helping Munster stretch the New Zealand All Blacks (1963) to the limit. He went on: 'Character is the hallmark of this side. I cannot say enough good things about them. They're a wonderful group of players and a credit to province and country.'

Nobody would argue with that, not least the 3,000 or so fans who made the journey to Bordeaux and who stood enthralled as Munster tore the form book to shreds. For three players, the occasion had a special significance. Dominic Crotty, Anthony Foley and Galwey had, just three years before, endured the greatest pain and suffering of their fledgling professional careers as Toulouse inflicted a huge defeat in a pool match.

For Galwey, the win in France was a major turning point.

The last thing that anyone wanted was to have to play them away from home, but in a sense it actually galvanised us. Another thing was that we had three years of training as professionals behind us, three years to catch up as we needed to catch up following that 1996 defeat. It took a few years to kick in and I suppose we hadn't factored in the reality that we had come on in leaps and bounds in the meantime. We were as strong, if not stronger, as fast if not faster, and as fit if not fitter than the rest of them; we just needed to believe that was the case.

That was a huge thing for us because fitness, particularly, was always an issue for Irish teams who tended to blow up towards the end of matches. All of a sudden, that was gone out the gate, and at that stage we were confident we could match anyone on that score. Also, I think, the fact that Ireland did so poorly in the World Cup might have helped; guys came home and they had a point to prove. They did, and it kicked on from there, the Munster success led to a lot of guys being picked on the Irish team, and success bred success farther up the line; things started to get better for Irish rugby in general.

Against that background, once we thought about playing Toulouse, once we convinced ourselves that we could match them I think some of the potential problems disappeared. To be honest, some of the younger lads helped considerably; they came into the game on the back of good performances and some stunning victories against high-class sides from England and France, they had no baggage and that was a huge positive. We had developed a good, all-round game and we believed in our own ability, notwithstanding the obvious respect we would have had for Toulouse.

A big bonus for us, as well, was the presence of Keith Wood, who had come back from Harlequins to join us that season. He was Irish captain, I was Munster captain; between us we had a bit of an advantage over our opponents because we had no hesitation in pooling our knowledge. But it was an easy team to captain; you had the likes of Peter [Clohessy], Axel [Foley], Langford and Killian Keane, all great natural leaders in their own right. Killian wasn't always in the starting side, but he was a superb team player and he was one of the mature guys who had that ability to suss out the opposition and spot weaknesses.

Mike Mullins had huge experience and Duchy [Jason Holland] made a huge impact when he joined us from Midleton. I sensed from the beginning that Jason would make an impact; he had those lovely deft touches that made him stand out from a crowd. He was a great man to spot an intercept, although we used to give him a bit of a hard time because he sometimes didn't have the pace to finish it off – we used to tease him about hitting quicksand at some stage of his breakaway runs. The good news was that we had worked out a certain move used by Toulouse and figured it was ripe to provide an intercept opportunity for Jason. He read it like a book and this time got away to gallop in for a try under the posts.

I think Toulouse must have underestimated us; I don't think they realised the weaponry we had in the backline, Mikey was a massive player for us and Anthony Horgan was totally underestimated. I remember that he marked Emile N'Tamack out of the game, an uncapped player against a guy with a host of French caps who was much bigger than Hoggy as well. Then you had John Kelly and Dominic [Crotty], two great footballers who were not always given the credit they deserved either.

It was a great day for the pack as well. We lost Woody at half time but Frankie Sheahan came on and had the game of his life. David Wallace was superb and John Hayes scored a remarkable try although I like to remind him of how laziness or exhaustion, or both, was a contributory factor.

Somebody noted that John, after carrying the ball through a phase, lay on the ground for seventeen seconds after being tackled. Play continued, he got up and the ball went back to the same place. He was perfectly positioned to take a pass from Dominic Crotty and he went through their scrum half; he didn't try to go around the player or try a side-step, he just went through him as if there wasn't anyone there, and he scored a great try. He didn't score too many tries after, but that was good enough at the time.

Galwey recalls Munster's superb preparation and attention to detail. 'Behind the scenes, we had water carriers, isotonic drinks lined up, wet towels at the ready for use whenever needed; as it transpired, there was no sign of similarities in the Toulouse camp, and at half time, looking at our opponents, they looked out for the count. It was just a hunch, but we figured we had them on the ropes anyway.'

Northampton, a side built upon similar foundations to Munster, secured a late victory over Llanelli in the second semi-final, thus providing an unlikely final pairing for the organisers. It was far from a classic, with both sides displaying obvious nervous tension throughout a closely fought decider that ended 9–8 to the English.

Munster will bemoan the fact that scoring the only try of the game was not enough; O'Gara missing the conversion and a late penalty chance; and Galwey being harshly sin-binned near the Northampton line for obstruction – at a time when the Munster challenge was in full flow. It was a heartbreaking end to a fairy-tale season, but Galwey believes his side left the title behind them in the dressing room, not on the pitch.

There was just a huge amount of hype about that game, hype that we wouldn't have been used to in any section of Irish rugby. Getting to the final

Desolation after losing to Northampton in the 2000 final at Twickenham. A tearful Munster captain Mick Galwey makes his way around the stadium to thank the Munster fans, accompanied by daughter Neasa.

was huge, there was a three-week break and there was a lot of media interest, stuff going on that we had no control over.

Even the day before the final, we went down to Twickenham and we found ourselves knocking around for too long. We had a meeting at which everyone made their views known; there was a lot of emotion and I think, ultimately, we were adversely affected by the whole show. It was a powerful thing at the time, but when we hit the pitch at Twickenham, we didn't appear to have the energy we would normally have had on matchday. It's hard to put a finger on it, maybe we were mentally drained, maybe it was stage-fright, maybe it was a bit of both, but it mattered, and we lost because we didn't do ourselves justice.

In the aftermath of the game, Galwey was worried that the Munster dream would die that afternoon in Twickenham.

The biggest fear we had was whether we would ever get back there again; we questioned ourselves as to whether our making the final was a flash in the pan, but thankfully it wasn't.

Instead, it was the start of Munster building a great team, building a product, building a support base. Yes, I will look back and regret not having won a Heineken Cup medal, but I'll never regret being involved with that team, that special team, who helped put Munster rugby on the map and created an environment to allow future teams and, hopefully future generations, enjoy the success we didn't.

The pain of letting that one slip away will never leave me, but the pain has dimmed. I must say we were consoled by the magnificent response of the Munster crowd shortly after the final whistle sounded.

We were out there in the middle of the pitch trying to let the whole thing sink in, not really believing it had happened; there were tears, for ourselves and for the fans who had given us such support throughout the campaign and with whom we built up such a magnificent bond, of friendship and mutual respect.

Then, out of the blue, a group started chanting Munster, Munster, Munster . . . leading to another group who struck up a chorus of 'The Fields of Athenry'. Within a couple of minutes, the whole stadium was rocking to the sound that had been so familiar to us during the pool games. We lost, but those people made us feel like winners. I knew then that we, Munster, would be back to fight another day.

Munster (v Northampton):

D. Crotty, J. Kelly, M. Mullins, J. Holland, A. Horgan, R. O'Gara, P. Stringer, P. Clohessy, K. Wood, J. Hayes, M. Galwey (captain), J. Langford, E. Halvey, A. Foley, D. Wallace.
Replacement: K. Keane for Crotty.

Northampton's Budge Pountney goes off to celebrate, leaving
Anthony Foley to reflect on a sad day.

Chapter 24:
2000/1: FOOT AND MOUTH

2000/1: FOOT AND MOUTH

Keith Wood was never going to hang around with Munster – not when he had a contract with Harlequins to honour – and so, after the drama of Twickenham on that May day in 2000, he packed his bags and did not even have to cross the pond to get home. Even on a very busy day at nearby Heathrow Airport you could hear the Twickenham roar at the Stoop.

But having come up short, Wood left with a heavy heart; he said he was indebted to Munster, and particularly to Declan Kidney, for giving him his rugby life back. Wood was gutted following Ireland's World Cup exit to Argentina at Lens; he felt he might never recover from the blow. But Munster, he said at the time, renewed his faith in the game and in himself.

I was never so down in my life as I was after Lens, but Munster and Declan helped me get the buzz back. I owe a big debt to the Munster spirit. Munster will be back. Just look at the bench, look at the guys who did not get a spin this time, but whose turn will come in the near future. I'm disappointed, I'm always disappointed to finish on a losing side, and a single point defeat is always a bummer but we have had many highs to get to this one point, so to dismiss all that because of a 9–8 loss would be stupid.

I've had a year that I couldn't have expected, I've loved every single minute of it; I couldn't get to the point of saying this is a low. We've lost a match that maybe we could have won and I refuse to bow my head, because we are still one of the two best teams in Europe and we helped bring over 70,000 people to a club match. Who could ever imagine, a few years ago, that would be the case one day?

Wood knew the future was in safe hands, and Frankie Sheahan was to be a significant part of that future for many more seasons. Sheahan had a good working relationship with Wood, but he was glad to see the back of him at the same time because it paved the way for a brighter future in the number 2 jersey.

It came as a surprise to Sheahan when Wood decided to leave Harlequins and rejoin Munster on a short-term contract the previous season. In fact, it still irks Sheahan that he heard news of the development on the radio. 'To be honest, I wasn't very pleased the way I found out; it was also a big shock because it affected my prospects of getting regular game time.'

It all worked out well, however, as Sheahan recalls. 'Thankfully, it didn't affect the situation with Ireland. I spent a lot of time on the bench with Munster but I also got into the Irish squad, and I got some game time as well. It was devastating news at the start, but I decided to get on with it and I think it's fair to say I learned a lot during Woody's year here. I got my opportunity in the 2000 semi-final when he was injured and I played the full second half. It was a challenge for me and I think I got through it well.'

Munster drew Castres Olympique, Newport and Bath in the 2000/1 season, and although they started the campaign by defeating Newport at home, the 25–18 victory did not inspire confidence for Munster's chances of making the knockout stages. It augured well for Sheahan, though – he grabbed one of Munster's three tries against a gritty Welsh side.

The general consensus among the Munster supporters was that the victory at Vicarage Road was the turning point in Munster's rise from wannabes to European champions. As coach, Kidney would never deny the importance of that win for a whole host of reasons, but he believes it was the second game of the 2000/1 campaign when everything changed forever.

For some, such as skipper Galwey, Peter Clohessy and Anthony Foley, the trip to Castres would have bittersweet memories. The 1996 visit ended in last-minute heartbreak when Munster took their eye of the ball momentarily; at half time on a crisp November night at Stade Pierre-Antoine, the now vastly experienced trio could only sit and wonder how on earth Castres had managed to pull clear by fourteen points.

Kidney explained to them that they had made two mistakes in a good forty minutes and urged them to put it all behind them, to start all over again and forget the scoreline. He reasoned that if Munster had made two mistakes in the first half, that Castres would, if Munster applied pressure, be forced into making even more. Alan Quinlan had been sent to the sin bin and returned shortly before the interval. That, says Kidney, was when Galwey proved to be a brave and inspirational captain.

We had a line-out inside our 22, and the obvious safe option was to call a throw to two; Mick, however, knew he had to get Quinny to focus back on the match and ordered that the ball be thrown to the back. Quinny caught a good ball, we cleared our lines and made more ground than we would if we had taken that safe option. It had a double beneficial effect.

That chat at half time was very important; the win over Saracens the previous year put us out stage and centre, it got us up and running, but it was in Castres where we had to ask hard questions of ourselves, questions that nobody else had asked. Having lost the final the previous year, people might have got on our backs, but they didn't. There was no pressure on us, other than pressure from within.

Those first-half mistakes weren't worth harping on because they made errors in the second half, as I felt they might, and we went three points up with three minutes left.

That's when Gaillimh and Anthony [Foley] kicked in; they had learned in Shannon how to close down games. There were three minutes in which to win a match and they closed it out efficiently, brilliantly. These days it would be called clinical, but back in 2000 it was something really special because you wouldn't have experienced it very often.

For me, that was the night Munster moved beyond being a one-season wonder, it was there we got momentum. Back then, the competition was stop-start and some teams never got it going after breaks in activity, but we learned how to get it going again. Gaillimh's leadership was often understated but always appreciated from within; he would be the first to admit there were key men at his side, Claw, Axel, Duchy, guys making calls when calls needed to be made.

The thing about Munster that was evident from an early stage was the friendship; maybe the players didn't see me as their friend as such because I was coach, but we genuinely were friends, we had great times, sometimes an absolute howl; it was an uncommon thing in the world of professional sport where teams are usually thrown together and where the common bond is that they want to win because they're being paid. This went beyond that, way beyond it.

Next up were Bath, who arrived in Limerick full of hope that reputation might be enough to end Munster's great home record. It was not to be; Anthony Horgan was in flying form and scored two tries, David Wallace another and O'Gara, once again, put the game beyond reach with a personal contribution of sixteen points as Munster secured an impressive 31–9 victory.

The following week the teams met again; Bath turned the tables and deservedly won by eighteen points to five.

But January was a fruitful month for Munster; an away win over Newport was crucial in securing their place in the quarter-finals. In a hard-fought victory, O'Gara was the scoring hero with a try, four penalties, three conversions and two drop goals. Mike Mullins and Horgan also scored tries as Munster eventually pulled away to secure a 39–24 win. A week later, Castres did their best to spoil the party at Musgrave Park, but Munster, thanks to O'Gara with eleven points, prevailed by twenty-one points to eleven to top the table and secure a home quarter-final against Biarritz. That game was certainly no stroll in the park, with Munster winning 38–29.

At this stage of the season, Munster had become accustomed to watching O'Gara take matches by the scruff of the neck. On 28 January 2001 he did it again, but this time he had to share joint billing with Foley. The big number 8, once described by Keith Wood as the most astute forward to have played in the modern game, scored a hat-trick of tries en route to a career Heineken Cup tally of twenty-three, while O'Gara finished Biarritz off with seven penalty goals and one conversion.

That victory gave Munster passage into the last four once again, but they were unfortunate to be drawn away to Stade Français, and unfortunate again to lose in the most controversial manner possible on 21 April.

It is normal these days to have video referees present at all Heineken Cup games; back in 2001 that was not always the case. In this game, held in Lille, there was none, and it was one of the main reasons why Munster lost out on a place in the final against eventual champions Leicester Tigers. While it was generally acknowledged that Stade looked the better side on the day and probably deserved their narrow 16–15 triumph, one of a number of decisions could well have cost Munster the match.

The game was fifty-two minutes old with Munster trailing 9–16 when Peter Stringer planted a perfectly weighted kick into the path of John O'Neill. The big winger took it in his stride and dived over, holding the ball away from the covering tackles to his right and touching it down about six inches inside the in-goal area. As O'Neill celebrated and the hordes of Munster supporters went wild with excitement, referee Chris White dashed from the direction of the goalposts and was about to signal a score. Then he looked to touch judge Steve Lander for confirmation but there was none; apparently Lander had been too far away from the touchdown to be positive. White then gave the benefit of the doubt to the defence and awarded a 22-metre dropout.

O'Neill recalls the sensational decision.

The referee looked at the touch judge, the touch judge looked at the referee – nothing. [Christophe] Dominici, [O'Neill's opposite number] had resigned himself to the fact that it was a try and had walked away. I was shocked, and I think he was shocked too. It was galling to stand there afterwards, knowing that I had scored a try and that we had been beaten by just one point. We should have been in the final, not thinking of how to get into another final some time in the future. It was amazing to think that there should have been such a breakdown in communication between the officials because, video referee or no video referee, that was a try; there was no contest, no doubt about it, that was a try.

It was not the only moment of controversy on a day when the match officials had an off-day and Munster suffered. O'Gara kicked a penalty in the sixty-sixth minute that was clearly good, but it was ruled out by the touch judges and the referee. And when Dominici was sent to the sin bin in the

John O'Neill gets the touchdown for the perfect try that never was. Match officials were badly positioned to see O'Neill get his hand to the ball and did not have the benefit of video analysis to confirm the view that it was a legitimate score. As a result, Munster lost that semi-final in Lille to Stade Français in heartbreaking circumstances. ERC urgently reviewed the rules following the subsequent furore.

seventy-second minute but allowed to return after eight minutes instead of the mandatory ten, referee White, reacting to Munster protestations, said he had no control over a decision made by the fourth official on the touchline.

After O'Gara's close call fourteen minutes from the end, he did kick two penalties to keep Munster in the hunt as they cranked up the pressure in the closing minutes. Eventually they ran out of time and were left to rue those bad decisions by the officials as well as their own inability to control the match as they had hoped to do.

'I guess we didn't keep possession for long enough or in the right positions on the field,' says captain Mick Galwey. 'Their defence was well organised and they managed to frustrate us; it was one of those days when just about everything went wrong for us.'

Kidney, however, believes it all went wrong a long time before that. He pointed to the disruption wreaked upon Irish teams when travel restrictions were put in place following an outbreak of foot-and-mouth disease. Those restrictions meant there was a serious lack of match practice for his players, as he outlined:

I think we should not play down the fact that our preparations were severely disrupted. What we had, as a squad, between the Biarritz and Stade Français matches was the odd club game and a Munster v Rest of Ireland match which was basically a trial for the Lions tour of 2001. We were undercooked because there was no rugby of any note.

The French league had been going on the whole time, so they had a huge advantage in terms of preparation. You could add in the fact that it was a horrible day, that we had injuries going into the game – Eddie Halvey and Quinny were both ruled out – we had to ask Donncha O'Callaghan to play out of position at a time when he was only developing as a player, and we had to enlist the help of Dion Ó Cuinneagáin to come over from South Africa and provide cover for us.

There were loads of reasons why we shouldn't have won that game, and the fact that there was no TMO [television match official] was one of them, but the single biggest factor was the outbreak of foot and mouth and the effect it had on our preparations.

We learned one thing that day, that we had the best supporters one could wish for, and ultimately ERC were to learn an awful lot about the competition that day and what they needed to do to improve it.

There would be joy down the line for those who survived until 2006, but this was the end of the road for Langford, who played his last game for Munster. Initially, he planned to stay in Ireland for a year, but extended that after vowing to help the side lift the Heineken Cup after the shattering loss in Twickenham the year before. He did not hide the tears as the final whistle sounded.

It really was emotional when we went over to the fans. In my time playing the game I have never experienced such great support for a team and I would like to think that somewhere, sometime, I'll experience something similar again.

The consolation in defeat is, I suppose, the knowledge that we gave it our best shot; we can't change the things that went against us. Whether we deserved to win or not based on the run of play over eighty minutes is immaterial; the fact is that while we scored a legitimate try and a legitimate penalty, they didn't count because of circumstances outside of our control.

As for the future, Langford knew that success would finally come. 'Munster are far from finished,' he said. 'We had some great times and played high-quality rugby. I will treasure the memories for the rest of my life. The last two years have been brilliant. It's time for me to go but for Munster to move on, and they will move on, I'm convinced. Two years of unfinished business will make them even more determined. Their day will come, I'm certain of that.'

It would take four years, but their day did come. And when it did, Langford's contribution to Munster's development, though five years before, was not forgotten by his friends. Nor will it ever be.

Munster (v Stade Français):

D. Crotty, J. O'Neill, M. Mullins, J. Holland, A. Horgan, R. O'Gara, P. Stringer, P. Clohessy, F. Sheahan, J. Hayes, M. Galwey (captain), J. Langford, D. O'Callaghan, A. Foley, D. Wallace.
Replacements: D. Ó Cuinneagáin for O'Callaghan, M. Horan for Clohessy.

*Declan Kidney and John Langford take it on the chin, but it proved to be a sad day –
an emotional Langford was heading back to Australia after two action-packed years
with Munster.*

Chapter 25:
2001/2: SO NEAR AND YET SO FAR

2001/2: SO NEAR AND YET SO FAR

When Declan Kidney and Niall O'Donovan took over the coaching duties at Munster in late summer 1998, the season was over almost before it began – 12 October to be precise.

The following seasons proved more demanding for the coaching team and for the players, with the 1997/8 programme of eleven games stretched to double that in 2001/2. This was partly due to Munster's success in getting to another Heineken Cup final, but also because of a progressively expanding programme of matches.

Every coach points to the necessity of winning games on the road in order to achieve success in Europe. Munster knocked down walls just about everywhere they went, and they smashed through another on 6 October 2001 at the Stoop.

It was the first year of the Celtic League, and it gave Kidney and his coaching team the ideal opportunity to give much-needed experience to the fringe players, albeit on a limited scale initially. Munster's growing reputation was enough to convince Wasps and Bath to travel to Limerick and compete in a round-robin tournament for the Brazen Head trophy as a build-up to the opening Celtic League fixture against Edinburgh in Myreside, a match Munster narrowly won before going on to win four of the next five games in the tournament and qualify for the quarter-finals.

Impressive victories over Caerphilly (61–18) and Cardiff (51–10) put Munster in the right place as they prepared for that opening Heineken Cup clash with Castres at Thomond Park. Although winning 28–23, Munster played nervously and had to rely on a Jason Holland try to seal the win.

As Munster prepared for a first away assignment to Keith Wood's Harlequins, there was a lack of confidence among supporters following the opening performance. However, Munster won by twenty-four points to eight;

better still, they won without playing very well, as Keith Wood reiterated afterwards. 'Munster didn't play outstandingly well but they won and that's the mark of a good side. They make very few mistakes and they appear to be able to cover up the mistakes they do make. They grind it out like a very good cup side. Munster played like Munster always plays – good defence, great tackles, time after time; we make the mistakes, they score the tries. It's clinical, low-error cup rugby and nobody does it better. We played some great rugby at times but it was no good; they were playing cup rugby, winning rugby, streetwise rugby.'

Harlequins coach John Kingston praised Munster's character. 'We went 5–0 up but their experience showed. We cut them open for that try and we felt we were playing some of our best rugby; we were the better side with respect, but they went 6–5 up against the run of play and then scored a try right on half time. At the end, you saw one streetwise side playing an inexperienced one. I've seen them getting their arses kicked at various stages of various matches, but they often tend to come out smelling of roses. It says a huge amount for their character.'

Mick Galwey tries to batter his way through the Leicester defence in the decider in Cardiff.

Marcus Horan celebrates another Heineken Cup victory; after some appearances off the bench he made his first start against Bridgend in 2002, a game Munster won easily, 40–6.

Kidney and O'Donovan had, over time, given ample praise to Holland, who once again scored a crucial try and a drop goal to help Munster on their way, but the man of the match on this occasion was Ronan O'Gara, who completed his side's scoring with a try, two penalties, a drop goal and a conversion.

It was O'Gara's all-round play that impressed Kidney. 'He is a smashing team player. In the out-half slot, you can be given undeserved praise and sometimes unfair criticism, but Ronan did his job as he always does; it was like a normal day for him.'

When John Langford returned to Australia, Jim Williams – seen here in action at Thomond Park – came in and made a huge impact.

Most observers saw that win at the Stoop as the key result of that particular campaign, particularly since Munster lost the last match away to Castres Olympique.

But Kidney, who always does his statistical homework, says the most important win on the road was at the Brewery Field. 'The competition is littered with examples of teams being unable to win both of those mid-pool fixtures; to get a win in Bridgend, a place that people might forget is a real old-school rugby venue, where pride and passion amongst the supporters is the norm, was very important.'

At the time, he described it as one of Munster's tougher matches. 'We looked a bit tired at times, but we've got to turn around and do it all again next week.' Munster did just that, proving much too good for the Welsh side at Musgrave Park with a facile 40–6 win.

The first three weeks of December were set aside for the knockout stages of the Celtic League and Munster, on the back of seven successive wins, powered on with a 13–6 win over Llanelli and a 15–9 victory over Ulster in a semi-final at Lansdowne Road.

Leinster were doing their own work at the other side of the draw and the teams met at headquarters on 15 December in a decider that produced great excitement. Munster appeared to be on their way to victory when Leinster struck twice to secure an amazing 24–20 win; it was a major disappointment for Munster, not only to lose in the manner they did but to lose to their most bitter rivals.

However, the defeat appeared to galvanise Munster over Christmas as they prepared for the rematch with Harlequins. It was a must-win match and Munster delivered the goods when so many doubted them. Running in six tries, they scored fifty-one points, their biggest ever European score.

Wood, who was sidelined with a calf muscle injury and had to watch the match from the stand in the company of Harlequins chief executive Mark Evans, was suitably impressed. 'It was a superb Munster performance; it must have been their best of the season and it augers well. I was impressed by Jim Williams; I doubted whether he was the right guy for Munster when he signed, but I was wrong. He has come in and is knocking guys out of the way and doing a lot of serious damage to opponents.'

It was a disappointing day, too, for Paul Burke, playing opposite O'Gara for the visitors. 'They gave us nothing and they now stand a good chance of winning the group and going all the way to the final, particularly if they manage to get a home draw.' Burke's prediction was correct up to a point. Munster did make it to the final but failed to get a home quarter after losing to Castres in the final match and finishing second to the French side.

That Castres game was hugely controversial – Ismaella Lassissi, the Castres flanker, was subsequently banned for a year for biting Munster prop Peter Clohessy. The alleged incident was enough to prompt an angry Munster to cite the player, and the mood did not improve when Lassissi persuaded Castres to counter-claim that Clohessy had subjected the Ivory Coast international to 'racial and discriminatory remarks'. The club withdrew the allegations during the initial hearing but went on to appeal the ban; the appeal proved successful, much to Munster's annoyance.

Munster had twelve weeks to let that annoyance fester and plot their revenge; of more pressing importance, however, was the meeting with Stade Français at Stade Jean Bouin in Paris. After losing in such controversial circumstances to Stade the previous season, this was just what the doctor ordered, although neither Kidney nor the team were keen to have to play that quarter-final in Stade's own backyard.

As in 2001, it was a tough battle with little or nothing between the teams. A gale blew throughout the game, in which Munster dominated the first half and Stade the second. Things became nasty during an early scrum, with Munster's John Hayes taking a blow to the head. But, as Kidney recalls, 'I think things were sort of settled early in the second half.' Anthony Foley remembers the incident well and relates the story in his book *Axel: A Memoir* (Dublin, 2008).

It was one of the most satisfying Munster victories, even though I was responsible for letting my opposite number, Christophe Juillet, slip over for a try early in the second half. The filthy looks I got for that can be imagined. We had worked our arses off to build up a 16–3 lead on the strength of a gale blowing straight down the pitch, and in the second half we were just going to protect that lead. Letting Juillet score wasn't a good start – but we all worked harder as a result.

Kicking into the gale wasn't an option, so our recycling had to be spot on, and it was. The key was not allowing Diego Dominguez any shots at goal and that meant putting up with all sorts of provocation. Ironically, the only one to lose his temper was Hayes. It's pretty hard to get him angry but, as one scrum broke up, he clocked Sylvian Marconnet an awful box, which stunned everyone, not just Marconnet, who was taken off a few minutes later.

In general, we kept our cool, defended hard and held on for an excellent win after which Gaillimh was chaired off by hundreds of very happy supporters. Paris had been taken by storm.

Foley was full of praise that day for young Paul O'Connell.

He was invited to train with Munster the previous summer, and just a few weeks after that Stade game he was due to make his international debut. I liked the cut of him. He was wiry and aggressive and, most of all, incredibly keen to play for Munster. He had turned down the offer of a full Connacht contract for an academy contract with us because he was so determined to join Munster. His only problem, maybe, was that he was almost too keen. I remember watching him play a Munster Senior Cup final between Shannon and the Cookies [Young Munster], when he charged off the bench so pumped up that he was in the sin bin three minutes later. Declan had to give him a stern talking-to about his discipline – another irony when you think of how big he is on discipline nowadays.

Kidney, always proud of his side's achievements, was particularly pleased that day. 'To beat them, considering the high-profile players they had, was a feat in itself. We were written off by everyone, except we didn't write ourselves off. It was a formidable task to protect our lead that was cut to just two points with plenty of time on the clock for Stade. The pitch was on the short side; they had a strong wind at their backs and a great goal kicker; had they got a penalty anywhere from their 10-metre line in they would probably have won it but we thrived because our discipline was so good.'

On the same day, Castres, with Lassissi in the side, overcame Montferrand (later renamed Clermont Auvergne) 22–21 and were favoured with a home semi-final against, of all teams, Munster. Although it was not quite a home draw, as the rules stipulated, and Beziers was chosen by ERC as the venue.

It certainly did not suit Munster to be without activity for so long between games, although a match against Leinster at Musgrave Park provided a timely warm-up. That game ended in a 6–6 draw after a tough encounter, which can't have done them any harm as they faced the French side yet again.

It was late April in the south of France, a sweltering day in the city of Beziers whose local authority recognised that Munster fans would arrive in numbers and catered accordingly. The city council erected tents around the heart of the town and there were plenty of bars and restaurants; it was a weekend when people fully realised just how much the Munster support had contributed to the growing popularity of the Heineken Cup. The place was a mass of red and white, with Castres' supporters barely getting a look in.

Donncha O'Callaghan came on for the injured Anthony Foley early on and played the game of his life. It was a match in which tensions, inevitably, ran high, as Kidney recalls.

Peter [Clohessy] and a Castres player were sent to the sin bin after about fifteen minutes; on the way off the pitch, Peter, who had been given a bottle of water, squirted the contents at the French guy, who wasn't at all pleased but couldn't afford to react. It was typical of Peter in taking the opportunity to let the other guy know what he thought of him. John Kelly got a great try that day, Rog [O'Gara] did a lot of damage and, overall, the team played well. It was very satisfactory to beat Castres; it was one that, as a team, the boys had to win after all that had happened earlier in the season.

Certainly it was a personal triumph for Clohessy, who wanted more than anything to put Castres to the sword after all the drama and controversy of the earlier game. Indeed the prop forward went through the pain barrier to ensure he could play. A few weeks before the match, he burned his arm and face in what was reported as a gardening accident, lighting a barbeque at his home. As recalled in Foley's book, he got no sympathy from his colleagues when he turned up for training a few days afterwards with his arm in a sling, his face badly scalded and his hair singed.

He turned up in an awful state; we stopped the session and walked over to look at him. There he was looking pretty sorry for himself when someone giggled and then we all burst out laughing. We couldn't stop; we showed no mercy, maybe because he'd have shown no mercy himself.

Still, his injuries were serious enough for people to wonder whether he'd ever play again, let alone play in the semi-final – he was retiring at the end of the year anyway. But those people didn't know Claw; he wasn't going to miss a rematch against Castres, He was told he would have to pass a fitness test a few days before the game but that was no bother. He played a game of indoor five-a-side soccer at UL, declared himself fit, and that was that – bitten, burned, but not beaten, as it said on the T-shirt!

John O'Neill was drafted in as a late replacement for the injured Anthony Horgan and came agonisingly close to scoring a try that might have helped win the game. It was the second time in a year that O'Neill was denied a try in the corner – this time Austin Healey did manage to get in a fruitful and legal challenge to stop him.

After two victories on French soil, Munster should have been feeling more confident about their chances in the final against Leicester Tigers, who triumphed the previous year over Stade in a 64-point thriller in Paris. But storm clouds had been gathering in the weeks between the semi-final and the decider. Foley was struggling to overcome a shoulder injury and Jim Williams was nursing a calf muscle strain. Munster went to Belfast to play Ulster and lost by five points.

Then, when Munster gathered in the Vale of Glamorgan Hotel on the Thursday night before the game, they played a game of tip rugby during which Anthony Horgan broke two bones in his hand. Ruled out of the final, Horgan was replaced by John O'Neill; although this had no negative effect on the performance, it was hardly what Munster needed forty-eight hours before the big day. On top of that, Kidney admitted that he had to make a big call, figuring that Foley would last longer than Williams but that neither could play a full eighty minutes. He went with Foley, who played fifty-five minutes before being replaced by Williams, who did manage to finish the game despite worries to the contrary.

Jim Williams never gave up in the pool game against Harlequins but his surge for the line was stopped short.

Then there was the incident involving Neil Back, who illegally handled the ball and scooped away possession from Munster in a scrum close to the Leicester line near the end of the game, with the Tigers leading 15–9. There was widespread condemnation of the English flanker, even from some Leicester supporters, in the days that followed, but for Munster there was no consolation. Neither the referee nor touch judge had seen it, despite vigorous protestations from scrum half Peter Stringer, and whatever chance Munster

Where Williams failed, Galwey succeeded and he was one of Munster's six try scorers in the 51–17 win over 'Quins.

had was lost. Back showed no remorse for some time, before eventually stating he regretted what he had done.

Foley, in his book, said he bore no grudge, even though he insisted that Munster had a move planned that they felt would yield a try at the posts to give O'Gara an opportunity to convert and kick Munster into a 16–15 lead. Foley also said, however, that he felt the better team won.

Maybe if the touch judge had seen him, we would have won the penalty, knocked it in the corner, driven over and Rog would have kicked the winning conversion. Maybe. But that would have been an even bigger steal than what Neil Back did to us.

Our preparation was generally far smoother than it had been in 2000 but this was still another of those Munster days overloaded with emotion. We knew Deccie [Kidney] and Niallo [O'Donovan] were moving on. Claw was definitely retiring, having agreed to play the season only because of the disappointment of the previous year in Lille. Gaillimh knew he was coming to an end, while Dom Crotty was emigrating to the USA.

So, of course, there was a lot of talk about this being Munster's year, almost as if we deserved to win because we had been unlucky in the past. Were Leicester going to do us a favour? I don't think so. They beat us because they scored two tries to zero, did a number on our line-out and were by far the better side. While we were heartbroken walking up to receive a second collection of losers medals, I think we all probably realised that.

It was a sad day for Kidney and O'Donovan, who were moving on to what some might describe as promotion with Ireland. As events transpired, however, neither would have felt they had been promoted.

Kidney says he will never forget that day, 25 May 2005 – and not for all the wrong reasons either.

Of course, we were all bitterly disappointed. Some of us were moving on; Peter was playing his last game for Munster; that's a big day in the life of any player. I'm sure he would swap everything had we got the required result, but otherwise he couldn't have picked a better day to go; I'll never forget the round of applause from everyone, including Leicester fans, in the stadium as he trooped off the pitch, all 72,000 of them.

He headed to the bench on the sideline and Luke, his son, was brought down to sit on his lap for the remaining ten minutes or so of the match, even though he might have been required to go back on the pitch had there been an injury to any of the other props.

Goodness knows how we would have coped with Lukie if that had been the case, but we would have had to deal with it. I guess people would have said it was a Munster thing.

Munster (v Castres):

D. Crotty, J. Kelly, R. Henderson, J. Holland, A. Horgan, R. O'Gara, P. Stringer, P. Clohessy, F. Sheahan, J. Hayes, M. Galwey (captain), P. O'Connell, A. Quinlan, A. Foley, D. Wallace.
Replacements: M. Mullins for Henderson, M. Horan for Clohessy, D. O'Callaghan for Foley.

Munster (v Leicester):

D. Crotty, J. O'Neill, R. Henderson, J. Holland, J. Kelly, R. O'Gara, P. Stringer, P. Clohessy, F. Sheahan, J. Hayes, M. Galwey (captain), P. O'Connell, A. Quinlan, A. Foley, D. Wallace.
Replacements: J. Williams for Foley, M. Horan for Clohessy, M. O'Driscoll for O'Connell, J. Staunton for Crotty, M. Mullins for Henderson, J. Blaney for Sheahan (temporary).

Chapter 26:
2002/3: GALWEY'S THOMOND

2002/3: GALWEY'S THOMOND

Michael Galwey started to wind down his professional career following the 2001/02 season; his biggest regret was that he failed to lead Munster to Heineken Cup glory, although he certainly gave it everything in a smashing career that brought him from the GAA fields in Kerry and beyond to rugby stadiums throughout the world, with Munster, Ireland and the Lions.

But ask him about favourite grounds and there is only one answer – Thomond Park. 'Irrespective of where we play in Europe, leading Munster out at Thomond Park has been my greatest thrill, my proudest moment as captain. All of a sudden, the crowd lifts you and if you're anyway iffy about the match, they give you that certainty that you'll do it, that they're behind you, and if you're struggling, they'll be behind you even more,' he wrote in *Galwey: The Autobiography* (Dublin, 2002).

Before the start of the 2002/3 season, knowing that time was catching up on him, Galwey relinquished the captaincy and there was a straight players' vote between Jim Williams and Anthony Foley for the job. Williams won by a single vote. Foley may have been disappointed but he offered Williams his full support and, in any event, he would have his day.

But this particular season was not just about Galwey or Williams; Munster had a new coach in Alan Gaffney, and most of the players would agree that it was a good time for change, even though they were sad to see Kidney go and would remember him with affection over the next three years until his surprise return. Gaffney was quickly accepted, even though, according to Munster's out-half in *Ronan O'Gara: My Autobiography* (Dublin, 2008), he made instant, sometimes unpopular, demands of the squad. Greater emphasis was placed on ball skills and new training drills that would allow Munster play a different style of game.

In the previous three years Munster's success had been based on cup rugby. We had a big man at 12 who set targets for our forwards to run off and then we drilled the ball to the corners. That way of playing had gotten us to two Heineken Cup finals but it wasn't good enough to win either of them. In the knockout stages of the 2002 competition we had scored two tries in three matches and one of those was in the last minute against Biarritz when the game was virtually won. We weren't going to win the Heineken Cup if we didn't score more tries.

Alan was very strong on video analysis and I felt the benefit of that. Back play was his speciality and he suggested things to me that made my game better. He was good on passing techniques and the kind of detail that makes a difference.

But O'Gara admits that not everyone felt the same about the new coach, who, he suggested, became frustrated at the lack of depth in the squad.

Peter Stringer rounds the Leicester Tigers defence to score a crucial try in the 20–7 quarter-final victory at Welford Road.

During his three years with us, feelings towards him in the squad were divided. Our pool of players wasn't as deep as it is now and when the internationals were away in camp Munster struggled for results. These players left behind felt that Alan took out his frustrations on them. They were beasted in training during the week and then given a really simple game plan at the weekend because he didn't think they were capable of executing anything more complex. The morale of the Celtic League team became poor after a while. Then we would come back from Irish camp and it was all smiles again. All I could do was take him as I found him and he was good for me.

Despite losing the vote for the captaincy to another Australian, it was clear that future leader Foley got on famously with both Gaffney and Williams. In his book, he constantly refers to Gaffney as Gaffer, not Alan. 'It was a brave move for Gaffer to come from Leinster; he said he took the plunge because his mantra in life is "don't die wondering". He could never have dreamt up some of the stuff that he experienced with us!'

Foley did criticise Gaffney for signing what he described as 'some dodgy imports': ' . . . as Claw would say, not naming names, but Clinton Huppert?' but praised him for employing good helpers such as Brian Hickey as assistant coach and Paul McCarthy as scrum specialist, before the arrival of Graham Steadman to work on defence. 'Gaffer was an outstanding technician and encouraged us to think about the game in terms of a process or a series of processes. He probably figured out soon enough that the emotional side of things would look after itself.'

Foley did concede that Gaffney, and the team, were probably fortunate that season to draw an Italian side in Pool 2 because it allowed them to pick up points at a time when the general form left something to be desired. Munster lost the opening tie of the Heineken Cup away to Gloucester – heavily – before stringing together three successive wins prior to losing again away to Perpignan on 11 January.

That left them in the most critical position in years, as Foley recalled. 'The changing room in Perpignan was like a morgue after we lost that game in round five, it seemed to close the door on qualification. The supporters we met in the airport on the way home were thanking us for the memories of the previous few seasons. All they asked from the following Saturday was that we beat Gloucester and preserve our unbeaten record at Thomond Park.'

That game – the drama, excitement and glorious celebration at the end when Munster won by thirty-three points to six, by the required twenty-seven points and the necessary four tries to give them advantage over Gloucester – is now part of Munster rugby folklore. It became known as 'The Miracle Match' and it was deemed important enough for Munster to endorse the production of a DVD by the same name; the Munster marketing machine was about to kick in. Foley described how the 'miracle' happened.

We were sorted on the emotional side, naturally. Gaillimh, who had stepped aside for Donners [Donncha O'Callaghan], got us going in the changing room with some well-chosen words. Claw even stuck his head around the door after receiving some award on the pitch designed to get the crowd going – Marcus [Horan], who had waited long enough to get his chance, had some choice words for him, as I remember. The fact that two of our tries would come directly off the scrum was a source of pride for Marcus, who had been criticised for not having a big enough arse, among other things.

But I don't need to go into detail about how each try came. What I'd love to be able to describe is the surge of energy that coursed through my entire being when Rog launched the first bomb for Gloucester's fullback Henry Paul and the crowd went ballistic. I'd love for the fans to see up close the look of bewilderment in the eyes of Ludovic Mercier as the impossible became increasingly possible, and I wish I could recreate the sheer hysteria when Rags [John Kelly] touched down for the fourth try.

That victory secured Munster's place in the knockout stages although the draw – an away fixture to Leicester – was greeted with muted enthusiasm by the supporters given the opposition and the location for the game. The team felt differently, however; they craved revenge and would find a whole host of reasons to motivate themselves twelve weeks down the line.

In the meantime there was other business to attend to, and they headed to Cardiff in pursuit of the Celtic League trophy. Munster and Neath had reached the decider in the Millennium Stadium and Munster's stirring triumph over Gloucester meant they went as favourites. Gaffney's men secured victory by thirty-seven points to seventeen in a game controversial only for what appeared to be a cynical foul by Brett Sinkinson on O'Gara, who had to be replaced by Rob Henderson in the twenty-sixth minute. With Munster in control, Sinkinson's act rebounded on Neath when Henderson scored a smashing 56th-minute try to put the game beyond reach.

Thus, Williams lifted Munster's first major trophy high in the air, but only after inviting former skipper Galwey to join him; the two got a standing ovation from the large crowd; a huge weight had been lifted from Munster's shoulders.

With eight victories from nine games, Munster could not wait to meet the Tigers – but they had to be patient. That Welford Road date was fixed for 15 April, and with a huge travelling support expected, it was suggested that the game be moved to the larger Walkers Stadium. Leicester's experienced board of directors considered it, but dismissed it just as quickly. Giving up home advantage, even at the expense of a bumper pay day, was not a runner. In any event, Munster supporters travelled in such numbers to Welford Road as to bring a totally new atmosphere to this grand old ground that has played host to many epic battles. And from Munster's point of view, it was another one of those.

There were scores to be settled, individual scores – with Neil Back for what had happened in Cardiff; with Martin Johnson, who earlier that year led England to a Grand Slam victory, insulting the President of Ireland and infuriating the Irish supporters in the process. At Lansdowne Road, Johnson stubbornly refused to adhere to standing in an assigned pre-match position in accordance with agreed protocol, forcing Mary McAleese to walk on the heavy pitch to greet the Irish team rather than on the red carpet provided for the purpose.

Seconds from the end of the Heineken Cup game, Johnson's Leicester team well and truly beaten, Munster were awarded a penalty near the Tigers' line. Williams told O'Gara to kick it into touch to finish the game, but before he got the chance there was a lull in the noise around the ground. Suddenly, an Irish voice was heard to shout, 'Aha, ya b*****d, Johnson – for sale, one red carpet, never used!'

The second row, caught on camera, even managed a wry smile as the fans at that corner of the pitch rocked with laughter. But for Johnson, and his

Peter Stringer is carried shoulder high from Welford Road by ecstatic Munster supporters, including John Madigan to his right offering a hand of congratulations. Madigan played for Munster against the All Blacks in 1973 (3–3) and 1974 (4–14).

What a day, what an achievement: John Kelly raises both hands and Ronan O'Gara jumps in the air to celebrate the end of the 'Miracle Match' against Gloucester, the result of which pushed Munster into the quarter-finals. Kelly's late try gave Munster a bonus-point win, and the conversion by O'Gara gave the team the required winning margin of twenty-seven points.

second-row partner Ben Kay, the second-rowers who had terrorised opponents for club and country, nothing was funny that afternoon, particularly as they were outplayed by two rookies by the names of Paul O'Connell and Donncha O'Callaghan.

An angry Munster is a most dangerous opponent. Fuelled by what Back had done in the Millennium Stadium and what he said afterwards – 'If the game had been a boxing match it would have been over at half time' – and further annoyed that Leicester had delayed the kick-off by ten minutes (to allow the fans take their seats) without informing Munster (who were on the pitch waiting for the game to start), the Irish team went for the jugular from the off.

Mike Mullins summed up the Munster mood. 'They tried a few things to upset us, but it only made us more determined. We wanted to put Cardiff behind us; for the week before the game we had said it would have nothing to do with revenge – but of course it had. We had a score to settle and there aren't too many more satisfactory wins than by beating the European champions on their own ground and booting them out of the competition.'

Munster led 6–0 and held the Tigers scoreless for sixty minutes until the champions struck with a converted try. Mullins believes Leicester's arrogance was their undoing. 'That should have been the makings of them, but it broke them instead. Judging from their reaction, they thought they had it won. But our belief never varied; we knew we had the capacity to score more, we got a try from Rog and that forced them to play catch-up again. They fell right into the trap; the pack was magnificent, our defence was aggressive and they couldn't find a way to cope. When they substituted Kay it was like an admission that they had got it wrong; we took that as something like waving the white flag.'

Vanquished coach Dean Richards believed Munster could go all the way and predicted 'a very closely contested match' against Toulouse. He was partly right.

Munster lost 12–13 in the south of France, due, effectively, to a lack of strength in depth. The starting fifteen would be a match for anyone, as they were for Toulouse, but Gaffney did not have enough experience on the bench, a luxury afforded to his opposite number, Guy Noves

At key moments, Noves could introduce high-quality, experienced players to the fray. This was the difference between winning or losing, as he admitted afterwards. 'We had to call on all of our experience; we thought we were prepared for Munster, but they pushed us all the way. In the end, it was really just the bounce of a ball.'

O'Gara had kept the scoreboard ticking over for Munster, who led 12–6 until Frédéric Michalak scored a try that substitute Jean Baptiste Elissalde converted to secure victory.

There was one happy Irishman in the ground, however. Trevor Brennan had put in a huge effort for Toulouse throughout the afternoon and for his

Munster's Anthony Foley (left) is backed up by captain Jim Williams about to hand off Perpignan's Sylvian Dereoux, as Peter Stringer (second from left) closes in to support,.

trouble sported a black eye. Diplomatically, he declined to reveal how it had come about. 'Let's put it this way, it was a tough game; neither team shirked from anything, it was my type of game.'

Intriguingly, Brennan said he felt he had played the game before. 'I had the most sleepless night of my life before the game; I dreamt that Quinny [Alan Quinlan] and myself beat the crap out of one another, that we were both sent off. I dreamt that they beat us, that we beat them, that it was a draw and went to extra time, all sorts of things; my mind was obviously all over the shop. Sitting here now, I'm still not convinced we won; it was that close.'

If there was any consolation, it was that the Munster supporters once again covered themselves in glory and endeared themselves to the partisan Toulouse following. The depression of losing was lifted temporarily as the fans demanded that Munster 'walk the walk', allowing the supporters to bid adieu for another season and to thank the team for their efforts.

In a remarkable development, sections of the ground housing only Toulouse fans erupted in chants of 'Munster, Munster, Munster' to give Williams' troops a sense of a changing world. Toulouse fans, as Declan Kidney's Munster had found in Bordeaux three years earlier, do not usually do tributes to the opposition, but this was a special occasion. Perhaps they also felt Munster might be a special team; something like them, maybe.

Munster (v Gloucester):

J. Staunton, J. Kelly, M. Mullins, J. Holland, M. Lawlor, R. O'Gara, P. Stringer, M. Horan, F. Sheahan, J. Hayes, D. O'Callaghan, M. O'Driscoll, J. Williams (captain), A. Foley, A. Quinlan.

Munster (v Toulouse):

J. Staunton, J. Kelly, M. Mullins, R. Henderson, A. Horgan, R. O'Gara, P. Stringer, M. Horan, F. Sheahan, J. Hayes, D. O'Callaghan, P. O'Connell, J. Williams (captain), A. Foley, A. Quinlan.
Replacements: J. Holland for Henderson.

Chapter 27:
2003/4: FIRE AND ICE

2003/4:
FIRE AND ICE

Frankie Sheahan spent many years toiling with Munster and Ireland – 'thirteen great years', as he was to describe his tenure in the red jersey prior to his departure at the end of the 2008/9 season.

It was not easy for him to pick out the highlights, aside, of course, from Munster's Heineken Cup victories in 2006 and 2008, but he did. One was the victory over Gloucester in the 'Miracle Match' in 2003; the other was the defeat to London Wasps in the semi-final of 2004.

Sheahan would also have reason to remember another game against Gloucester in 2004, when his team was pitched against the English team, Bourgoin and Treviso in Pool 5 of the Heineken Cup. Once again, Gloucester put it up to the Irish side, and were the only side to beat them in a pool battle that went down to the wire.

Before all the European drama, Munster had a share of disappointment in the early part of the season, despite starting with three consecutive victories – friendlies against Rotherham and Connacht and a Celtic League win over Leinster. It went downhill after that over a six-week period, however, as they lost five Celtic League matches on the bounce. Still, the opening Heineken Cup game provided Munster with a welcome, if uneasy, victory over Bourgoin in Stade Pierre Rajon, followed by a 51–0 win over Treviso.

Gloucester exacted revenge for the previous season's loss in Limerick with a 22–11 win at Kingsholm – but Munster turned the tables at Thomond Park the following week. 'Fire in the belly, ice in the mind', a phrase coined by Sheahan, was employed as Munster's mantra as they recorded a 35–14 win. Gaffney's side enthralled a capacity attendance and the display prompted the coach to say, 'It was the most complete performance I have experienced with this side. We let ourselves down in England and were confident we would put that behind us. By virtue of the defeat in Kingsholm, we were being written

Anthony Horgan (right) and Jim Williams on the charge during the 2004 encounter with Gloucester at Thomond Park. Munster won the game 35–14 to avenge the 22–11 defeat a week earlier.

off but one loss doesn't make for a bad team, particularly when it relates to this particular side.'

Munster scored four tries and earned a bonus point as a result. In the overall context, it was crucial, for over the two matches Munster had the better record. That counted at the end of the pool campaign; Munster earned a home quarter-final against old rivals Stade Français, while Gloucester had to travel to London to take on Wasps. It was a bridge too far for the West Country side.

Nigel Melville, Gloucester's director of rugby at the time, said after the Thomond Park game: 'It's impossible to win games without the ball.' Under pressure scrum half Andy Gomersall won the admiration of the crowd for one brilliantly executed reverse pass with half of the Munster pack bearing down on him in the second half, but he was not in the mood for praise. 'Me having to do reverse passes, that's a sign I wasn't getting the quality of ball I wanted, no matter how well the execution of the pass may have looked.'

Both Melville and Gomersall agreed on one thing – Munster had set the standard for a lot of clubs around Europe. 'They've come a long way in the last few years, put it up to all of us to follow suit,' said Melville, with Gomersall adding, 'Great club, great side, streetwise and battle hardened; they're always hard to beat and they keep coming at you even when you think they have been beaten. Once they get on top, they have that ruthless streak that's associated with winners.'

It was Shaun Payne's first season in Munster, following his arrival after two seasons with Swansea; the signing of the South African proved to be inspirational in the years that followed. And, of course, there was the introduction of Christian Cullen midway through the season on a thirty-month contract.

Payne slipped in quietly, whereas Cullen arrived in a blaze of publicity, which was not to his liking as he was not a limelight seeker. He was spotted at Cork airport one Sunday afternoon and the news spread quickly. For the first time in their history, Munster had to host a press conference to introduce a player publicly; Cullen was in the glare of a thirty-strong media corps, while airport security had some work to do in keeping an increasingly excited young crowd calm.

As it transpired, Cullen would not have many days in the sun with Munster as he was beset by one injury after another from the moment he arrived. He did manage to get through the quarter-final at Thomond Park against Stade Français that season, a match in which Payne scored an early try to send Munster on their way to the last four. There were no wild celebrations following the 37–32 win, however; Munster knew there was plenty of improvement needed in defence having leaked four tries, as many as they scored. The difference was in the goal-kicking; O'Gara slotted all four conversions and three penalties, while his counterpart, Diego Dominguez, missed a crucial penalty and a relatively simple conversion.

Payne was rational in his assessment of the game.

We won, so we're happy but I've sure we will be well reminded of our shortcomings in the days ahead. There were positives and negatives, but the positives outweighed anything and helped get us the all important result. We weren't happy that we threw away such a big lead [seventeen points] and that's something we have to look at seriously, how it happened. We just didn't seem to be able to cope with going so far in front so early [eleven minutes].

I'm sure we will take on board the circumstances of this win, how we deserved it and how we might have thrown it away. From now on, we will respect everyone, but fear nobody. That's the way it has got to be.

Shaun Payne (left) and Mike Mullins, pictured here leaving the pitch together after another Munster victory, and Christian Cullen (far right), all of whom played huge roles en route to another semi-final in 2004, this time getting a home draw against London Wasps at Lansdowne Road. Unfortunately Munster lost another match in controversial circumstances, Wasps scoring a late try that was afterwards proved to be invalid.

Many talked up Munster's chances of beating Wasps, their semi-final opponents, but management and players kept feet firmly on the ground in the two weeks that followed. The game was held in Lansdowne Road in front of 48,000, with Wasps only able to sell 4,000 tickets of a promised allocation of 20,000. Thus, it was a real home fixture for Munster and a huge opportunity to secure a place in yet another final.

But it was not to be. In his autobiography, Anthony Foley outlined what he believed were some of the reasons for the defeat: O'Gara was forced out early in the game with a hamstring injury, Donncha O'Callaghan was sin-binned – very harshly according to the back-rower – and referee Nigel Whitehouse failed to ask for a TMO ruling on Trevor Leota's crucial late try which helped secure a 37–32 win for Wasps; had he done so, according to Foley, the try would have been disallowed and the game gone to extra time. 'Either we suffer because there is no TMO, or we're losing out because he's there but they won't use him.'

But Foley did not make his name through moaning.

The bottom line is that we were ten points up with ten minutes to go, in front of something like 45,000 Munster supporters and we couldn't close the deal. We didn't hold our discipline and our defence just wasn't good enough – we leaked five tries that day and four in the quarter-final against Stade Français. I'm not a subscriber to the Kevin Keegan philosophy of 'you score four, we'll score five'. Basically, Wasps were ruthless and efficient, and we weren't. After three losing semi-finals and two losing finals, the sense of debt to our supporters was truly overwhelming.

Cullen, for all his potential, would never get to repay much of that debt due to injury, and he had nothing but sympathy from his Munster colleagues, among them Foley, who insisted that the legendary All Black did everything humanly possible to pay his way during his time in Ireland.

Although Foley, like others, recognised that Cullen had not given the province a good return on the financial outlay needed to bring him here, he described the run of injuries as cruel. 'It was never the case that he wasn't pulling his weight; if that had been so he would have been eaten alive.'

Foley said there was a certain irony that Cullen was signed in the same season as 'a supposed journeyman' by the name of Shaun Payne. 'He ended up being one of our two best imports ever. For what Payne brought to the cause, and will continue to bring as manager, he has to rank up there with Jimmy [Williams], even ahead of John Langford. I think of him as a modern-day Pat Murray – and although he won't know who the hell Pat Murray is, he can take it as a massive compliment.'

So the season ended in heartbreak and the game in Dublin marked the start of a winding down process for Williams. He would continue to play for a good portion of the 2004/5 season, but he relinquished the captaincy to the man destined finally to lead Munster to the Holy Grail – Foley – and made

Christian Cullen in action against Stade Français in the 2004 quarter-final at Thomond Park.

room in the team for a youngster with a big reputation from County Tipperary. Behind the scenes, Williams invested a lot of his time coaching Denis Leamy in the finer points of back-row forward play. Down the line, Williams would see that work bear a rich harvest as Leamy took his place among the giants of the Munster game – people like Williams, Foley, Wallace and Quinlan, and others before them.

Munster (v Gloucester):

S. Payne, J. Kelly, M. Mullins, R. Henderson, A. Horgan, R. O'Gara, P. Stringer, M. Horan, F. Sheahan, J. Hayes, D. O'Callaghan, P. O'Connell, J. Williams (captain), A. Foley, D. Wallace.
Replacements: G. McIllwham for Horan, S. Keogh for Williams.

Munster (v Stade Français):

C. Cullen, J. Kelly, R. Henderson, M. Mullins, S. Payne, R. O'Gara, P. Stringer, M. Horan, F. Sheahan, J. Hayes, P. O'Connell, D. O'Callaghan, J. Williams (captain), A. Foley, D. Wallace.
Replacements: A. Horgan for Mullins, J. Holland for Kelly.

Munster (v Wasps):

C. Cullen, J. Kelly, R. Henderson, M. Mullins, S. Payne, R. O'Gara, P. Stringer, M. Horan, F. Sheahan, J. Hayes, P. O'Connell, D. O'Callaghan, J. Williams (captain), A. Foley, S. Keogh.
Replacements: J. Holland for O'Gara, A. Horgan for Kelly.

Chapter 28:
2004/5:
A MIXED BAG

2004/5: A MIXED BAG

Like a bad penny, Castres turned up in Munster's group yet again as Anthony Foley began his tenure as Munster captain. And yet again, Castres threw a spanner in the works by beating Munster 19–12 at Stade Pierre Antoine on 3 December 2004.

This time, though, it did not deny Munster, who emerged from the group with six points to spare at the top of the table. However, the twenty-two points total from five victories with two bonus points was not enough to guarantee them a home quarter-final.

The season started slowly, with a mixed bag of results in the early stages. But then Munster put together a run of nine successive wins between the Heineken Cup and the Celtic League. Ironically, Castres brought that run to an end, the consolation being that Munster picked up a bonus point.

Given the shaky performances in Munster's opening games of the Heineken Cup, a 15–9 win over Harlequins at home and a 20–18 win over the Ospreys at the Knoll, a fall was probably on the cards; instead it appeared to galvanise Alan Gaffney's troops, who pushed on with six consecutive wins in both competitions; true enough, none apart from the return fixture against Castres was executed with a massive degree of flair, but both coach and captain were pleased all the same. The sixth, and most important, match, following a 20–10 win over the Ospreys, was against Harlequins, who volunteered to move from the restricted surrounds of the Stoop to Twickenham. There were 34,000 people at the match – most of them shouting for Munster!

Young Denis Leamy made his first Heineken Cup start at home to Harlequins and impacted immediately by scoring one of the two all-important tries. He had to wait his turn after that until the return fixture against Castres, when he produced a display to provide a compelling argument for regular selection; the performance was marked by another try from Munster's captain

Paul O'Connell in a facile 36–8 victory. The win was so comfortable that Gaffney used all of the twenty-two squad members for the first and last time in the tournament that season.

Christian Cullen scored one of his few tries of real importance for Munster in the 20–10 win over Ospreys at Thomond Park on 8 January 2005. It was greeted with huge enthusiasm, because everyone wanted the former All Black to feel part of the party; the fans recognised, as much as his colleagues, that he was doing his best to overcome that unreal litany of injuries.

A week later, everything was to play for at Twickenham; Munster had to win, while Harlequins were only in it for the money they lost over the years in their encounters with the Irish side. Well, they got the money but Munster secured the vital result, if not quite the glory they would have sought.

Questions were asked afterwards of Munster; the question of pace and absolute power in the back division being one of them. Jeremy Guscott, the hero of 1997 for the British and Irish Lions on the tour to South Africa, suggested

Rob Henderson and Frankie Sheahan in action during the 2005 clash against Harlequins at Twickenham. The game attracted 33,000 and gave Harlequins a pay day, but Munster won the game 18–10.

Christian Cullen trying to break through a tackle from Andy Reay against Harlequins.

that Munster could have a huge representation on the 2005 Lions when he championed the chances of Marcus Horan making the squad. Interestingly, however, of the Munster backline, Guscott only gave Ronan O'Gara and Peter Stringer a sniff of a chance. And the injured O'Gara was not even playing!

Without doubt Munster had underperformed, as Gaffney recognised.

A win is a win, we will be hard on ourselves in the clear light of day. Obviously we didn't perform to our capabilities, but if anyone had offered us a guaranteed spot in the quarter-final before the competition began we would have taken it.

Still, there is a new desire within this squad; guys would have been delighted a few years back to beat teams like the Ospreys and Harlequins in successive weeks, in fact to beat them at all; it goes to show that expectations have changed. We look at ourselves more critically these days; we turned over too much possession, we made too many mistakes. Yes, we had enough of the ball but, no, we didn't actually make the best use of it. We have to improve.

Unfortunately, Munster did not secure a home draw in the quarter-final. They had to travel to play Biarritz Olympique, close to the peak of their powers at the time, who hosted game across the Spanish border in San Sebastian. It was another new situation for ERC, the first match to be held in Spain, and the governing body milked it like never before. So too did the tourism bodies in Biarritz and San Sebastian; it was certainly an exemplary cross-border exercise that sporting bodies in our own country could take note of.

But despite the huge Munster support at the 32,000-capacity stadium, Munster never got going in the match; they fell nineteen points behind early

Gotcha! Peter Stringer hands on for dear life to Harlequins captain Tony Diprose.

on and the game was over at the interval. That the Irish side hit back to score ten unanswered points in a fairly heavily contested second half meant little. All of us scribes present, including the experienced rugby analyst Donal Lenihan, believed it was another case of so close, but yet too far.

The decision to move the game to the Basque region of northern Spain proved a resounding success. The atmosphere within the stadium was a magnificent advertisement for an outstanding competition. For Munster, however, the quest for the ultimate European prize becomes more difficult with each passing year.

On the basis of Munster's second-half performance, one was left to wonder if they had paid too much respect to Biarritz in the opening forty minutes. They were left with a mountain to climb although their character could never be called into question, a point made at the end when the supporters stood in unison to acknowledge those efforts in the second half, albeit also acknowledging that the better side won.

Gaffney, in his last season before returning to Australia, was in no doubt that the ultimate prize would come Munster's way. He must have felt it cruel that it happened months after his departure, but as Foley would say – 'Gaffers wasn't like that.' After that match in San Sebastian, the coach was full of hope. 'I am positive that Munster will be a force for years to come. I have no doubt about that; they will win the Heineken Cup and they will win it soon; there are some very high-quality players coming through. Maybe some of the current squad are getting on but if they're the best players then you keep playing them. Age doesn't come into the equation when players are on the top of their game; the structures are there for Munster, the players are coming through, they will develop and they will blossom.'

Horan's five-star display yielded little recognition beyond Irish shores, but Munster had some consolation for the efforts that season. With Gaffney about to depart, the side produced a stunning end-of-season extravaganza of results.

Munster hammered the Borders and Edinburgh in quick succession to reach the knockout stages of the Celtic Cup. Edinburgh provided the opposition in the quarter-finals just a couple of weeks after being beaten in Thomond Park; Munster got the better of Leinster in the semi-final at Lansdowne Road and then of Llanelli Scarlets in the final, again at Lansdowne Road, on 14 May.

It was the last chapter in the Alan Gaffney era and, even though it was not a Heineken Cup victory it was close enough to provide a perfect script for departure. Gaffney's burning desire over three seasons was to see Munster play a more expansive game; in part he saw his charges carry out his instructions with a victory that was more comprehensive than the scoreline might suggest.

Ronan O'Gara returned after injury and, with all due respect to a most capable deputy in the form of Paul Burke, he made a difference. Within minutes of the start, Anthony Horgan got in for a try at the corner and Llanelli, despite all the bravery, faced a catch-up game against a team that packed too much experience. O'Gara moved the game on a notch with a second try, while Mike Mullins grabbed the third; the out-half, with a personal tally of seventeen points, proved to be the major difference as Llanelli pushed the boat out in an effort to save the match.

At Gaffney's going-away party, Foley promised the Australian that his legacy would be remembered when Munster finally found the Holy Grail.

I was still slightly euphoric after our triumph over Llanelli; it was Gaffer's second trophy in three years. No doubt, Munster's critics would have laughed at the idea of us never winning the Heineken Cup, especially around Christmas of that season when we were losing Celtic League games to Leinster and Ulster, when we were long odds even to get out of our pool.

That Christmas was a time for straight questions and honest answers. I didn't lose faith, because I simply couldn't afford to lose faith. Munster was now the sole focus of my professional life, so winning the Heineken Cup was my only real objective. I knew I was running out of time so that added a certain amount of urgency.

Munster (v Harlequins):

C. Cullen, S. Payne, M. Mullins, R. Henderson, A. Horgan, P. Burke, P. Stringer, M. Horan, F. Sheahan, J. Hayes, D. O'Callaghan, P. O'Connell, A. Quinlan, A. Foley (captain), D. Leamy.
Replacements: J. Williams for Quinlan, J. Holland for Henderson.

Munster (v Biarritz):

S. Payne, J. Kelly, M. Mullins, R. Henderson, A. Horgan, P. Burke, P. Stringer, M. Horan, F. Sheahan, J. Hayes, D. O'Callaghan, P. O'Connell, A. Quinlan, A. Foley (captain), D. Wallace.
Replacements. P. Devlin for Mullins. J. Williams for Quinlan, J. Holland for Burke.

Munster (v Llanelli, Celtic Cup final):

S. Payne, P. Devlin, M. Mullins, R. Henderson, A. Horgan, R. O'Gara, P. Stringer, M. Horan, F. Sheahan, J. Hayes, D. O'Callaghan, P. O'Connell, A. Quinlan, A. Foley (captain), D. Wallace.
Replacements: G. McIllwham for Horan, D. Leamy for Devlin.

The final curtain. Paul O'Connell consoles Rob Henderson after the 2005 quarter-final defeat by Biarritz in San Sebastian. It was Henderson's last Heineken Cup appearance for Munster.

Chapter 29:
2005/6:
CROWNING GLORY

2005/6: CROWNING GLORY

Former Irish skipper Keith Wood was never one to dispense praise wildly; certainly he would never offer it where it was not deserved. But in describing Anthony Foley, Wood once said, 'He is the smartest rugby player I have had the honour of playing with and against. There were more talented, more skilful players, but none that maximised their talent so fully. Foley invariably did the right thing on a rugby field because he understood the game. He rarely had to think about what to do; he knew what to do.'

Foley was the real deal. It was right that he should find himself centre stage one day, holding aloft the Heineken Cup to the masses of supporters enthralled by Munster's glorious first victory over Biarritz Olympique, the pride of France. Yet, when it happened finally in 2006 there were many who spared a thought for the men who went before him, particularly Mick Galwey, who had led Munster so brilliantly and for so long without savouring the ultimate reward.

One of those was Foley, who relates the following post-match story in his autobiography. 'Lots of things were going through my mind as I walked in for the press conference after the match, but I'm just in the door when I hear a familiar bark from the back of the room. 'Go on, Foley' – it's none other than Gaillimh, who has been doing radio commentary. The press conference can wait. We go to each other and there's a big hug, maybe even a few tears. This trophy belongs to more than the eighteen fellas who were on the pitch.'

The celebration of Munster's long-awaited first Heineken Cup victory does not, however, tell the story of heartbreak suffered by the squad after the untimely death of their young rugby colleague, Conrad O'Sullivan.

Ronan O'Gara admits that the two weeks before the quarter-final against Perpignan, following Conrad's tragic death, was the worst period of his life. It had been a good season, with the emergence of youngsters Barry Murphy and Ian Dowling, and Munster felt secure in the knowledge that they would play a home quarter-final after David Wallace scored a late fourth try for a bonus-point victory over Sale Sharks in the last pool match.

Conrad O'Sullivan died less than a fortnight before that game; the first O'Gara and the Munster players knew about the fate of their young colleague was when they turned up to training one day at Thomond Park. O'Gara remembers candles being lit in a room normally reserved for snacking after training, he remembers a priest, grief counsellor and sports psychologist being present to help them through it.

In his book, he recalls the moments before the Perpignan match as he stood through a minute's silence; standing next to Donncha O'Callaghan, he heard the big second row whisper to himself, 'hold it together; hold it together.'

Coach Declan Kidney spoke of how the funeral, a week before the big game, put everything in perspective. 'Conrad's death was a massive blow to everyone; I remember standing around the grave after he had been buried and nothing mattered to any of us, the quarter-final didn't matter. We won the game, but still it didn't matter in the context of that terrible tragedy.'

Life went on for Munster, however; perhaps it helped galvanise them as the weeks went by, with just two giant steps now needed to bring those long-cherished dreams of glory to fruition.

The first obstacle was Leinster – and the men in red were ready and able for the semi-final challenge. The battle of Ireland attracted a capacity attendance to Lansdowne Road and Foley described it as a ferocious contest, the difficulty not reflected at all in Munster's 30–6 margin of victory. 'To put it in perspective, we were just ten points ahead going towards the last quarter and then it opened up for us; Rog got a try to push us well clear and Trevor Halstead finished Leinster off with an intercept try near the end.'

Foley has talked his way through the 20 May final over and over again; prior to the game he caused consternation in Cardiff when he declined to lift the trophy with Biarritz captain Thomas Lièvremont for a publicity picture. The Munster skipper was not being awkward, however, just superstitious. 'I don't believe you should lift a trophy until you've earned the right to do so. Besides, we've enough people in the side who would have lost it if they heard I'd been putting my paws on the European Cup the day before the final!'

That was at 3 p.m. on the Friday; by 5.15 p.m. on the Saturday, Foley did have his hands on the trophy; in between he had helped spirit Peter Clohessy on to the pitch, looked after his young son Tony, who was wearing a Munster jersey with the word 'Dad' written on the back, and celebrated amid the tears, laughter, hugging and kissing.

He recalled that the Heineken Cup was heavier than he expected, but no matter. 'The noise might have lifted it anyway because none of our supporters appeared to have left the building. It's a moment we have watched on DVD on countless occasions and it still brings a lump to the throat.' And so it does to thousands of others.

Munster captain Anthony Foley (right) and Denis Leamy start the drinks party at the presentation of the 2006 trophy.

Munster's Path to Glory

Sale Sharks 27 Munster 13

Sale Sharks skipper Jason Robinson raced 60 metres to score his side's second try and finally condemned mighty Munster to a pointless trip across the Irish Sea to Edgeley Road in a firecracker opening to Pool 1.

A record crowd of 10,641 witnessed a closely fought first-half in which the boots of British and Irish Lions outside half team-mates Charlie Hodgson and Ronan O'Gara dominated proceedings.

Hodgson's territorial game looked to be giving the Sharks the extra edge, but the Irishmen battled back to lead 10–9 at the break. Three Hodgson penalties accounted for the Sharks' points; for Munster, a penalty from O'Gara was followed by a driving line-out try by Frank Sheahan while the home side's Argentinian international lock Ignacio Fernandez Lobbe was in the sin bin. O'Gara added the conversion.

Even though Munster led at half time, the Sharks had had the majority of the territory and their French number 8 Sebastien Chabal and prop Andrew Sheridan were already making major dents. By the end of the game Chabal had picked up the Heineken man of the match award, and had sent the Munster prop Federico Pucciariello into orbit with the tackle of the night that set up Robinson's kick and chase score.

While that try sealed the game and denied Munster a bonus point, it was the ten points the home side picked up while Sheahan was in the bin after fifty minutes that really turned the fortunes. No sooner had Sheahan departed than the Sharks followed the Munster lead by driving a close range line-out and hunting a try. But somehow the visitors kept them out and then turned the Sharks' scrum to claim their own put-in 5 metres out. They struck the ball well enough, but Foley couldn't control possession at the back, scrum half Tomás O'Leary failed to touch down over his own line and could only watch in horror as his opposite number Sililo Martens followed up to score a sucker try. Hodgson added the conversion to his earlier penalty and the Sharks were in the driving seat.

As brave as Munster were in defence, they could not match the power of Chabal and company in attack and when Pucciariello lost control of the ball in the tackle inside the Sharks' half, Hodgson kicked long and Robinson easily won the chase for the decisive second try.

Munster 42 Castres 16

Munster's Thomond Park fortress remained intact after Declan Kidney's men sent Castres home to France without a point. Munster led 19–13 at half time, despite playing into a swirling wind, and cruised to an impressive 26-point victory. It was a much-needed victory after the loss to Sale Sharks, and Munster received the perfect boost to kick-start their campaign.

O'Gara controlled the game beautifully from fly-half, and the fourteen points from his boot kept the home side in front throughout. Fellow Lion Donncha O'Callaghan was driven over the try line in the opening minutes, and things looked ominous for the visitors. Laurent Marticorena pegged back some lost ground with two penalty goals, but the famous Munster maul was soon in evidence again as it carried hooker Jerry Flannery over the line for their second try.

Winger Anthony Horgan made it three before Castres hit back through impressive outside half Romain Teulet, but the French side had the wind at their backs for the first half and they were never going to overturn a 19–13 deficit at the break. Marticorena and O'Gara (two) swapped penalties as the weather worsened, and Munster confirmed their bonus point in the sixty-fourth minute when winger John Kelly collected a pinpoint O'Gara cross-kick to score. O'Gara converted from the touchline to make it 32–16 and seal the victory.

Inside centre Trevor Halstead used his power and pace to add Munster's fifth try, and the home side could even afford to lose winger Shaun Payne to the sin bin without conceding any points. In fact, their defence in the final ten minutes was just as effective as their attack in the first seventy.

Newport Gwent Dragons 8 Munster 24

All coaches point to away results as being crucial in the success, or otherwise, of a Heineken Cup campaign. Munster did not set the world on fire at Rodney Parade in the first of a back-to-back fixture with the Dragons, but they did enough to secure a well-deserved victory.

Munster could have won by more but coach Declan Kidney was relatively happy with the outcome. 'A win was the most important thing, it was important that we keep it tight because Newport would be one of those teams capable of punishing any mistakes.'

It was a contrasting view to Newport's coach Paul Turner, who described the game as 'a step up for some of our younger players'. In the absence of the injured Paul O'Connell, Munster need not have worried about not dominating up front. 'They're just so good,' said Turner. 'Experience was the key from start to finish.'

Munster did have a great start, with Mossie Lawlor striking with a drop goal early in the match, O'Gara knocking over two penalties and a drop goal, adding to a try by Denis Leamy. Craig Warlow kicked a penalty for the Dragons and Gareth Chapman scored an 87th-minute try, after Marcus Horgan had got in for Munster's second, converted by O'Gara, midway through the second half.

Munster 30 Newport Gwent Dragons 18

Newport Gwent Dragons came mighty close to destroying Munster's unbeaten Heineken Cup record at Thomond Park, but ultimately left Ireland without even a losing bonus point as the home side racked up the points in the final minutes.

Paul Turner's side led 18–17 with ten minutes to play, but two penalty goals from Ronan O'Gara gave the Irish side the lead and hooker Jerry Flannery scored an eightieth-minute try to break Welsh hearts. Munster had led 10–8 at half time, and had looked to be gaining control when Anthony Foley weaved a bit of magic down the touchline. The back-row forward took the ball on the wing, kicked ahead and re-gathered to score his twenty-first Heineken Cup try.

But Turner – who obviously spotted the chance to upset mighty Munster – made astute changes at the break and his side battled back into the match. O'Gara restored the traditional order of things at Thomond Park, however, with a penalty goal from in front, and made up for several mistakes with a superb 52-metre effort that ricocheted off the left-hand upright and over the bar.

The match erupted in the 73rd minute with both packs wading into each other. Dragons hooker Jones and Munster prop Horan were singled out by referee Chris White and sent to the sin bin, and the fourteen remaining Dragons had nothing left. The home side dominated the final ten minutes, kicking for touch instead of going for goal in an optimistic push for two more tries, and hooker Jerry Flannery was duly shoved over the line in the eightieth minute.

Castres 9 Munster 46

Munster scored seven tries on their way to a superb 46–9 win over Castres Olympique in a red-jersey day in the south of France.

Marcus Horan and Shaun Payne both crossed early in the first half before the visitors conceded sloppy tries before half time. But Paul O'Connell and Tomás O'Leary scored two each in the second half, with John Kelly also going over, to help Munster record a comfortable victory – and an all-important bonus point ahead of the crunch clash with group leaders Sale.

Laurent Marticorena started the ball rolling with a penalty before Ronan O'Gara replied as Munster dominated the early stages, culminating in Horan's try after thirty-two minutes. Payne soon followed with another crossover to capitalise on expert team play by the Irish side. Marticorena would not be denied, though, and kicked two more penalties to peg back Munster and give Castres a foundation upon which they failed to really build.

Munster responded gallantly after the break and Kelly quickly went over to take advantage of O'Gara's incisive kick. O'Connell soon went over for his first try of the match and wasted little time adding a second, having secured the bonus. With Castres disillusioned, O'Gara set up O'Leary with some alert play close to the line before the latter completed the rout late on.

Munster 31 Sale Sharks 9

On a day when Sebastian Chabal felt the full brunt of angry Munster forwards, the Heineken Cup specialists did the impossible once again, as an 82nd-minute try from David Wallace clinched the bonus point that enabled them to overtake Sale Sharks at the top of the pool.

This was Munster's twenty-fourth successive victory at Thomond Park, and, by reversing their defeat at Sale in the opening round, they became only the second side in Heineken Cup history to register fifty victories.

The game got off to a lively start and French referee Joel Jutge issued the first of three yellow cards for fighting to Sale Sharks Argentinian lock Ignacio Fernández Lobbe after only four minutes. O'Gara opened the scoring with a sixth-minute penalty, which his outside half rival Charlie Hodgson matched five minutes later.

But just before Lobbe returned, Munster struck the first telling blow when they drove inspirational skipper Anthony Foley over for his twenty-second try in what was also his fiftieth personal European victory. O'Gara added the conversion and did the same on the half hour when Ian Dowling dived in at the left corner.

Now Munster really were on a roll and two minutes after Sale's England lock Chris Jones and Munster's Irish international prop Marcus Horan had fought their way into the sin bin, Heineken man of the match Barry Murphy ran 50 metres to score the try of the game. O'Gara converted to stretch the lead to eighteen points, and the only consolation for Sale was a third Hodgson penalty on the stroke of half time.

Munster were unable to maintain their momentum in the second half as they went in search of the fourth try they needed to clinch the bonus point and steal top place in the pool. But all things come to he who waits and the 13,000 Munster faithful, fingernails chewed down to their knuckles, were able to celebrate in style when Wallace rounded off a flowing move in the eighty-second minutes to notch the try they all wanted. O'Gara added the conversion and Munster were on their way to the quarter-finals as pool winners.

Munster 19 Perpignan 10 (quarter-final)

Munster guaranteed Ireland's part in the Heineken Cup semi-final with a workmanlike 19–10 victory over Perpignan at Lansdowne Road. Ronan O'Gara kicked fourteen points including the conversion after man of the match Paul O'Connell's try to set up an all-Irish semi-final against rivals Leinster.

Munster had to come from behind after trailing 10–7 at half time to Mathieu Bourret's try, conversion and penalty. But the wing missed two crucial kicks in the second half as Perpignan indiscipline cost them men to the sin bin and helped ease Munster's passage to the last four.

Munster came closest to breaking the deadlock in a cagey opening quarter when Paul O'Connell spilled the ball as he crossed the line following Donncha O'Callaghan's break. But after Perpignan prop Nicolas Mas was sent to the sin bin for illegally slowing a Munster attack, the giant Ireland lock went one better to grab the opening score. Line-out force O'Connell set up a scoring position for Munster yards from the line, and he was also was on hand to crash over on twenty-one minutes after Perpignan had repelled a series of drives. O'Gara, a doubt until a late fitness test before the game with a hamstring problem, converted to make it 7–0.

But Perpignan, who made their only Heineken Cup final appearance at the same venue in 2003, showed they were not about to roll over by racing into a 7-10 lead. The Catalans capitalised on Munster's errors, and after France centre David Marty seized on a loose ball in midfield, Mathieu Bourret had a clear path to the corner. The young wing converted from the touchline on

It takes two to stop Trevor Halstead in the quarter-final win over Perpignan.

thirty-one minutes and added a penalty to leave Perpignan ahead.

O'Gara, however, got Munster back in front with two penalties in five minutes straight after the break to steal a 13–10 lead. Perpignan pressed as Nicolas Durand went close but let Munster off the hook with their lack of discipline. Moments later the scrum half was shown the yellow card by Welsh official Nigel Whitehouse, while Julien Laharrague missed two speculative drop goal attempts and Bourret sliced two penalties from much closer range. O'Gara, in contrast, kept his cool to slot over two more penalties and ease Munster through.

Taking no prisoners: Donncha O'Callaghan ploughs on in the quarter-final victory over Perpignan at Lansdowne Road in 2006.

Munster 30 Leinster 6 (semi-final)

Ronan O'Gara scored twenty points as Munster brushed aside Leinster at a packed Lansdowne Road. Skipper Anthony Foley celebrated his seventy-fifth Heineken Cup match with a powerful performance to propel his side into the final against Biarritz Olympique. O'Gara kicked regular goals to keep his side in front throughout, and his eightieth-minute try was just reward for a fine performance.

Munster went straight on to the attack from the kick-off, and O'Gara opened the scoring with a penalty goal in only the second minute. A Paul O'Connell steal at a Leinster line-out set up a royal try-scoring opportunity and Denis Leamy was shoved over the line to extend his side's lead.

The visitors lost centre John Kelly to a shoulder injury after fifteen minutes, and Leinster gradually got back into the game. Fly-half Felipe Contepomi kicked a penalty goal from in front, but the good work was undone when O'Connell was taken out at a line-out and O'Gara converted the penalty. A controversial decision to penalise Contepomi gave O'Gara the chance to slot his fourth goal of the match, and Contepomi's poor game got considerably worse when he dragged a simple shot at goal well wide.

The Munster-dominated crowd started a fourth rendition of 'The Fields of Athenry' as their side took a 16–3 lead into the final exchanges of the first half, and that remained the score as a late O'Gara attempt sneaked past the wrong side of the upright.

Contepomi had the first chance to open the second-half scoring, but his angled attempt hit a post, and it seemed to sum up Leinster's afternoon as their opponents dominated territory and possession in the third quarter.

Kelly's replacement, Rob Henderson, limped off after sixty-five minutes, and Contepomi narrowed the margin to ten points with a point-blank penalty goal. Munster prop Federico Pucciariello was sin-binned for repeated infringements, but Contepomi's kick was wide and Munster fans began planning their trip to Cardiff. Munster attacked until the final whistle and they were rewarded when O'Gara brushed off some tired tackle attempts to score behind the posts. His conversion seemed to have sealed a famous victory, but Munster were not finished yet. Centre Trevor Halstead intercepted a Leinster attack and ran 70 metres for the final try of the game.

Leinster might have lost, but Brian O'Driscoll (centre) is always a threat and it takes desperate measures from Ronan O'Gara and the inrushing Trevor Halstead to slow him down in the semi-final at Lansdowne Road.

Paul O'Connell (left) and Denis Leamy (far right) provide the possession for Peter Stringer in the semi-final.

Munster 23 Biarritz 19 (final)

Munster were crowned European champions for the first time after winning a gripping final against Biarritz in Cardiff. Heartbreaking defeats in the finals of 2000 and 2002 had upped the stakes for Munster but it was a case of third time lucky after producing the performance of a lifetime.

A packed Millennium Stadium erupted in a sea of red after Trevor Halstead and Peter Stringer both scored tries to savour. And Ronan O'Gara kicked a perfect five-out-of-five to clinch an historic win for the Irish giants and spark wild celebrations that were heard all the way back in Limerick and Cork.

Sereli Bobo had given Biarritz hope with a controversial try after two minutes and Dimitri Yachvili kicked fourteen points – including three second-half penalties – as the French champions roared back late on. But after so many disappointments in the final – including the 2002 defeat at the same venue – Munster were not to be denied a thrilling victory.

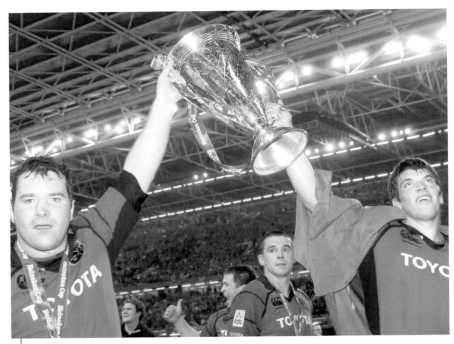

Anthony Foley (left) and Donncha O'Callaghan show off the Heineken Cup, with Alan Quinlan and Marcus Horan (giving the 'thumbs up') suitably enjoying the occasion in the background.

They had to recover from the blow of conceding that early try to dominate the first half of this tenth Heineken Cup Final. Biarritz had been criticised by some for failing to carry their thrilling form from the French Championship into the knockout stages of the Heineken Cup. The French champions had managed just one try in 160 minutes – scored by Bobo – against Sale Sharks and Bath in the quarter-final and semi-final respectively. But it took them little more than two minutes to find a way through Munster's defence – and once again it was Bobo who tiptoed inside (officially) the touchline to score.

Biarritz had Munster under pressure right from the kick-off, and when Philippe Bidabe shrugged off John Kelly on the narrow side the Fijian Bobo had enough room to squeeze over in the corner to stun the huge Munster contingent. O'Gara narrowed the gap with a seventh-minute penalty and then began the move that saw Halstead lift the roof off the Millennium Stadium by giving Munster the lead. Biarritz looked to have survived a red siege on their try line before Anthony Horgan raced onto O'Gara's neat chip. Jerry Flannery and Paul O'Connell burst forward before the ball was worked out wide for Halstead to crash over from close range.

Yachvili levelled the scores with a 22nd-minute penalty after O'Gara had added the conversion but that could not stop the red machine, by now in fifth gear. The power of the Irish forwards saw Munster rumble their way once more to within 10 yards of the Biarritz line but it was a moment of thrifty opportunism that got them over.

Ireland scrum half Stringer saw opposite number Yachvili out of position and left Serge Betsen grasping air as he rounded the blindside of the scrum untouched to score. O'Gara's conversion put Munster 17–10 ahead before the break and a second penalty gave them the perfect start to the second half.

Yachvili kept a cool head to bang over two penalties in response, the second after Denis Leamy's high tackle on Imanol Harinordoquy. That kept this final on a knife-edge with just four points separating the sides and half an hour still to play. Biarritz lost two key players in centre Damien Traille and skipper Thomas Lièvremont to injuries but a fourth penalty for Yachvili narrowed the gap to a single point ten minutes from time. But ice-cool O'Gara was calm under pressure in front of goal to kick another penalty and help Munster hold out until the final whistle.

Munster (v Biarritz):

S. Payne, A. Horgan, J. Kelly, T. Halstead, I. Dowling, R. O'Gara, P. Stringer, M. Horan, J. Flannery, J. Hayes, D. O'Callaghan, P. O'Connell, D. Leamy, A. Foley (captain), D. Wallace.
Replacements: F. Pucciariello for Horan, M. O'Driscoll for O'Connell, A. Quinlan for Foley.

Protecting the Heineken Cup from the rain: Marcus Horan brings his brolly to the party in Limerick.

Chapter 30:
2006/7: TIGERISH SPIRIT NOT ENOUGH

CHAPTER 30

2006/7: TIGERISH SPIRIT NOT ENOUGH

In that way of his, Declan Kidney's shrug of the shoulder and a smile at Welford Road in the winter of 2006 was enough to reveal how he rates Ronan O'Gara in the greater scheme of things in Munster rugby.

O'Gara had shortly before kicked a monster penalty goal to give Munster a sensational 21–19 victory over Leicester, smashing through an unbeaten home record the Tigers had enjoyed for thirty-three months.

Again, in that way of his, Kidney praised O'Gara for securing the result but emphasised that it was essentially a team effort, pointing to a tremendous first-half display that had them 15–6 ahead at the break. During that first half, Donncha O'Callaghan and David Wallace went in for tries, with O'Gara converting one and also kicking a penalty; Leicester had to make do with two penalties from former Munster fly half Paul Burke.

It was not a good day for Burke in the teeming rain; he missed two relatively straightforward penalty attempts and was replaced in the second half by Andy Goode, whose prodigious boot enabled the Tigers to turn the battle for territory in their favour; Goode's penalty after fifty-two minutes raised the stakes for the home side and their vociferous fans.

O'Gara replied with his second penalty on the hour to keep Munster two scores ahead, but the Tigers pack turned up the pressure, and the game on its head, when they made a mess of the Munster scrum to earn a penalty try with ten minutes to go. Goode's conversion and a subsequent penalty changed everything, but Munster refused to capitulate.

They trundled their way up the pitch in a last throw of the dice; when they won a penalty on their 10-metre mark, O'Gara was readying himself to kick for the corner in the hope of launching one last offensive. Unfortunately for Leicester, the replacement back row Shane Jennings offended referee Nigel Owens, who penalised the Tigers a further 10 metres, and O'Gara did not need to be asked his view on what should happen. The out-half placed it, studied it, ran up and kicked it straight and true: 21–19 to Munster.

At Thomond Park, Munster were never going to lose to Bourgoin, the French club that had caused more controversy than any other through an apparent lack of interest in the competition – on more than one occasion.

This time they did look interested; certainly the former Munster scrum half Mike Prendergast was not going to oversee a lacklustre Bourgoin display in front of his family and friends. Ultimately, it was not a good day at the office for Prendergast, who was yellow carded for a professional foul and whose side eventually lost 23–41. At least they played, and Prendergast was pleased with that. Munster got the bonus-point victory they wanted, but they were made to work hard for it.

Back on the road, Munster went to Cardiff and wrote a new chapter in Heineken Cup history by becoming the first side to record six straight away wins. The then reigning champions passed Leicester's record of five to go top of Pool 4 with this third consecutive victory.

Denis Leamy scored a first-half try and O'Gara added seventeen points with the conversion and five penalties in a 22–12 win; it was a personal contribution that pushed O'Gara's Heineken Cup grand total to a massive 803 points.

Mick O'Driscoll wrapping up an opponent against the Scarlets in the 2007 quarter-final backed by Donncha O'Callaghan (third from right). John Hayes (left) and Marcus Horan (second left) are on the way to support.

Tomás O'Leary was picked on the wing for the game against Cardiff Blues,
a pool match Munster won.

Kidney's fears about the return fixture at Thomond Park were unfounded. Cardiff gave it their best shot, but Munster were in no mood to be trifled with even if they had to scrap to score four tries and secure the bonus point. Denis Leamy (two), Alan Quinlan and Barry Murphy were the try scorers; O'Gara kicked three conversions and two penalties to push the victory out to 32–18 and leave Munster in contented mood over the Christmas holiday.

Munster have often adopted the mantra that records are made to be broken – they would shortly experience the negative of their positive spin on that – but on the 14 January trip to Bourgoin, the viewpoint was that records are there to be stretched. And so it was that they hit a run of seven consecutive victories on the road, an achievement that has yet to be matched, when they fought a tough rearguard action and emerged smiling with a 30–27 win over the French side at the Stade de Genève in Geneva.

Bourgoin had opted to move the game from their home stadium of Stade Pierre Rajon (capacity 8,100) to Geneva where the ground had a capacity of 23,000 and attracted an attendance of 16,255. Bourgoin went for the big pay

*Lifeimi Mafi, seen here in a later appearance, made his first Heineken Cup start
for Munster in the same game against Cardiff at the Arms Park.*

day above facilitating their fans, who had to make a ninety-minute journey by
road to get to the game. ERC were happy; their view was that the hosting of a
Heineken Cup fixture in Switzerland broke new ground; Bourgoin were happy
with the extra cash and Munster were happy with the win, however difficult
it was for them to achieve.

Munster conceded four tries and only scored three (one penalty try), which
prompted this reaction from O'Gara: 'We're trying to develop a fifteen-man
game and at times it looked good. At other times it was terrible. There was
some suicidal passing. It was looking hairy for a while but I felt we did enough
to deserve the win.' Maybe, but the danger signs had been posted for the

return fixture with the Tigers six days on. It was to provide a big wake-up call for the champions, who lost the opportunity to secure a home quarter-final when the Thomond Park record fell.

Leicester played into the wind and rain in the first half and shocked Munster by establishing an 8–6 lead at the break. With conditions in their favour in the second half, they extended the lead with an unconverted try and held out to top the pool. Apart from the loss of revenue from hosting a quarter-final at Thomond Park – it would have been against Stade Français – Munster had to travel to Stradey Park to take on a Llanelli side that had blitzed their way through Pool 5 with an unbeaten six-match run – and that against quality sides like Toulouse, Ulster and London Irish. Munster had every reason to be fearful, especially when new captain Paul O'Connell had to withdraw through injury.

Munster's international players were coming off the back of a dramatic Six Nations Championship run when Ireland lost the title on points difference to France on the last day of the season. It was a heartbreaking finale as Italy scored a late try in Rome in Ireland's big win, and France grabbed another late score in the victory over Scotland. The combination of both tries turned Ireland's advantage on its head and France took the title by a whisker.

Back with Munster, O'Gara was named as replacement captain for O'Connell and, writing in his autobiography, he frankly admits that he did not do a very good job as Munster slumped to a 24–15 defeat.

For the previous season I had been joint vice-captain with Paulie but when Axel stepped down there was only one man for the job. Now, in Paulie's absence, it was down to me. I thought I was ready for it. I was wrong.

I didn't think there was any great mystery to it. Decision-making had always been part of my job on the field and as a senior player with Munster and Ireland I had been consulted about strategy for years. I believed that the most important thing I could do for the team was to get my performance right and the captaincy would look after itself.

I spent half of the next season as captain and only then did I realise how far off the pace I'd been on the week of the Llanelli match. Most of all, I neglected the needs of other people. I should have done more to make sure that other players were in the right frame of mind and I failed to do that.

On the field my decision-making was poor. They got an early try, I missed a couple of penalties in the first half and we didn't chase the game with enough patience. I turned down three shots at goal before the break and another couple later on. I wouldn't have got all of those kicks but I should probably have attempted three or four of them. The upshot was that we didn't score for over an hour and by the time we did we were 17–0 behind. People said that being captain had affected my performance and they were probably right.

There were bigger issues in our performance that night, though. There was no heart in it. They wanted it more than us, which should never happen to a Munster team in the Heineken Cup. We played like lame ducks. Not enough desire, intensity, aggression – all the things that made us so hard to beat. We got a late try but they were worth more than a nine-point win.

O'Gara revealed how Munster dealt with the defeat – and it was more than allowing tears to flow into pint glasses!

As a group we had to confront this. Something wasn't right and there was no sense waiting until the beginning of the following season to address it. We had issues that could only be sorted out with honest, hard, straight talking. A day-long meeting was organised for the Radisson Hotel near Limerick. Our old team-mate Killian Keane was brought in to facilitate the meeting, with the management coming in and out of the process at different stages. Management were part of the problem too.

Video analysis needed to be better, fitness needed to be better. One of the conditioning coaches [Damien Mednis] seemed to want full control over our

The mammies make the best supporters: Margaret Horan, Marie O'Callaghan and Mary Quinlan enjoy a day out on the road – one of many.

physical preparation and that wasn't possible; in our system we had a speed coach, a strength coach, we had people based in Cork and Limerick and he wanted to run all of it. This led to rows and to the players it looked like there was a bad atmosphere in the management [set-up]. He [Mednis] left at the end of that season.

Even Kidney did not escape the scrutiny many were put through that day in the Radisson.

Deccie's role was another issue. He had taken charge of attack but that wasn't playing to his strengths. He excels at man-management, at getting a team of coaches working around him, at making everybody feel included; he excels at team selection, at creating the environment in which we can succeed. But being an attack coach is a highly technical and specialist job. That wasn't his strength. At the end of that meeting Deccie knew the players' feelings on that issue and he accepted it in the right spirit.

I don't know how other teams operate but in the Munster setup there is a huge emphasis on honesty. If something needs to be said nobody is too big or too important to hear it. Without that ethos we couldn't be who we are. That day in the Radisson, we needed to find ourselves again.

We had no chance of winning the Magners League and in a World Cup year the international players could have coasted until the end of the season. We decided, though, that Munster needed a positive end to the season and we won our last four games [including, ironically, a facile 20–0 win over Llanelli].

For those few weeks Munster probably needed us. The next time we put on the jersey six months later [after Ireland's disastrous World Cup showing] we needed Munster.

Munster (v Llanelli):

C. Cullen, J. Kelly, L. Mafi, T. Halstead, I. Dowling, R. O'Gara (captain), P. Stringer, M. Horan, J. Flannery, J. Hayes, D. O'Callaghan, M. O'Driscoll, A. Quinlan, D. Leamy, D. Wallace.
Replacements: B. Murphy for Kelly, T. O'Leary for Dowling, D. Ryan for O'Driscoll, F. Pucciariello for Horan.

Chapter 31:
2007/8: NO ONE-HIT WONDERS

2007/8: NO ONE-HIT WONDERS

As Declan Kidney contemplated life without Munster, or a part of Munster at least, he bade farewell to provincial rugby at the top; it was a pretty emotional afternoon for him at the Millennium Stadium on Saturday 24 May 2008 as the champagne corks popped and he had to duck and dive as his charges sprayed him with pints of foamy liquid.

As he surveyed the scene he declared, 'I'd like to thank all those guys over these past ten to twelve years, come to think of it the people over more than a hundred years of Munster rugby for giving us those lessons that have put us in this very privileged position; we're just the lucky ones to have done it, it has happened through what has been done in the underage, the schools, the clubs, and the cream certainly does come to the top.'

Never one to steal the limelight, Kidney was in it a bit more than usual, but this was a day for the masses to sit back and enjoy one of the greatest moments in Irish sporting history. For those involved a decade before, it would have been impossible to dream of Munster beating a team like Toulouse in a European final; it was close, it was hard-fought, but it was deserved, with heroes on the pitch and heroes on the terraces on a day when Munster supporters turned the Millennium Stadium, not for the first time, into a home from home.

Rugby writer Aymeric Marchal, commenting on the game in the French newspaper *L'Équipe*, described it thus: 'Munster promised Toulouse hell, and Toulouse weren't disappointed!' Marchal was stunned by the influence of the Munster crowd. 'There was more red in the stadium than when Wales won the Six Nations; the atmosphere was indescribable and that was due as much to Munster's approach to the game as anything. Far from being the predicted trench warfare, we saw an exciting and spectacular encounter, because Munster too decided to have a go, as if to give evidence of their new approach to the game.'

Former international player and manager Donal Lenihan went further. 'Two years before, I left the Millennium Stadium content I had witnessed a day that would never be surpassed in the history of Munster rugby. I was wrong; the victory over Toulouse was even better. To win the Heineken Cup for the second time in three seasons is a feat that elevates Munster to the pantheon of greats in the European game. To defeat a team like Toulouse in a game that will go down as one of the classic contests of the professional era reflects even better on this outstanding group of players.'

Summing up the achievement, Lenihan singled out Kidney's contribution. 'Six years before, Declan left Munster for national duty at a time when the province was at a dangerous crossroads. Two final defeats in three seasons meant that his team was very much a work in progress. On this occasion, he leaves with mission accomplished. There is simply nothing more to prove. Munster are a genuine European superpower.'

Those involved with Munster will tell you that this second victory had to happen; Munster delighted in the inaugural victory over Biarritz but hurt badly at a failure to repeat it in 2007. The players pledged after 2006 that they would not settle for just one European title; the mantra was that good teams win competitions, great teams win them again. Munster would, at one time, have looked at Toulouse in awe; the French side went into the game with three European titles. This was Munster's opportunity to catch up rather than fall further behind; they grasped the opportunity well.

For John Kelly, who was involved in all three previous finals, it was a new experience – his first simply as a supporter. Had it been a year or so before, Kelly would have been handed an aircraft boarding pass and a room key on arrival in some far-flung hotel. He now had to see how the other half lived and he was enthralled by the experience.

I got into Cardiff early to soak up the atmosphere among the crowd and it was incredible. I walked around in a daze, amazed by the colour, the noise and vibrancy of the supporters. As a player you only get a taste of the intensity in a few manic moments as the bus pushes its way into the stadium, swamped by supporters roaring encouragement.

As players, we always respected the role of the supporters but this was a whole new perspective for me. For each Munster player who wears the jersey on match day, there is a massive sense of obligation to the huge following. It is this obligation that drives the team through difficult passages in the match and helps them edge to victory in the tightest of games. That sense of duty will always be innate in every Munster player as long as the support continues to follow them all over Europe. Long may it last.

On days like this, the evidence to suggest it will was absolutely compelling.

The players milk the moment as the fans lift the roof off the Millennium Stadium. (L–r): Jack Kiely (kit manager), Frank Sheahan, Ronan O'Gara, Lifeimi Mafi, David Revins (masseur), Tony Buckley.

Munster's Path to Glory

Wasps 24 Munster 23

London Wasps served notice to the rest of Europe that they would not be giving up their Heineken Cup crown without a fight after an epic 24–23 win over Munster. The battle of champions turned into a real thriller at the Ricoh Arena before a crowd of over 20,000.

In a match of huge intensity and great technique, Wasps were forced to come from behind no fewer than three times before finally getting their title defence off to a winning start. Munster went ahead early when Ronan O'Gara kicked a fourth-minute penalty, and after Danny Cipriani levelled matters the men in red stormed into the lead. O'Gara's second penalty boosted the confidence and then Lifeimi Mafi paved the way for a Heineken Cup debut try for his centre partner Rua Tipoki. O'Gara's conversion extended the lead to ten points and the 2006 cup winners were flying.

But Wasps are made of stern stuff and they were back on level terms within ten minutes. Cipriani chipped over his second penalty before Riki Flutey pounced on an unusual error in the Munster defence to race up the right touchline to score a try, which Cipriani converted.

It looked as though that was how things would stay until the second half, but O'Gara had other plans. A neat chip kick to the line presented Shaun Payne with the chance to mark his fiftieth Heineken Cup appearance with a try, and a brilliant touchline conversion from the Munster skipper gave the visitors a 20–13 interval lead. A third penalty from O'Gara four minutes after the restart gave Munster a ten-point cushion once again and forced Wasps to chase the game, which they did with a degree of assurance.

They powered forward and Cipriani kicked a third penalty, before Wasps closed in when Marcus Horan was sent to the bin for a technical offence. Cipriani punished Horan's indiscretion with his fourth penalty to cut the gap to four points, and then Wasps scored through George Skivington, a try that proved crucial despite Munster's best efforts.

Munster 36 Clermont Auvergne 13

Munster ran in five tries in a clinical Heineken Cup victory over Clermont Auvergne at Thomond Park, a combination of forward power and an in-form Ronan O'Gara proving crucial.

Clermont had the better of the early exchanges, but the game was turned on its head in the eighth minute when Welsh referee Nigel Owens sin-binned the visiting winger Vilimoni Delasau for not rolling away at a ruck. As the French side complained to Owens, O'Gara took a quick tap and chipped across the field for fullback Shaun Payne to score. Delasau's Fijian team-mate Seremaia Bai pegged back three points for the visitors, and Clermont scrambled well to limit the damage to 7–3 in Delasau's absence.

Errors were the order of the day as both sides struggled to put a series of phases together, and World Cup-winning hooker John Smit was having a game to forget as Clermont's line-out disintegrated. O'Gara and Bai traded penalties, before Munster scored what was to be a vital try in the last play of the half. Back-rower Alan Quinlan charged down a Bai clearance and from the ensuing scrum, centre Rua Tipoki scampered over. O'Gara's superb sideline conversion gave Munster a 17–6 lead at the break, with the boost of having the wind at their backs in the second half.

Munster's league convert Brian Carney opened the second-half scoring after a slick backline move, but the home side went for a bonus point too early and Clermont centre Marius Joubert brought them back to earth with a thump when he charged down a Tipoki kick to score on his debut for the French club.

But just as Clermont looked to have denied Munster an important home bonus point, fullback Julien Malzieu failed to clear at the base of the scrum, and Quinlan dived on the bouncing ball to score. With the pressure off, Munster ran straight back from the kick-off and Marcus Horan scored the home side's fifth side in the corner.

Llanelli 16 Munster 29

Munster avenged the 2007 quarter-final defeat with a well-deserved victory in Wales that effectively knocked the Scarlets out of the competition. Regan King's first-half try gave Phil Davies' side a glimmer of hope but nineteen points by fly half Ronan O'Gara and tries by David Wallace and Marcus Horan put the 2006 winners top of the pool.

O'Gara was in imperious form at a rain-soaked Stradey Park; indeed, the conditions forced English official Wayne Barnes to stop the match for thirty seconds in the second half as he considered abandoning the fixture altogether.

Munster started brightly and O'Gara scored two early penalties to put his side in command. Four minutes later, Wales scrum half Dwayne Peel was denied by Lifeimi Mafi's last-ditch tackle after breaking through the Munster defence, but when Mafi was sin-binned shortly afterwards, Rhys Priestland kicked a penalty and Regan King scored the first try of the match, which Priestland converted.

Two penalties from O'Gara put Munster back in the lead before Peter Stringer's quickly taken line-out allowed David Wallace to crash over. O'Gara duly converted and then kicked his fifth penalty on the stroke of half time to put Munster into a 22–10 lead at the break. Priestland reduced the deficit to six points with two penalties before Horan's converted try on seventy-four minutes, following a series of powerful forward drives, sealed the win.

Munster 22 Llanelli 13

Munster ground their way to a hard-earned 22–13 victory in the return fixture at Thomond Park, nothing less than Declan Kidney expected. Kidney has always feared these back-to-back fixtures, pointing to the benefit he feels accrues to the team beaten in the first game.

Yet Munster enjoyed the perfect start; with the wind at their backs in the first half they took immediate advantage when a floated pass from O'Gara gave hooker Jerry Flannery the space to power over in the corner. The Scarlets hit straight back, however, when Stephen Jones found space around the fringes, and his conversion gave the Welsh side a shock 7–5 lead.

It did not last long, though, and two O'Gara penalty goals were good reward for some dangerous Rua Tipoki breaks. The Munster fly half added a third when Scarlets prop Ben Broster was sin-binned for a professional foul and the home side took a 14–7 lead into the break.

Consecutive high tackles from Scarlets forwards Adam Eustace and Alix Popham gave O'Gara the chance to kick his fourth goal of the match, but Jones struck for another two penalties to send the match see-sawing into the final quarter. Munster secured victory when a superb hand-off from Flannery helped set up a try for winger Brian Carney.

Clermont Auvergne 26 Munster 19

English referee Rob Debney sent three Clermont Auvergne players to the sin bin as Munster grabbed what proved to be a vital bonus point in a 26–19 loss at Michelin Stadium. Munster's losing bonus point meant Clermont could not top the pool and they needed a remarkable series of results in other pools as they attempted to go through as one of the best runners-up, a task that proved beyond them.

The home side raced into a 23–6 lead, but they were rocked by the yellow cards and the boot of Ronan O'Gara brought the visitors back into the match. The first quarter belonged to Clermont as the Munster players consistently failed to clear their line. The Irish province made one David Wallace-inspired visit to Clermont territory from which O'Gara opened the scoring with a penalty goal, but the home side hit straight back with a try from scrum half Pierre Mignoni.

Fly-half Brock James converted Mignoni's effort, and added two penalty goals as the Munster pack struggled to cope with the Clermont unit. And James had barely thrown the kicking tee off the field when he was called on to convert a try from hooker Mario Ledesma.

Clermont lock Loic Jacquet was sin-binned for a professional foul, and the home side were rocked in the opening minute of the second half when impressive winger Julien Malzieu was also yellow-carded for a professional foul. But such was Clermont's dominance at that stage of the game that Munster could not score even against thirteen men. To twist the knife, Malzieu returned to the field in time to watch James' penalty goal put his side twenty points clear, but a break inspired by Munster's replacement prop Tony Buckley gave centre Lifeimi Mafi a clear run to the posts, while O'Gara's conversion and a further penalty gave the visiting fans a glimmer of hope.

Back-rower Alexandre Audebert became the third man to see referee Rob Debney's yellow card, and O'Gara's penalty from in front of the posts moved the visitors into the all-important bonus-point territory. O'Gara and James swapped late penalty goals, and the Clermont players were the sorrier-looking as they trudged off the field having wasted the perfect opportunity to put Munster out of the competition.

Munster 19 Wasps 3

Munster killed off the then defending champions with a controlled masterclass to emerge as winners from a sector that had been dubbed the Pool of Death ever since the draw was made. The 2006 winners defeated the 2007 champions in dreadful conditions at Thomond Park on a night that suited Munster's style.

Munster and Clermont Auvergne both finished on nineteen points in the pool, but Munster secured a quarter-final place on a count back of match points between the two sides. It was the tenth straight season that Munster made the play-offs, a Heineken Cup record.

Wasps found their line-out demolished by man of the match Donncha O'Callaghan. More often than not, he was responsible for disrupting the set piece, meaning the visitors found it impossible to establish any rhythm, particularly in the second half.

The English side went into the match without flanker Joe Worsley, winger Paul Sackey and inspirational centre Riki Flutey, but they opened the scoring when Cipriani ignored the conditions to slot a long-range penalty goal. A couple of quick-fire penalties awarded by Welsh referee Nigel Owens gave Munster some much-needed territory, and O'Gara made no mistake with his first shot at goal before showing his pace to rescue his side from a David Doherty chip through. Cipriani's second shot at goal drifted wide of the left-hand upright, and the game became heated as referee Owens struggled to retain control of two fired-up packs.

Wasps skipper Lawrence Dallaglio was at the centre of several of the illegal confrontations, but it was Munster back-rower Denis Leamy who saw the first yellow card of the match, although he returned without any change having been made to the scoreline. Indeed, Munster sneaked ahead when O'Gara converted a penalty that came after Wasps lock Simon Shaw had been sent to take a ten-minute rest, and the out-half kicked a third to help his side into a 9–3 lead at the break.

O'Gara's fourth penalty goal came after Dallaglio was sin-binned for a professional foul – much to the delight of the home crowd – but Wasps knew they needed only a try to sneak into the quarter-finals on count back.

The visitors played better without Dallaglio, dominating large periods of play, but their line-out continued to be the Achilles heel and another lost throw was their downfall. Munster marched upfield, retained possession through an incredible twenty-one phases of play before O'Gara found the space to put Leamy over for the match-sealing try; O'Gara made no mistake with the conversion to send Wasps packing.

Gloucester 3 Munster 16 (quarter-final)

Paul O'Connell's Munster heroes powered their way into a seventh Heineken Cup semi-final with a devastating display of rugby to see off the Guinness Premiership leaders. The victory secured a semi-final meeting against Saracens, who defeated the Ospreys in their quarter-final clash.

Playing into the stiff breeze at a packed Kingsholm, the visitors were thankful that Scottish international wing Chris Paterson uncharacteristically left his kicking boots at home. The man who recorded 100 per cent kicking

All up in the air for Denis Leamy (second from left) and Donncha O'Callaghan as they get to grips with an attempted clearance by Gloucester scrum half Rory Lawson in the Heineken Cup quarter-final at Kingsholm.

records at the Rugby World Cup and the Six Nations somehow managed to miss with three first-half penalties, which meant none of the early Gloucester pressure was converted into much-needed points.

Munster spent the first twelve minutes of the game locked in their defending territory without the ball, yet their rock-solid defence held firm and it was O'Gara who struck the first blow with a point-blank penalty after fifteen minutes. Better was to follow for the visitors as half time approached when former All Black Doug Howlett turned deep defence into daring attack

Rua Tipoki's explosive power was a key ingredient in Munster's success in 2008.
Here he charges through a Gloucester defender in the quarter-final.

and Ian Dowling sped up the left wing. The Munster forwards joined forces and the move eventually led to Dowling crossing in the right corner for a try that gave Munster an 8–0 interval lead.

With the elements in their favour and their pack growing in stature, Munster piled on the pressure with another O'Gara penalty and a second try. This time it fell to the other wing, Howlett, as he raced on to an inch-perfect chip ahead by fullback Denis Hurley to cross for the decisive score in the right corner. Ryan Lamb landed a consolation penalty for Gloucester, but by then their European dreams were well and truly shattered.

Saracens 16 Munster 18 (semi-final)

Munster used all their experience and skill to hit back from a fifth-minute setback and reach their fourth Heineken Cup final, booking their return to the Millennium Stadium thanks to two first-half tries.

Yet the English Premiership outfit started superbly at a near-full Ricoh Arena when fullback Richard Haughton launched a blistering attack early on, and the excitement mounted before Kameli Ratuvou scored an opening try that Glen Jackson converted. The Munster response came two minutes later from the boot of O'Gara with a simple penalty and then the Irish outside half edged his side in front with a great dummying try at the end of the first quarter.

The game ebbed and flowed until the last move of the first half when Howlett exploded from halfway to the edge of the Saracens 22 and the ever vigilant Alan Quinlan arrived to pick up and race unopposed to the posts for a try, which O'Gara converted. That gave the Irish side a handy lead to take into the interval, but the eight-point gap was cut to two in the third quarter as Jackson knocked over two more penalties against an increasingly nervous Munster.

O'Gara punished Saracens to push Munster into a five-point lead, but Jackson was on target with ten minutes to go and there were anxious moments in the Munster camp as they had to stand firm to book their place in the final.

Munster 16 Toulouse 13 (final)

Munster won their second Heineken Cup title in three seasons with a nail-biting 16–13 triumph over Toulouse. Denis Leamy's first-half try was supported by eleven points from the ice-cool O'Gara as head coach Declan Kidney was handed the perfect send-off en route to his new job as Irish coaching director. Yves Donguy gave Toulouse a lifeline with his second-half score but O'Gara clinched victory with his third penalty with fifteen minutes remaining.

Toulouse came to Cardiff in search of their fourth Heineken Cup title while Munster returned to the scene of their 2006 triumph, backed by thousands

Alan Quinlan on the way to scoring a crucial try in the semi-final win over Saracens . . .

. . . and congratulated by Donncha O'Callaghan.

Jean Bouilhou of Toulouse and Paul O'Connell contest possession in the Heineken Cup final.

Paul O'Connell (left) and Jerry Flannery appear to have time for a quick chat during the Heineken Cup final.

of fans that helped pump £20 million into the Cardiff economy. Munster had tasted both joy and despair at the Millennium Stadium on their previous two visits. Declan Kidney's men snatched victory for their first Heineken Cup title against Biarritz but also suffered heartbreak to Leicester Tigers in 2002. And Kidney's last stand came against the Real Madrid of rugby and legendary Toulouse coach Guy Noves, who was also at the helm when the French outfit won their first title in Cardiff back in 1996.

Captains Fabien Pelous and Paul O'Connell led their sides into a cauldron of noise, and as the 2008 final got under way the early opportunities fell to Toulouse. Munster were relieved to see Jean-Baptiste Elissalde pull his fourth-minute penalty attempt wide, although he coolly slotted a drop goal two minutes later to hand Toulouse the lead.

It was one-way traffic from Toulouse, who continued to pile on the pressure in the opening quarter. But Munster remained just three points adrift thanks to their committed defence, and in the first attack after thirty minutes Denis Hurley was stopped just short of the line after Doug Howlett's mazy run.

Munster were gathering momentum and number 8 Denis Leamy was denied by video referee Derek Bevan after he dropped the ball with the line at his mercy. But after a series of close-range drives, Leamy powered over for the first try of a compelling encounter. O'Gara extended the lead with the

There is a God: Denis Leamy celebrates again.

conversion and then a penalty to nudge Munster seven points clear before Ellisalde narrowed the gap with a penalty. And Kidney's men were handed a boost when Pelous was yellow-carded for kneeing Alan Quinlan in the backside in the fiftieth minute.

O'Gara kicked another penalty, but a moment of genius from Cédric Heymans brought the three-times champions back into the contest. Donguy produced the finishing touch after Heymans' delightful chip and chase released Jauzion, who beat O'Gara to the punch. Elissalde converted to tie the scores, but O'Gara was having none of these dramatic French comebacks and he booted his third penalty fifteen minutes from time to secure a nervous, but well-deserved, second title for Munster.

Munster (v Toulouse):

D. Hurley, D. Howlett, R. Tipoki, L. Mafi, I. Dowling, R. O'Gara, T. O'Leary, M. Horan, J. Flannery, J. Hayes, D. O'Callaghan, P. O'Connell (captain), A. Quinlan, D. Leamy, D. Wallace.
Replacements: T. Buckley for Horan, M. O'Driscoll for O'Connell.

Jerry Flannery takes the flag.

Coach and captain savour the moment.

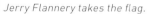

The 'Bull' Hayes takes centre stage with Denis Leamy.

Chapter 32:
2008/9: CAN'T WIN THEM ALL

2008/9: CAN'T WIN THEM ALL

When sights were set on the highest peak, winning the Magners League title might be construed as scant consolation in replacing a European crown; except somebody forgot to tell the loyal fans of Munster, close to 20,000 of them, at Thomond Park in the last game of a busy 2008/2009 season.

The atmosphere was never going to match big European days, but the supporters took the opportunity to thank this Munster team for their efforts throughout the season. They hailed the contribution of departing favourites Anthony Horgan, Frankie Sheahan and Freddie Pucciariello and stayed to enjoy the presentation of another trophy to the squad.

There was even a touch of the romantic about it when Horgan signed off on a high with a marvellous try ninety seconds after his introduction as a seventy-third-minute replacement. Sheahan was not so fortunate and he had to depart shortly after his introduction as a substitute with a shoulder injury, but he too got a rousing send-off along with popular Argentinian prop forward Pucciariello.

With the title already in the bag, Munster did not need a result but got it anyway; it was a comprehensive win in the end. Having struggled to pull away from a gritty Ospreys side in the opening half, a two-try salvo in three minutes early in the second established total control and assured a bonus-point win.

The Ospreys came to play, but had to play second fiddle for most of the contest and Munster finally broke their spirit as they piled up the scores. O'Gara and Hook exchanged penalties early on before Paul Warwick scored under the posts and O'Gara converted to give Munster a 10–3 lead before the visitors pegged it back with a converted try from James Hook. That was the end of their scoring, however, and three tries, a double salvo from David Wallace and one from Leamy, two of them converted by O'Gara, helped push Munster into a 29–10 lead before Horgan rounded off a spectacular movement by grabbing his try, which O'Gara converted.

Munster's New Zealand stars (l–r) Rua Tipoki, Doug Howlett and Lifeimi Mafi throw down the challenge to the All Blacks by performing the haka prior to the challenge game at Thomond Park in November of 2008 in front of a captivated Munster squad.

The relatively easy victory was in contrast to some hard-earned wins over the course of the season. Indeed Munster had to fight for their lives to achieve their first European victory, Ronan O'Gara coming to the rescue in the 19–17 win against new boys Montauban in the first game of the campaign at Thomond Park. Twice in the second half the French visitors edged their noses in front to give their travelling army of 200 fans, among the record 23,500 crowd at the new Thomond Park, the chance to dream the impossible dream. No French team had ever won on Munster soil, either in Cork or Limerick, and only Cardiff and Leicester Tigers had managed to lower the colours of the twice champions and four-times finalists at home.

So when Romanian international scrum half Petre Mitu punished an offence by Peter Stringer with his fourth penalty at a scrum 35 metres out with the clock showing seventy-four minutes, the champions faced defeat. That Mitu strike made it 17–16 to the visitors and they only needed to run down the clock to make history on their debut in the top-flight European tournament.

But having secured the O'Gara restart, the forwards lost the ball in their 22; they compounded the problem by conceding a penalty and then fell foul of English referee Wayne Barnes, who marched them down the field a further 10 metres and within O'Gara's kicking range. The Heineken Cup's record scorer hit the mark – taking his overall tally for Munster and Ireland through 2,500, including 968 in Europe – and the penalty steered his side to a nervy victory.

With skipper Marc Raynaud and Scottish legend Scott Murray to the fore up front, the Montauban pack delivered plenty of quality possession for their side and turned over Munster a surprising number of times in the loose. That led to frustration and indiscipline among the home ranks.

Mitu drew first blood with the first of his four penalties after six minutes and the visitors held the lead for the next twenty-six. Then O'Gara landed his first penalty, and five minutes later replacement Barry Murphy raced over for a try which O'Gara improved upon to make it 10–3 at the break. A flurry of penalties in the third quarter saw the score move on to 13–9 before Sylvain Jonnet ran in a try for Montauban that edged them ahead by a point just before the hour; it took another O'Gara penalty on sixty-five minutes to regain the lead before the drama of the last few minutes.

If Munster were flattered with victory that night, they proved that no team fights harder in difficult situations when they secured another great win on the road with a stunning 24–16 triumph over Sale at Edgeley Park.

The champions dominated the first half after selecting to play into the wind and were 13–6 to the good thanks to a try and a remarkable drop goal from fullback Paul Warwick and five points from the boot of O'Gara to two penalties from Luke McAllister.

But as soon as Sale rang the changes at halfback early in the second half, bringing on Charlie Hodgson and switching Richard Wigglesworth from

Paul Warwick dives over for a crucial first-half try against Sale at Edgeley Park.

David Wallace is congratulated by Ian Dowling (left) and Lifeimi Mafi as he scores another to help Munster win the game 24–16.

Marcus Horan scores a crucial try away to Clermont Auvergne that helped Munster secure a bonus point in the 19–25 defeat.

outside half to scrum half, they began to gain field position and dominate. O'Gara and McAlister swapped penalties in the third quarter to take the score to 16–9, but then Hodgson inspired a move which led to a converted try that brought the record 10,928 crowd to its feet.

But with their backs firmly against the wall for the second week in a row, Munster managed to regain their composure, grab some possession and snatch the scores needed to see them through. David Wallace crashed over for a try that O'Gara converted and the out-half sealed the deal with a magical drop goal from 40 metres.

As Munster prepared for the home and away games with Clermont Auvergne in December, there was the small matter of a challenge game against the touring All Blacks to consider, and coach Tony McGahan had little say in the players he could choose to face them.

National coach Declan Kidney had dictated – obviously given the history between the two countries and the necessity for Ireland to retain ranking points to secure seeding in the next World Cup – that eight Munster players would start against Argentina the following Saturday. Therefore McGahan had to plan without Marcus Horan, Jerry Flannery, John Hayes, Donncha O'Callaghan, Paul O'Connell, David Wallace, Ronan O'Gara and Tomás O'Leary.

Munster, even against a second-string Kiwi side, could have expected to be swept aside; instead this was one of the great performances in modern-day rugby, a match won by New Zealand only in the last couple of minutes when they scored a try by Joe Rokocoko to sneak home by 18–16.

The New Zealanders were stunned as Rua Tipoki, Doug Howlett, Lifeimi Mafi and Jeremy Manning threw down a challenge when they led Munster in the haka; from there a spirited Munster produced another challenge on the pitch and were only beaten at the death.

New Zealand scored from a set-piece move, but Munster strongly disputed the penalty that gave them field position in the first place when captain Mick O'Driscoll was deemed to have joined a ruck from the side. Even New Zealand fans considered the decision by French referee Roman Poite to be harsh, although they were happy to take it.

It was a night to remember – even in defeat – as not so well established Munster players by the names of Timmy Ryan, James Coughlan, Niall Ronan, young Billy Holland and more threatened to turn this game upside down.

Paul Warwick was at the peak of his form and kicked two penalties, dropped a goal and converted Barry Murphy's try. But the key moment in this hotly disputed tie came after Poite's decision to penalise Munster, and the All Blacks grabbed that try to add to one earlier from Stephen Donald, who also kicked a conversion and two penalties.

Not for the first time in defeat, Munster were pushed by the crowd to accept the plaudits by walking the pitch afterwards. Frankie Sheahan described it as one of the most emotional nights of his career, and few would disagree with the view that it was one of the most memorable occasions in the colourful history of Munster rugby.

Munster left it late but scored twice in the closing minutes. Niall Ronan gets the final score to put the game completely beyond Clermont's reach, watched by a delighted Ronan O'Gara.

Munster did not have
matters their own way in the
return fixture against the French side in Limerick.
Paul O'Connell and Jamie Cudmore failed to see eye to eye,
culminating in Cudmore's dismissal and O'Connell's cooling off period
in the sin bin. O'Connell has the look of an angry man as Cudmore sees red.

Beyond that, Munster had to get down to the business end of the season and the challenge was not long coming in the form of Clermont Auvergne. Clermont got the victory but Munster took a crucial bonus point for finishing within seven points. Once again, they could thank O'Gara for kicking a 74th-minute penalty to put them within striking distance. The home side would regret yielding 10 metres for disputing Wayne Barnes' decision to award Munster that penalty; it brought O'Gara into the strike zone and he made no mistake.

Munster looked set to take all four points when Marcus Horan scored a tremendous try to open a 13–6 lead on twenty-five minutes. O'Gara and Brock James had traded two penalties apiece when the Ireland international received the ball out wide following Alan Quinlan's break and David Wallace's pass. Horan had two defenders to beat yet managed to bat both aside with a ferocious hand-off to open enough space to touch down with authority in the corner. O'Gara converted and added a third penalty to open a 16–9 lead, after Doug Howlett was denied in the right-hand corner by a desperate goal-line challenge by France wing Julien Malzieu.

However, Munster were made to pay a heavy price for a series of penalties that allowed Clermont to remain in touch through the pinpoint accuracy of James. Penalties either side of half time cut the lead to a point and the tide had turned in Clermont's favour.

French number 8 Elvis Vermeulen came off the bench as the home side stepped up a gear, and within a minute James beat two tackles for a crucial score. Julian Bonnaire marshalled a powerful line-out drive, Mario Ledesma tore headlong into the Munster midfield before James stepped inside O'Gara and out of the grasp of Paul O'Connell to give Clermont the lead on forty-seven minutes. James kicked two more penalties but O'Gara had the last word with a penalty that Munster would be very grateful for down the line.

The return fixture at Thomond Park was another personal triumph for O'Gara as he edged past the 1,000-point Heineken Cup barrier when helping his side to a 23–13 win. But the real heroes were Horan and Niall Ronan, who scored late tries to edge Munster past a determined Clermont side who overcame the loss of Jamie Cudmore – sent off after eighteen minutes – and made light of having to play with fourteen men for over an hour.

Munster led 11–3 at the break through a David Wallace try and a couple of penalties from O'Gara to a penalty from Brock James, who added another in the second half before converting a try from Julien Malzieu. Clermont held that 13–11 advantage as time ticked on, but Munster saved their season with two tries, one converted by the out-half, in the final three minutes.

Munster then charged through to the quarter-finals with an emphatic 37–14 win over Sale Sharks with six tries in their most convincing performance of the campaign.

Ian Dowling scores in the 37–14 triumph over Sale Sharks at Thomond Park.

Sale had boasted the best defence in the English Premiership, but Munster made a mockery of that and romped to victory despite the fact that, for once, O'Gara left his kicking boots in the changing rooms.

Sale were still in the match after fifty minutes when they trailed by just five points, but Munster got better as the game went on. The tries came from Paul O'Connell, Jerry Flannery, David Wallace, Ian Dowling, Tomás O'Leary and Paul Warwick, two of which were converted by O'Gara, who also kicked a penalty.

Taking heart from that, Munster set about teaching Montauban a lesson of sorts in the final game. Lifeimi Mafi, Barry Murphy, with two apiece, and Tomás O'Leary scored tries; O'Gara converted three of them and also kicked two penalties, while Paul Warwick also kicked a conversion.

The tie had been postponed by twenty-four hours on safety grounds following gale force winds in the region and it did not upset Munster in the slightest; the only goal being to secure a home tie in the quarter-finals, for which they had already qualified.

The demolition of the Ospreys might or might not have been a good thing for Munster as they marched confidently into the semi-finals with a 43–9 win. The Welsh region had hoped to join rivals Cardiff Blues in the last four for the first time in their history. But Seán Holley's men were comprehensively out-thought, out-muscled and out-played as the Red Army celebrated their 100th Heineken Cup tie in emphatic style.

Paul Warwick's first-half strike set the tone before Paul O'Connell scored, and a brace of tries from Keith Earls piled on the Ospreys' misery after the interval. While the manner of the defeat will have caused embarrassment at the Liberty Stadium, the Ospreys were always most likely on a loser in their attempt to emulate Leicester Tigers and Cardiff, the only teams to have beaten Munster in forty-four games on home territory (Thomond Park and Musgrave Park).

The visitors held their own until the turning point came in the thirty-fourth minute. With the scores level at 6–6 (two penalties each from O'Gara and James Hook), Warwick scored a try that O'Gara converted and the fullback then dropped a goal to establish a 16–6 lead at the interval.

The red tide kept coming, despite Hook managing to add a third penalty straight from the kick-off for the second half; after O'Gara's third penalty in the forty-ninth minute, Munster were out of sight when O'Connell scored the crucial second try that O'Gara converted to make it 26–9.

Warwick added his second excellent drop goal before the floodgates opened as Earls added a double with Munster's third and fourth tries. The first came in the sixty-first minute following a brilliant flick-pass from Lifeimi Mafi, while the centre displayed pace and stamina to beat Mike Phillips' despairing tackle three minutes later to spark wild celebrations in Limerick.

There was to be no repeat of such Munster heroics at Croke Park, where the semi-final clash with Leinster set a world record attendance for a club game – 82,208. This clash was more about Leinster, en route to their first final, than about the men in red, who failed to rise to the challenge posed by a side highly motivated by captain Leo Cullen and coach Michael Cheika.

Leinster gained ample revenge for their defeat to Munster at the same stage of the 2006 competition, as tries from Gordon D'Arcy, Luke Fitzgerald and man of the match Brian O'Driscoll helped them run out comfortable 25–6 victors.

D'Arcy's thirtieth-minute score contributed to an 11–6 half-time lead for the Pool 2 winners, with Fitzgerald crossing early in the second period and O'Driscoll finishing the rout with just over an hour played. Munster had nothing left in the tank against a side inspired by Cullen and Australian Rocky

In his last game for Munster, Anthony Horgan shows blistering pace to get past an Ospreys defender on the way to a sensational try in the May 2009 Magners League encounter at Thomond Park . . .

. . . he scores . . .

. . . and is congratulated by Ronan O'Gara (left) and Frankie Sheahan (right) as Tony Buckley (far right) heads away after offering his words of praise. Sadly, since then another great Munster and Ireland stalwart – Sheahan – has also had to announce his retirement owing to injury.

Colleagues gather around triumphant skipper Paul O'Connell to celebrate as the champagne flows (above), and (below) the entire Munster squad accept the acclaim of the fans and cherish an opportunity to finish the season on a high note with the official acquisition of the Magners League trophy.

Elsom. Leinster certainly dominated the majority of the match despite playing for sixty-five minutes without starting fly-half Felipe Contepomi.

A Contepomi drop goal from the edge of the Munster 22 had Leinster in front after a quarter of an hour but Munster hit back with a penalty from O'Gara. Replacement Jonathan Sexton kicked a penalty before Isa Nacewa carved out the opening to send D'Arcy in for his try, and Munster were left to rely on a second penalty from O'Gara to keep them in touch at the interval.

Munster needed to score first in the second half but instead conceded another try to Luke Fitzgerald and Sexton added the conversion to establish an 18–6 lead. Munster had time to respond but displayed little signs of composure as they rushed every challenge in an effort to turn the match around. They merely succeeded in giving Leinster an opening to put the game beyond reach, O'Driscoll intercepting an O'Gara pass before racing 80 metres for a try that Sexton converted.

Paul O'Connell was clearly gutted, not just that the defeat came at the hands of Munster's oldest and fiercest rivals but that the standards set from the outset had not been adhered to. 'We were a long way from reaching the standards we expected of ourselves; they really raised their game and unfortunately all those calculations happened on the same day.'

But those in the mood to write off Munster would do so at their peril, insisted the captain. 'It was a bit strange to hear suggestions that we're gone past it because of that semi-final defeat. Clearly, those who say that have a lack of knowledge about the strength and the resolve within this Munster squad. Let them say it; people are entitled to their opinions, but I don't take too much notice of comments like that, and next season will be business as usual, with the same goals. It might sound old fashioned, a bit old school if you like, but all we set out to do any season is to do the jersey proud; we will continue to do that.'

Coach Tony McGahan also insists that nothing major will change.

We sat down after the Leinster game and assessed the way the season had gone; we had management meetings, we met with the players, we looked at our strength and conditioning preparations and came to the conclusion that the process was correct in the build-up to the game.

What wasn't right was the performance on the day; we came up short and that was very disappointing. It's difficult to accept but we have to accept it; Leinster played extremely well while we didn't take the opportunities that came our way in the early part of the game. We just bombed too many of them and it was one of those days when, with a combination of factors, we came up second best.

Look, we chased both the Heineken Cup and Magners League and, if you take it from just one perspective, we came up short, but the Magners League was worth winning. We had an excellent start to the season and a great spell during the time when the Six Nations was being played; winning the Magners League was more a representation of the whole squad because we used the full squad to get us there. On the broader issue, I believe we have moved our game forward, some young guys have come in and made a mark and I am confident we have the capacity to go further next time.

McGahan is not alone in believing Munster will bounce back; his views have been strongly endorsed by highly respected journalists, former top players/rugby analysts and some of the most experienced and best coaches around. Read on . . .

Munster (v Leinster):

P. Warwick, D. Howlett, K. Earls, L. Mafi, I. Dowling, R. O'Gara, P. Stringer, M. Horan, J. Flannery, J. Hayes, D. O'Callaghan, P. O'Connell (captain), A. Quinlan, D. Leamy, D. Wallace.
Replacements: D. Fogarty, T. Buckley, M. O'Driscoll, N. Ronan, M. Prendergast, B. Murphy, D. Hurley.

Munster (v Ospreys, Magners League):

P. Warwick, D. Howlett, K. Earls, L. Mafi, I. Dowling, R. O'Gara, P. Stringer, F. Pucciariello, D. Fogarty, T. Buckley, M. O'Driscoll, P. O'Connell (captain), D. Leamy, D. Wallace, N. Ronan.
Replacements: D. O'Callaghan for O'Connell, D. Ryan for Pucciariello, F. Sheahan for Fogarty, A. Horgan for Dowling, K. Lewis for Earls, J. O'Sullivan for Wallace, M. Prendergast for Stringer.

Chapter 33:
THE FUTURE

THE FUTURE

Edmund van Esbeck, former rugby correspondent of *The Irish Times* and author of *Irish Rugby 1874–1999: A History* (Dublin, 1999), has his own insightful views on how the southern provinces should have fared so well this last decade; he is also convinced that Munster will stay close to or at the summit.

The Ireland team currently stands at the summit of European rugby, Triple Crown, and Six Nations Grand Slam champions. Allied to those achievements are three other Triple Crown successes since 2004. It is the most productive period in the history of the game in this country, eclipsing that of the 'golden era' 1948–51.

Central to Ireland's current achievements has been the contribution of the Munster players and the names come readily to mind: Ronan O'Gara, Peter Stringer, Tomás O'Leary, Marcus Horan, Jerry Flannery, John Hayes, Paul O'Connell, Donncha O'Callaghan, David Wallace and Denis Leamy all played a very significant part in the Grand Slam success, with Mick O'Driscoll on the bench.

As we acclaim their contributions, let us not forget the outstanding service rendered to Munster and Ireland by players such as Mick Galwey, Peter Clohessy, Anthony Foley, Keith Wood, Anthony Horgan, Alan Quinlan, Ian Dowling, Rob Henderson et al.

I must stress, too, that the Ireland coach was and is Declan Kidney, a man steeped in the Munster tradition who also led Munster to two Heineken Cup successes. There is no doubt whatsoever that Munster's exploits in the competition, dealt with so admirably in this book, were vital to the elevation of Irish rugby to the top of European affairs.

Munster's success in the Heineken Cup and indeed Celtic/Magners League illustrate just how formidable recent teams have been, and how much the game has progressed in the province in the professional era. No province

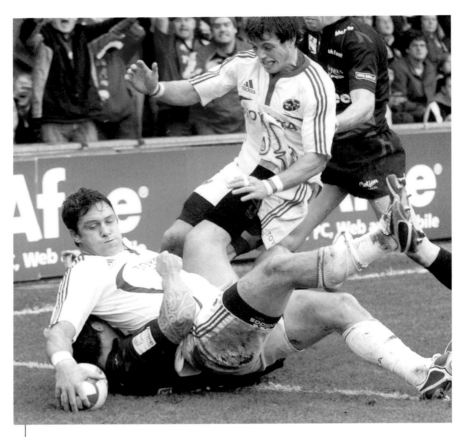

David Wallace has been central to Munster's success, says Edmund van Esbeck. Wallace is seen here scoring against Sale Sharks.

and very few teams on the European scene have risen to the challenge or embraced the change required to move from amateur to professional rugby like Munster. This, I believe, is tellingly illustrated by reference to the number of Munster players on the Grand Slam squad of 2009 compared to the number of Munster players who helped win the four matches when Ireland had last won the Grand Slam in 1948. Just six Munster players were involved – Jimmy Corcoran, Ernie Keeffe, Paddy Reid, Bertie O'Hanlon, J.C. Daly and Jim McCarthy. And both Corcoran and O'Keeffe played in just one match – that against France.

Munster rugby has never been less than competitive and the intensity of the annual Munster Cup campaigns through the years was unequalled in any of the other provinces. But Munster in the broader aspect of Irish rugby laboured under the handicap of a lack of numbers compared to Leinster and Ulster.

While Munster has been competing in the Interprovincial series since the

1870s and did enjoy some notable victories, both Ulster and Leinster were stronger forces overall. I would stress, too, that through the years Munster still produced some great players in every era, while the performances against major touring teams are of legendary proportions.

That tradition was first established in December 1947 when Australia came to these shores and met Munster at the Mardyke. I was a schoolboy at PBC Cork at that time and watched that match from the Wellington Bridge end of the ground. I have vivid memories of the atmosphere and the excitement as time was running out and Munster led – an historic win was imminent, and then came heartbreak in the form of an injury-time try by Australia's John Hardcastle.

While defeat was the portion that afternoon, I have never had any doubt that a pattern and precept were established that afternoon that were to find glorious expression in the years ahead when Munster met major touring teams.

It was Munster who first beat a major touring team, Australia at Musgrave Park in 1967; there had been some outstanding performances against the Springboks and All Blacks before that breakthrough, and a few very near misses. Then in 1973 it took a late penalty to earn New Zealand a 3–3 draw at Musgrave Park before the most famous win of all at Thomond Park in October 1978.

In 1981 and 1992, Munster beat the Wallabies, who were then world champions again, and those wins sent shockwaves through the world of rugby. Most recently that superb tradition was further embellished when a Munster team without its international players gave a superb performance against the All Blacks at Thomond Park in November 2008 only to lose in the last minute.

Now I revert to that point made earlier about the lack of numbers compared to Leinster and Ulster. In the early 1930s there were only seven senior clubs in Munster; four in Cork – UCC, Cork Constitution, Dolphin and Sunday's Well – with Bohemians, Young Munster and Garryowen in Limerick.

In the important area of schools level, too, Munster compared very unfavourably to Leinster and Ulster with regard to numbers. CBS Limerick was a powerful entity on the schools scene at that time but subsequently the game was not played there. The powers in the land were Presentation Brothers College (PBC) and Christian Brothers College Cork and Rockwell College. The Abbey School faded from the scene after a Senior Cup win in 1921. Mungret won the cup in 1941 and PBC Cobh once just before the Second World War. Alas Mungret is long since gone and PBC Cobh is no longer a force.

Colleges such as Midleton and Waterpark kept the flag flying but were not strong enough to compete with the big three. But matters have changed in the modern era at club and schools levels. It seems remarkable that Shannon did not attain senior status until 1953 and Highfield and Old Crescent also in the 1950s. At schools level Crescent and St Munchin's began to make an impact and still do, and Ardscoil Rís and Castletroy College are now challenging with the best;

Castletroy did the senior–junior double in 2008, a magnificent achievement – and the number of schools and clubs affiliated to the Munster Branch has risen dramatically.

The inauguration of the All Ireland League in 1990 has had a profound impact on Irish and most particularly Munster rugby. It is very significant that as the Munster senior clubs have dominated the scene so also the Munster side has prospered. Shannon, nine times, Garryowen and Cork Constitution, three times each and Young Munster once have all won the First Division title, and only three times has the championship been won by clubs outside the province – St Mary's College, Dungannon and Ballymena have each won one title.

What a contrast to Munster clubs' fortunes in the old Bateman Cup – the all-Ireland club championship that ran between 1922 and 1938 and contested by the four provincial senior cup winners. Only two Munster clubs won it, Young Munster in 1928 and UCC in 1936. It is also significant that so many members of the Ireland side have come through the All-Ireland League. The league, through its divisions, is based on merit and that enabled clubs such as Thomond, Clonakilty, Midleton, Waterpark, Bruff, Nenagh and Richmond to play in the league. Unfortunately both Waterpark and Richmond have also had to endure relegation.

There have been major changes in the game most notably since the advent of professionalism. Munster rugby has embraced those changes with commendable vision and foresight.

The name Munster has earned the respect of every club and country in Europe and the deeds of the province have spread across the global rugby scene. They have known the lean times; now they're entitled to glory in the riches that have come their way.

Sunday Times columnist Denis Walsh was ghost writer for *Ronan O'Gara: The Autobiography,* published in 2008. He has been a keen observer of Munster's gradual but dramatic rise into the top echelons of European rugby, as outlined recently when he wrote:

When Munster started out it was an unusual Irish sports story with some familiar themes. They were underdogs with attitude. Their limitations were clear but their ambitions were empowering. We shared in their journey, delighted in their triumphs and excused their defeats. Time and again they came close to the ultimate prize and in the grand Irish tradition we bathed them in glorified failure. As a sporting nation we were practised in the ways of making failure viable. At that point, though, we were no good for them.

They changed in spite of us and made something new. What Munster are now is unrecognisable from what they were ten years ago and it is unique in the history of Irish sport. They were neither broken by defeat nor weakened by success. They built a culture and a mentality that could accommodate both and take strength from either.

In many ways their response to triumph has been more impressive than their many recoveries from heartbreaking defeats. After they won the Heineken Cup in 2006 they told themselves that it wasn't the end of the journey, just another stop on the road, but that was easy to say and hard to do. The problem was that the quest had become inseparable from their identity and now the quest was over.

They often spoke about the value of 'bitterness' and, coming back from losing years, that fuel was freely available. But it was a finite resource and as winners they couldn't hope to be moved by it. They made a poor first defence of the Heineken Cup because they were struggling to redefine themselves. They needed to find a motivation that was unrelated to desperation or longing. They suffered that process and came out on the other side.

Now, winning is what happens when they set off in honest pursuit of the standards they have set for themselves. Increasingly, winning is what happens even when they fall short of those standards.

After they beat Saracens in the semi-final of the 2008 Heineken Cup, nobody celebrated in the Munster dressing room. Instead, there was a broody silence normally reserved for defeats. They knew they had played poorly in the second half and carelessly put the game at risk. In a big game, they hadn't produced a big performance; they hadn't produced the performance they demanded of themselves. Eventually, Declan Kidney tried to break the ice. 'Give the fella next to you a pat on the back,' he said. 'You're going to the final.' But nobody was in the mood to have their spirits lifted. The attitude they have cultivated is full of intolerance: for sloppiness, for mental laziness, for the age-old absolution of 'what harm, we won'.

Occasionally you will hear Munster players say they are too hard on themselves, but it is not a fault they are minded to correct. They are happy to err on the side of excess. No allowances.

For the continued evolution of this culture Tony McGahan was the perfect successor to Kidney. He inherited a group of winners and challenged them to be better. The players respect him because they know he's in the gym doing his workout at seven o'clock and at his desk before they've finished their cereal. On the training pitch he is hands on, fully briefed and sharp. Players respect that direct engagement. They must feel that the coach understands what they need and how it needs to be done. They must feel he understands it better than they do. McGahan has taken a group of battle-hardened professionals and furthered their warlike education.

He also understood that to take the team to the next level there could be no hiding place for anybody. Over the years the Magners League was an arena where Munster gave themselves permission to coast a little; to lose and not beat themselves up about it. McGahan withdrew that permission.

Over the years excuses were quietly made and widely accepted. Without

Tony McGahan is pictured here. The Munster coach, says writer Denis Walsh, has taken a group of battle-hardened professionals and furthered their warlike education.

their international players, for example, they didn't have a squad that was deep enough to compete all season in the Magners League. And even with a full squad to pick from they couldn't be expected to play with the kind of emotional intensity that always characterised their finest performances in the Heineken Cup. All of that stuff was a cop-out. We didn't say it, they didn't say it, but it was.

That has changed. Naturally, Munster's performances in the Heineken Cup still reach a higher emotional pitch, but in the Magners League they have found a way to be intense in cold blood. The fringe players that were wheeled out for the league used call themselves the 'muppets'. Ian Dowling was one of them a few years ago and he says he can't remember the last time he heard that phrase.

Notwithstanding a 2009 semi-final defeat to arch-rivals Leinster, the Munster squad has never been deeper or more integrated or more equipped for the week-in, week-out challenge of being Munster in the hugely demanding world they created for themselves.

Quite apart from the new expansiveness and behind-the-scrum electricity of Munster's performances, the results tend to tell a tale too.

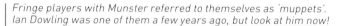

Fringe players with Munster referred to themselves as 'muppets'. Ian Dowling was one of them a few years ago, but look at him now!

It's not all about big one-off wins any more; it's about a pervasive and continuous culture of winning all the time. It is what they expect now and it is what their fans expect. Just as there used to be a different Munster team for the Magners League, there used to be a Magners League crowd too. They were much smaller, more faithful, less demanding. Now every game in the new Thomond Park is a major sporting event, with crowds in excess of 20,000 coming to see a show. Like global warming, the shift in temperature only needs to vary a couple of degrees to produce a different climate altogether.

Coping with that is a challenge but it is not an issue. We no longer see Munster as perpetual underdogs or desperate men chasing a cause, or gallant losers. They abandoned all that for something more powerful and permanent. It has nothing to do with us. It is all about them.

Donal Lenihan is better placed than most to judge the Munster merits and achievements through from the amateur era to professional rugby. Lenihan was first capped for Ireland in 1981 at the age of twenty-two; he went on to become part of Irish rugby folklore when he participated in the Triple Crown victories of 1982 and 1985 and was on the British and Irish Lions tours to New Zealand in 1983 and Australia in 1989, missing out on a third when the 1986 tour to South Africa was cancelled. Since retiring as a player, he has been team manager for Ireland and the 2001 Lions; these days, the Cork-based financial consultant is co-commentator on radio and television and is rugby analyst with the *Irish Examiner.* The following is his take on the modern-day Munster.

The first time it really dawned on me that a seismic change was happening to Munster rugby was the morning of that first Heineken Cup final appearance against Northampton back in May 2000. At 6.30 a.m. Cork Airport was not only thronged with patrons wearing red jerseys, hats, scarfs and tracksuit tops, but four chartered aircraft dominated the runway waiting to transport an ever-increasing red army to Heathrow. Similar scenes were in evidence at the same time in both Shannon and Dublin airports as Munster rugby followers descended on Twickenham.

While the tears flowed freely, both on and off the field, after that heartbreaking one-point defeat, the response of the Munster faithful lit a desire that would only be satisfied when the Heineken Cup was finally captured.

When Anthony Foley finally lifted the famed trophy in Cardiff six years later, having endured many more heartaches and narrow defeats, including another final defeat to Leicester in 2002, it sparked scenes that will stay with all the Munster men, women and children fortunate enough to be there for the rest of our lives.

Of even more importance, in the bowels of the stadium dressing room less than an hour after Munster's coronation, the players made a pact that this triumph marked the beginning and not the end. To be categorised as one of the greatest sides in Europe along with Toulouse, Leicester and Wasps, that victory could not remain as a one-off. They have been true to their word.

The 2008 final afforded Munster the opportunity of replicating that magnificent achievement within a two-year period, which they truly delivered on against tournament giants Toulouse. For much of the following season Munster looked odds-on to become only the second team after the Leicester Tigers to retain the trophy but great rivals Leinster burst that balloon with a sterling performance on a day that highlighted more than any how far rugby had come in this country. An attendance of 82,500 in Croke Park with several thousand more left marooned outside without a ticket said everything about the popularity of the sport in this country. Truly remarkable.

Despite that result, the Munster phenomenon is one that is now recognised and admired far and wide. Even the 2009 British and Irish Lions chose to build their template around the special mantra that Munster brings to the table.

What makes Munster special is the warmth, affection and clear sense of identity the team has with its supporters. Having been privileged to wear the red jersey for well over a decade, I find it heartwarming, even emotional, to see the manner in which this team has captured the hearts and minds of so many people. In the amateur days when Munster participated in the Inter-provincial Championship coupled with one or two warm up games, the players, drawn mainly from Cork and Limerick clubs, never had the opportunity to maximise the sum of all their undoubted talents.

The one time when the real passion and commitment that epitomises all Munster teams was seen at its imperious best was with the arrival of the big touring sides. For any Munster player prior to the professional era, playing against New Zealand, Australia or South Africa represented the pinnacle. Even then supporters from all over the province packed Musgrave Park, Thomond Park or the old Mardyke and displayed a fervour that has since grown to monumental proportions with the advent of the Heineken Cup.

Munster's famous 12–0 defeat of the All Blacks in 1978 after a number of close encounters over the previous two decades elevated the status of rugby in the province to a new high. Three years later I was fortunate to be a member of a Munster side which included several of the victorious 1978 team when Australia fell in Musgrave Park. Munster had back-to-back victories over southern hemisphere tourists, which was a great achievement; it instilled a belief in later generations that anything was possible once everyone was focused and aligned in the same direction. Munster have always been capable of punching above their weight.

That tradition and heritage was replicated once more with the heroic performance against the All Blacks which heralded the opening of the magnificent new Thomond Park in November 2008. The viewing facilities, pre-match pageantry, corporate hospitality boxes and stadium museum may well have ushered in a new era for rugby in the province but the performance *of a team shorn of their Irish international contingent demonstrated that all the old values were very much alive and well.*

What is especially pleasing for players of my era and before is the respect that the current squad have for the history and tradition of the jersey. They have never lost sight of where they come from and there is recognition that they are part of something way bigger than any one individual. Over the years some outstanding overseas players have bought into the characteristics that make Munster special, Jim Williams and John Langford immediately springing to mind.

This is further in evidence in recent squads with the outstanding contributions of Doug Howlett, Rua Tipoki and Lifeimi Mafi adding to the mix that make Munster special. While acknowledging their special input, it was even more satisfying to note that seventeen of the 22-man squad selected for the final against Toulouse in 2008 were born and learned the game in the province.

The 2006 final was special for all kinds of reasons, none more so than that seminal moment when the images of a crowded O'Connell Street in Limerick were beamed to the Millennium Stadium. At a time when Munster were vulnerable, the fans in the stadium recognised the significance of the moment and stood in unison. It was an inspirational response, certainly from my seat in the stand, and one can only imagine what it was like for the players on the pitch.

While those scenes from Limerick were extraordinary, that fanaticism was repeated in every home, rugby club and public house across Cork, Kerry, Limerick, Waterford, Tipperary, Clare and indeed in many outposts around the world.

Munster rugby has united all sports in the province, a point forcibly brought home to me when I asked a ten-year-old from Tipperary prior to the Saracens semi-final in 2008 who his favourite Munster player was. His response was immediate: 'Denis Leamy is from our parish.' Enough said. For me, that simple statement provided the essence of what Munster has become; the team of the people.

As a sporting nation (and with some justification), the English have often been accused of being overbearingly patriotic – hence, maybe, a reason why every other country in the world, big or small, loves to beat them.

Sky Sports pundit and *Sunday Times* columnist Stuart Barnes, the former English and Lions international out-half, is sometimes perceived as biased by Irish and French fans particularly. Barnes would argue strongly against the validity of that assessment and believes a close examination of what he has said and written shows he has no axe to grind with Irish rugby. He backs his view by referring to this written assessment of Ireland's thrilling 2009 Grand Slam victory.

| We are the men: Rua Tipoki and Lifeimi Mafi, says Donal Lenihan, were indispensable.

Ireland's second Grand Slam – the first since 1948 – has its origins far further back than the opening weekend win against France. Further indeed than the prescient decision to replace Eddie O'Sullivan with the shrewdest coach the nation has produced in living memory.

No, Brian O'Driscoll and his triumphant colleagues owe a huge debt to a different tournament, the parvenu of European rugby championship. The Heineken Cup is the competition that set Ireland en route to the 2009 Grand Slam.

It was the Heineken Cup that galvanised Irish rugby in a way that the old parochial Munster and Leinster clubs could not. For all the charm of a few pints in Garryowen, Ballymena or Blackrock, it needed a surge of something special to lift Ireland from the spirited (in every possible sense, from my Five Nations experiences in Dublin) masters of the up and under and at the English to Grand Slammers.

And that something special, for all that Dublin and Ulster supporters will hate it being said, is Munster. The magic province of the Irish game, the heartlands of the hard man, the home of the mythic conquerors of the All Blacks in the days of Tony Ward; Munster restored what Irish rugby had lacked for so long, the belief in its own powers.

The sport has often been a buried backwater but Munster and their European Cup adventures lifted the game to a new level.

The early episodes in Europe played their part. Men like Mick Galwey, Peter Clohessy and Anthony Foley prepared the next generation of Irish forwards for glory. Paul O'Connell and David Wallace were forged in the heat of European battle. All those epic wins and narrow losses in France helped. Slowly but surely, the men of Munster started to believe that Europe and any side within its borders could be conquered.

A serious analysis of the Grand Slam and its roots will mark one day where expectations became, in the minds of the so long underachieving Irish rugby fraternity, something to hunt down, not drown in a well-humoured jar of grog. That day was when Munster finally grasped the crown of European champions. The 2006 final against Biarritz was forgettable enough bar the turbulence of the emotions, but the result was all that mattered. Munster proved that Ireland could be more than the union bridesmaid.

Ireland was a devastated rugby nation when failure followed in the 2007 World Cup, but the belief never left and the second triumph in 2008 against the might of Toulouse was of equal significance. It guaranteed that when Eddie O'Sullivan's departure came, Declan Kidney would be ready to take up the challenge that had beaten every Irish coach, manager and player since Jackie Kyle. Like his players, he believed his men had what it took to beat any side in Europe. His belief was not of the 'we can beat anyone on our day' type, but rather it was the silence of the strong man.

When O'Sullivan said Ireland could beat anyone, some of the team always doubted. When the hush-toned Kidney whispered similar words, the Ulster and Leinster lads looked in the direction of the Munster men and believed both the words of their coach and the conviction of their team-mates.

Peter Stringer could think back to the daring originality of his critical break to set up Jamie Heaslip for the only try in Edinburgh. John Hayes could ruminate on how his beloved Munster regularly survived the battle of the scrum and came out stronger. Donncha O'Callaghan merely had to count the times he and his mate O'Connell had stared in the abyss of defeat and won, against the odds.

This is the history of success that fuelled the belief; that turned desire into deep conviction and made the Munster men believe they could get away with below-par performances and still come out on the winning side.

'John Hayes could ruminate on how his beloved Munster regularly survived the battle of the scrum and came out stronger,' said Stuart Barnes to those who have constantly questioned Munster's ability (and come out the wrong side of the argument) in the set pieces. Hayes pictured happily after another good day at the office in May 2008, with daughter Sally.

Most of Ireland's Six Nations efforts have been a studied imitation of those cussed, clever Munster men. Beauty has never been high on the list of Munster rugby priorities, although they can do beauty too. Achievement and victory is more the currency of this great rugby region.

The Coaches

Guy Noves is the longest-serving club coach in Europe and has plenty of personal experience of Munster, not least when his Toulouse side had to settle for the role of bridesmaid in that 2008 Heineken Cup.

Twelve years earlier, Noves had overseen the slaughter of innocents as Toulouse smashed Munster into submission in a European tie. 'In 1996, I remember Munster as being essentially an unknown team who were in the process of constructing themselves a new history. Actually, they have really caught us by surprise in a way since then; we didn't expect, I think, that they could become what they have become – one of the most attractive and high-performing teams in the competition.'

Even if Noves has reservations about Munster's provincial (as against his view of club) status – indeed the status of the Welsh regions as well – he does hold them in the highest regard.

They are now one of the teams everyone wants to beat, and they have got to that point by reinforcing the areas where they have felt they might be weak; that they have done very successfully.

Since 1996, they've acquired a wealth of experience. Personally, I've seen the progression year after year. Munster have the capacity to keep raising the bar while at the same time respecting the fundamentals of rugby. They're a machine of war up front with a solid tight five and an impressive captain in O'Connell. They also manage to keep their performance ticking over at a very high level; a team that don't make many mistakes, a team of great substance.

As a coach, I admire their discipline more than anything else. They're extremely well organised and that is something that is a reflection generally on the current quality of Irish rugby. They've tried to progress their game and have found a balance between the forward game and more width. Whilst they haven't dominated Europe every year, they're one of the best clubs over the last decade and have come a very, very, long way from those early days when you would maybe have feared for them.

Dai Young played against Munster as a prop forward and he coached Cardiff against them many times. He is a fan who is impressed with everything he has seen over the last decade.

Munster have been a model that many of the Welsh regions have looked to in recent years seeking success both on and off the field.

When Welsh rugby went regional in 2003 it was a new era for all of us, so people were looking at templates to follow. Teams looked at the likes of Leicester Tigers and Toulouse for their success on the pitch, teams who were capable of gaining success and repeating it.

But of more relevance to Wales was the achievement of Munster as a team that had grown to the stretch where it could compete year in and year out at the highest level. Of more importance was the whole product that Munster had developed; how it had successfully tapped into the local communities, had brought together the cities of Limerick and Cork and had such an affinity with the local people throughout the region, both in urban and rural areas. It is a model that all four Welsh regions have looked at and tried to emulate, although Munster are still a few years ahead.

On the field, the two main ingredients that have made Munster so successful in Europe are quality and passion. They work from a quality base with players who have been together for a number of seasons. These guys have been through the mill, knocking on the door for so long and they've learned from the experience, the disappointments and the joy; they have grown together and those early defeats just made them stronger year after year.

They work well on the basis of making minimum but necessary changes to the squad year after year, thereby ensuring there is always a strong unit at their disposal with fresh faces to keep the pot boiling at all times.

It is clear to everyone how they retain their ethic and pride in the jersey; they play for each other, for the province, and for the fans; with that quality and success comes a huge responsibility that the players are expected to uphold. Any new players are quickly reminded of what is expected of them, either by the other players or by the fans who follow them faithfully throughout Europe every year. It must surely be a great thing to be part of.

Finally, in terms of coaching experience, not too many can match Ian McGeechan, who has been to the forefront of club and international rugby for three decades. With a coaching CV the envy of all to back his view, the British and Irish Lions expert looks on Munster's development into a European power as one of the success stories of our time. McGeechan says he has never ceased to be amazed at Munster's achievements over the last decade and hopes, one day, that a Scottish team can emulate them.

It's nine years ago that Munster played my old club Northampton in the European final; they were starting to make their mark back then, having taken one step at a time. Now the Munster product has reached the point where others are looking to be like them.

What really impresses me is how they overcame the difficulties associated with having to work out of two centres, with the tremendous commitment of the players, with the huge loyalty and support they have built up over the years; that didn't happen by accident, that happened because they worked hard to generate it and developed a relationship with their supporters that is probably unprecedented throughout Europe.

Toulouse was probably the team everyone looked to in awe in the early stages of the European Cup; Toulouse is a great club, no doubt, but the people involved in Irish rugby have to be credited with the way in which they have managed the professional game; they're an example to everyone really.

Europe's top coaches, Ian McGeechan, Guy Noves and Dai Young, believe the Munster fans are unique. Young is convinced that the supporters have played a huge role in Munster's drive to the top of the European order of merit.

The way the people in Munster managed affairs has to be lauded; Munster would always be seen as having access to strong forwards and without question a competitive side right throughout every section of the team. But in order to challenge for the big prizes, they did have to look beyond the province and they managed that part of their business very well.

The signings they have got from abroad have, generally, been inspirational. It's not just that they bought in people; they bought in very good people with a view to looking at a larger picture. These overseas players are worth a place in the side, but they're also very good in helping the development of home-grown talent too. The benefits will be seen in time to come, but it's already being seen and is reflected in the emergence of young guys like Keith Earls.

McGeehan is convinced that Munster will remain a strong power in the years to come. Defeat in the 2009 semi-final does not, he argues, signal a shift in the balance of power; he firmly believes that very good teams do not become bad teams overnight.

Each season is a challenge; Munster have gone through tough times as well as good times, but they've been there or thereabouts like no other team in the last decade.

In my view they are unique for a professional team in that they have that undying spirit so hard to find in this game of ours. Munster have taken that spirit and allowed it to be used to best effect as the professional game evolved. They have maximised their potential with the development of a great new rugby stadium at Thomond Park; what has been achieved is absolutely sensational in a country where rugby is only the third or fourth most popular team sport.

APPENDIX 1

Munster's Heineken Cup History

1995/96

v:	Swansea
Venue:	Thomond Park
Result:	Won 17–13
Munster:	P. Murray (captain), R. Wallace, D. Larkin, S. McCahill, K. Smith, P. Burke, D. O'Mahony, J. Fitzgerald, T. Kingston, P. Clohessy, G. Fulcher, M. Galwey, E. Halvey, A. Foley, D. Corkery.
Replacements:	B. Toland for Halvey. Temporary replacement, M. Fitzgerald for J. Fitzgerald.
Scorers:	R. Wallace and P. Murray tries; K. Smith penalty, two conversions.

v:	Castres
Venue:	Mazamet
Result:	Lost 12–19
Munster:	P. Murray (captain), R. Wallace, D. Larkin, S. McCahill, K. Smith, P. Burke, D. O'Mahony, J. Fitzgerald, T. Kingston, P. Clohessy, P. O'Connor, G. Fulcher, M. Galwey, A. Foley, D. Corkery.
Temporary replacement:	B. Toland for Galwey/Corkery.
Scorer:	K. Smith four penalties.

1996/97

v:	Milan
Venue:	Musgrave Park
Result:	Won 23–5
Munster:	D. Crotty, R. Wallace, B. Walsh, S. McCahill, B. Begley, K. Keane, S. McIvor, J. Fitzgerald, T. Kingston, P. McCarthy, M. Galwey (captain), G. Fulcher, A. Foley, B. Cronin, L. Toland.
Replacements:	P. Murray for Crotty, B. O'Meara for McIvor.
Scorers:	B. Begley try, five penalties; K. Keane, penalty.

v:	Cardiff
Venue:	Cardiff Arms Park
Result:	Lost 18–48
Munster:	D. Crotty, R. Wallace, B. Walsh, S. McCahill, B. Begley, K. Keane, S. McIvor, I. Murray, T. Kingston, P. McCarthy, M. Galwey (captain), G. Fulcher, A. Foley, B. Cronin, L. Toland.
Replacements:	L. Dinneen for Foley, P. Murray for Begley.
Temporary replacement:	Dinneen for Galwey.
Scorers:	B. Begley try, penalty, conversion; A. Foley try; K. Keane penalty.

v:	Wasps
Venue:	Thomond Park
Result:	Won 49–22
Munster:	P. Murray, R. Wallace, B. Walsh, S. McCahill, D. Crotty, K. Keane, S. McIvor, J. Fitzgerald, T. Kingston, N. Healy, M. Galwey (captain), G. Fulcher, A. Foley, B. Cronin, D. Corkery.
Scorers:	K. Keane try, 2 penalties, 4 conversions; B. Cronin, D. Crotty, A. Foley, M. Galwey, R. Wallace tries, penalty try.

v:	Toulouse
Venue:	Stade Les Sept Deniers
Result:	Lost 19–60
Munster:	P. Murray, R. Wallace, B. Walsh, S. McCahill, D. Crotty, K. Keane, S. McIvor, J. Fitzgerald, T. Kingston, N. Healy, M. Galwey (captain), G. Fulcher, A. Foley, B. Cronin, D. Corkery.
Replacements:	P. McCarthy for Healy, L. Dinneen for Cronin, I. Murray for McCarthy.
Scorers:	D. Corkery try; K. Keane four penalties, conversion.

1997/98

v:	Harlequins
Venue:	The Stoop
Result:	Lost 40–48
Munster:	D. Crotty, J. Lacey, C. Burke, R. Ellison, A. Horgan, R. O'Gara, B. O'Meara, I. Murray, M. McDermott, P. Clohessy, M. Galwey (captain), S. Leahy, E. Halvey, G. Tuohy, A. Quinlan.
Replacements:	A. McSweeney for Murray, S. McIvor for O'Meara, U. O'Callaghan for Leahy. Temporary replacement: S. McCahill for Ellison.
Scorers:	C. Burke, M. Galwey, A. Horgan, J. Lacey, A. Quinlan tries; R. O'Gara three penalties, three conversions.

v:	Cardiff
Venue:	Cardiff Arms Park
Result:	Lost 23–43
Munster:	D. Crotty, J. Lacey, K. Keane, R. Ellison, A. Horgan, R. O'Gara, B. O'Meara, I. Murray, F. Sheahan, P. Clohessy, M. Galwey (captain), U. O'Callaghan, E. Halvey, A. Quinlan, A. Foley.
Replacement:	G. Walsh for Murray.
Scorers:	J. Lacey (two), A. Quinlan tries; R. O'Gara two penalties, one conversion.

v:	Bourgoin
Venue:	Thomond Park
Result:	Won 17–15
Munster:	D. Crotty, J. Lacey, C. Burke, R. Ellison, A. Thompson, K. Keane, B. O'Meara, I. Murray, M. McDermott, P. Clohessy, M. Galwey (captain), S. Leahy, E. Halvey, A. Quinlan, A. Foley.
Scorers:	J. Lacey try; C. Burke four penalties.

v:	Cardiff
Venue:	Musgrave Park
Result:	Lost 32–37
Munster:	D. Crotty, J. Lacey, C. Burke, R. Ellison, J. Kelly, K. Keane, B. O'Meara, I. Murray, M. McDermott, P. Clohessy, M. Galwey (captain), S. Leahy, E. Halvey, A. Quinlan, A. Foley.
Replacements:	S. McCahill for Keane, G. Walsh for Murray. Temporary replacement: S. McIvor for Ellison.
Scorers:	A. Quinlan, A. Foley, J. Kelly tries; C. Burke five penalties, one conversion.

v:	Bourgoin
Venue:	Stade Pierre Rajon
Result:	Lost 6–21
Munster:	D. Crotty, J. Lacey, A. Thompson, R. Ellison, J. Kelly, K. Keane, B. O'Meara, I. Murray, M. McDermott, P. Clohessy, M. Galwey (captain), S. Leahy, E. Halvey, A. Quinlan, A. Foley.
Replacements:	A. McSweeney for Murray, R. O'Gara for Kelly, G. Walsh for Clohessy.
Scorer:	R. Ellison, two penalties.

v:	Harlequins
Venue:	Thomond Park
Result:	Won 23–16
Munster:	D. Crotty, J. Lacey, M. Lynch, R. Ellison, J. Kelly, K. Keane, B. O'Meara, I. Murray, M. McDermott, P. Clohessy, M. Galwey (captain), S. Leahy, E. Halvey, A. Quinlan, A. Foley.
Replacement:	S. McIvor for O'Meara.
Scorers:	R. Ellison, E. Halvey tries; K. Keane, three penalties, two conversions.

1998/99

v:	Padova
Venue:	Musgrave Park
Result:	Won 20–13
Munster:	D. Crotty, J. Kelly, B. Walsh, M. Lynch, A. Horgan, R. O'Gara, T. Tierney, P. Clohessy, M. McDermott, J. Hayes, M. Galwey (captain), S. Leahy, A. Quinlan, A. Foley, E. Halvey.
Replacements:	B. O'Meara for Tierney, I Murray for Hayes, D. Wallace for Leahy, D. Corkery for Foley.
Scorers:	E. Halvey, J. Kelly tries; R. O'Gara penalty, two conversions; M. Lynch penalty.

v:	Neath
Venue:	Musgrave Park
Result:	Won 34–10
Munster:	B. Roche, J. Kelly, M. Lynch, C. Mahony, A. Horgan, B. Everitt, B. O'Meara, P. Clohessy, M. McDermott, J. Hayes, M. Galwey (captain), M. O'Driscoll, A. Quinlan, A. Foley, E. Halvey.
Replacements:	D. Wallace for O'Driscoll, I. Murray for Hayes, D. Corkery for Foley.
Scorers:	M. Lynch try, three penalties; M Galwey (two), A. Quinlan, tries; B. Everitt penalty, conversion.

v:	Perpignan
Venue:	Stade Aime Giral
Result:	Lost 24–41
Munster:	B. Roche, J. Kelly, K. Keane, C. Mahony, A. Horgan, B. Everitt, P. Stringer, P. Clohessy, M. McDermott, J. Hayes, M. Galwey (captain), M. O'Driscoll, A. Quinlan, A. Foley, E. Halvey.
Replacements:	I. Murray for Hayes, D. O'Callaghan for O'Driscoll, D. Corkery for O'Callaghan, F. Sheahan for McDermott, B. Walsh for Mahony.
Scorers:	B. Everitt, M. Galwey tries; penalty try; K. Keane, three conversions, penalty.

v:	Neath
Venue:	The Knoll
Result:	Drew 18–18
Munster:	B. Roche, J. Kelly, K. Keane, R. Ellison, A. Horgan, B. Everitt, P. Stringer, P. Clohessy, M. McDermott, J. Hayes, M. Galwey (captain), M. O'Driscoll, A. Quinlan, A. Foley, E. Halvey.
Replacements:	B. Walsh for Horgan, D. Wallace for Quinlan, M. Lynch for Everitt.
Scorers:	P. Stringer, M. Galwey tries; K. Keane, two penalties, conversion.

v:	Perpignan
Venue:	Musgrave Park
Result:	Won 13–5
Munster:	B. Roche, J. Kelly, K. Keane, R. Ellison, A. Horgan, B. Everitt, P. Stringer, P. Clohessy, M. McDermott, J. Hayes, M. Galwey (captain), M. O'Driscoll, A. Quinlan, A. Foley, E. Halvey.
Replacements:	D. Corkery for Quinlan, T. Tierney for Stringer, S. Leahy for O'Driscoll, D. Clohessy for Hayes, F. Sheahan for McDermott.
Scorers:	P. Clohessy try; K. Keane, two penalties, conversion.

v:	Padova
Venue:	Stadio Plebiscito
Result:	Won 35–21
Munster:	B. Walsh, J. Kelly, K. Keane, R. Ellison, A. Horgan, B. Everitt, P. Stringer, D. Clohessy, M. McDermott, J. Hayes, M. Galwey (captain), M. O'Driscoll, D. Corkery, A. Foley, E. Halvey.
Replacements:	M. Lynch for Ellison, T. Tierney for Stringer.
Scorers:	K. Keane try, two penalties, two conversions; D. Corkery, E. Halvey, J. Kelly, B. Walsh tries.

Quarter-final

v:	Colomiers
Venue:	Stade Selery
Result:	Lost 9–23
Munster:	B. Roche, J. O'Neill, K. Keane, R. Ellison, M. Lynch, B. Everitt, P. Stringer, P. Clohessy, M. McDermott, J. Hayes, M. Galwey (captain), M. O'Driscoll, D. Corkery, A. Foley, E. Halvey.
Replacements:	D. Clohessy for Hayes, T. Tierney for Stringer, D. Wallace for Corkery, S. Leahy for O'Driscoll.
Scorer:	K. Keane three penalties.

1999/2000

v:	Pontypridd
Venue:	Thomond Park
Result:	Won 32–10
Munster:	M. Mullins, J. Kelly, K. Keane, C. Mahony, A. Horgan, R. O'Gara, P. Stringer, P. Clohessy, K. Wood, J. Hayes, M. Galwey (captain), J. Langford, A. Quinlan, A. Foley, D. Wallace.
Replacements:	J. Staunton, M. Horan T. Tierney, D. O'Callaghan, E. Halvey.
Scorers:	A. Quinlan, K. Keane tries; R. O'Gara, five penalties, two conversions, drop goal.

v:	Saracens
Venue:	Vicarage Road
Result:	Won 35–34
Munster:	J. Stanton, J. Kelly, K. Keane, M. Mullins, A. Horgan, R. O'Gara, P. Stringer, P. Clohessy, K. Wood, J. Hayes, M. Galwey (captain), J. Langford, A. Quinlan, A. Foley, D. Wallace.
Scorers:	K. Keane, M. Mullins, A. Foley, J. Staunton tries; R. O'Gara, three penalties, three conversions.

v:	Colomiers
Venue:	Stade les Sept Deniers
Result:	Won 31–15
Munster:	J. Staunton, J. Kelly, M. Mullins, J. Holland, A. Horgan, R. O'Gara, P. Stringer, M. Horan, K. Wood, J. Hayes, M. Galwey (captain), J. Langford, A. Quinlan, A. Foley, D. Wallace.
Replacements:	I. Murray for Hayes, T. Tierney for Stringer, D. Crotty for Staunton, F. Sheahan for Murray.
Scorers:	J. Holland (two), K. Wood, M. Horan tries; R. O'Gara three penalties, two conversions.

v:	Colomiers
Venue:	Musgrave Park
Result:	Won 23–5
Munster:	J. Staunton, J. Kelly, M. Mullins, J. Holland, A. Horgan, R. O'Gara, P. Stringer, M. Horan, K. Wood, J. Hayes, M. Galwey (captain), J. Langford, A. Quinlan, A. Foley, D. Wallace.
Replacements:	J. O'Neill for Horgan, D. Crotty for Staunton, F. Sheahan for Wood, T. Tierney for Stringer, D. O'Callaghan for Langford.
Scorers:	K. Wood (two), D. Crotty tries, R. O'Gara, two penalties, conversion.

v:	Saracens
Venue:	Thomond Park
Result:	Won 31–30
Munster:	D. Crotty, J. Kelly, J. Holland, M. Mullins, A. Horgan, R. O'Gara, P. Stringer, P. Clohessy, K. Wood, J. Hayes, M. Galwey (captain), J. Langford, A. Quinlan, A. Foley, D. Wallace.
Temporary replacements:	T. Tierney for Stringer, J. O'Neill for O'Gara, M. Horan for Hayes.
Scorers:	M. Galwey, J. Holland, K. Wood tries; R. O'Gara, four penalties, two conversions.

v:	Pontypridd
Venue:	Sardis Road
Result:	Lost 36–38
Munster:	D. Crotty, J. Kelly, J. Holland, M. Mullins, A. Horgan, R. O'Gara, P. Stringer, P. Clohessy, K. Wood, J. Hayes, M. Galwey (captain), J. Langford, A. Quinlan, A. Foley, D. Wallace.
Replacements:	E. Halvey for Quinlan, M. Horan for Hayes.
Scorers:	A. Quinlan, A. Foley, D. Wallace tries; R. O'Gara, four penalties, three conversions, drop goal.

Quarter-Final

v:	Stade Français
Venue:	Thomond Park
Result:	Won 27–10
Munster:	D. Crotty, J. Kelly, K. Keane, M. Mullins, A. Horgan, R. O'Gara, P. Stringer, P. Clohessy, K. Wood, J. Hayes, M. Galwey (captain), J. Langford, E. Halvey, A. Foley, D. Wallace.
Replacements:	M. Horan for Hayes, A. Quinlan for Halvey.
Scorers:	A. Horgan, D. Crotty tries; R. O'Gara, five penalties, one conversion.

Semi-Final

v:	Toulouse
Venue:	Bordeaux
Result:	Won 31–25
Munster:	D. Crotty, J. Kelly, M. Mullins, J. Holland, A. Horgan, R. O'Gara, P. Stringer, P. Clohessy, K. Wood, J. Hayes, M. Galwey (captain), J. Langford, E. Halvey, A. Foley, D. Wallace.
Replacements:	F. Sheahan for Wood, M. Horan for Hayes, D. O'Callaghan for Galwey.
Scorers:	R. O'Gara try, four penalties, two conversions; J. Hayes, J. Holland tries.

Final

v:	Northampton
Venue:	Twickenham
Result:	Lost 8–9
Munster:	D. Crotty, J. Kelly, M. Mullins, J. Holland, A. Horgan, R. O'Gara, P. Stringer, P. Clohessy, K. Wood, J. Hayes, M. Galwey (captain), J. Langford, E. Halvey, A. Foley, D. Wallace.
Replacement:	K. Keane for Crotty.
Scorers:	D. Wallace try; J. Holland drop goal.

2000/2001

v:	Newport
Venue:	Thomond Park
Result:	Won 25–18
Munster:	D. Crotty, J. Kelly, M. Mullins, J. Holland, A. Horgan, R. O'Gara, P. Stringer, P. Clohessy, F. Sheahan, J. Hayes, M. Galwey (captain), J. Langford, A. Quinlan, A. Foley, D. Wallace.
Scorers:	F. Sheahan, M. Galwey, A. Horgan tries; R. O'Gara, three penalties, one conversion.

v:	Castres
Venue:	Stade Pierre-Antoine
Result:	Won 32–29
Munster:	D. Crotty, J. Kelly, M. Mullins, J. Holland, A. Horgan, R. O'Gara, P. Stringer, P. Clohessy, F. Sheahan, J. Hayes, M. Galwey (captain), J. Langford, A. Quinlan, A. Foley, D. Wallace.
Scorers:	R. O'Gara try, five penalties, conversion; D. Crotty, A. Horgan tries.

v:	Bath
Venue:	Thomond Park
Result:	Won 31–9
Munster:	D. Crotty, J. Kelly, M. Mullins, J. Holland, A. Horgan, R. O'Gara, P. Stringer, P. Clohessy, F. Sheahan, J. Hayes, M. Galwey (captain), J. Langford, A. Quinlan, A. Foley, D. Wallace.
Replacements:	K. Keane for Mullins, J. Staunton for Holland, M. Horan for Clohessy, M. O'Driscoll for Galwey, C. McMahon for Wallace.
Scorers:	A. Horgan (two), D. Wallace tries; R. O'Gara, three penalties, two conversions, drop goal.

v:	Bath
Venue:	The Recreation Ground
Result:	Lost 5–18
Munster:	D. Crotty, J. Kelly, M. Mullins, J. Holland, A. Horgan, R. O'Gara, P. Stringer, P. Clohessy, F. Sheahan, J. Hayes, M. Galwey (captain), J. Langford, A. Quinlan, A. Foley, D. Wallace.
Replacements:	M. O'Driscoll for Galwey, K. Keane for Kelly, C. McMahon for Wallace. Temporary replacement: M. Horan for Wallace.
Scorer:	D. Wallace try.

v:	Newport
Venue:	Rodney Parade
Result:	Won 39–24
Munster:	D. Crotty, J. O'Neill, J. Kelly, K. Keane, A. Horgan, R. O'Gara, P. Stringer, P. Clohessy, F. Sheahan, J. Hayes, M. Galwey (captain), J. Langford, A. Quinlan, A. Foley, D. Wallace.
Replacement:	M. Mullins for Keane.
Scorers:	R. O'Gara try, four penalties, two drop goals, three conversions; M. Mullins, A. Horgan tries.

v:	Castres
Venue:	Musgrave Park
Result:	Won 21–11
Munster:	D. Crotty, J. Kelly, M. Mullins, K. Keane, A. Horgan, R. O'Gara, P. Stringer, P. Clohessy, F. Sheahan, J. Hayes, M. Galwey (captain), J. Langford, A. Quinlan, A. Foley, D. Wallace.
Replacements:	J. Holland for Kelly, J. Staunton for Crotty.
Scorers:	A. Foley, D. Crotty tries; R. O'Gara, three penalties, one conversion.

Quarter-final

v:	Biarritz
Venue:	Thomond Park
Result:	Won 38–29
Munster:	D. Crotty, J. Kelly, M. Mullins, J. Holland, A. Horgan, R. O'Gara, P. Stringer, P. Clohessy, F. Sheahan, J. Hayes, M. Galwey (captain), J. Langford, A. Quinlan, A. Foley, D. Wallace.
Scorers:	A. Foley 3 tries; R. O'Gara seven penalties, one conversion.

Semi-final

v:	Stade Français
Venue:	Lille
Result:	Lost 15–16
Munster:	D.Crotty, J. O'Neill, M. Mullins, J. Holland, A. Horgan, R. O'Gara, P. Stringer, P. Clohessy, F. Sheahan, J. Hayes, M. Galwey (captain), J. Langford, D. O'Callaghan, A. Foley, D. Wallace.
Replacements:	D. Ó Cuinneagain for O'Callaghan, M. Horan for Clohessy.
Scorer:	R. O'Gara five penalties.

2001/2002

v:	Castres
Venue:	Thomond Park
Result:	Won 28–23
Munster:	D. Crotty, J. Kelly, M. Mullins, J. Holland, A. Horgan, R. O'Gara, P. Stringer, P. Clohessy, F. Sheahan, M. Cahill, M. Galwey (captain), M. O'Driscoll, J. Williams, A. Foley, D. Wallace.
Replacements:	P. O'Connell for O'Driscoll, M. Horan for Cahill.
Scorers:	J. Holland try; R. O'Gara six penalties, drop goal, one conversion.

v:	Harlequins
Venue:	The Stoop
Result:	Won 24–8
Munster:	J. Staunton, J. Kelly, M. Mullins, J. Holland, A. Horgan, R. O'Gara, P. Stringer, P. Clohessy, F. Sheahan, J. Hayes, M. Galwey (captain): M. O'Driscoll, J. Williams, A. Foley, D. Wallace.
Replacements:	P. O'Connell for O'Driscoll, M. Horan for Clohessy, D. O'Callaghan for Galwey, C. McMahon for Wallace.
Scorers:	R. O'Gara try, two penalties, conversion, drop goal; J. Holland try, drop goal.

v:	Bridgend
Venue:	Brewery Field
Result:	Won 16–12
Munster:	J. Staunton, J. Kelly, M. Mullins, J. Holland, A. Horgan, R. O'Gara, P. Stringer, P. Clohessy, F. Sheahan, J. Hayes, M. Galwey (captain), M. O'Driscoll, J. Williams, A. Foley, D. Wallace.
Replacements:	P. O'Connell for O'Driscoll, M. Horan for Clohessy.
Scorers:	M. Mullins, J. Kelly tries; R. O'Gara two conversions.

v:	Bridgend
Venue:	Musgrave Park
Result:	Won 40–6
Munster:	J. Staunton, J. Kelly, M. Mullins, J. Holland, A. Horgan, R. O'Gara, P. Stringer, M. Horan, F. Sheahan, J. Hayes, M. Galwey (captain), M. O'Driscoll, J. Williams, A. Foley, A. Quinlan.
Replacements:	P. Clohessy for Hayes, R. Henderson for Kelly, M. O'Driscoll for Galwey, K. Keane for Staunton, C. McMahon for Foley.
Scorers:	J. Horgan, J. Kelly, J. Staunton, J. Holland, M. Mullins tries; R. O'Gara three penalties, three conversions.

v:	Harlequins
Venue:	Thomond Park
Result:	Won 51–17
Munster:	D. Crotty, J. Kelly, M. Mullins, J. Holland, A. Horgan, R. O'Gara, M. Prendergast, P. Clohessy, F. Sheahan, M. Horan, M. Galwey (captain), M. O'Driscoll, J. Williams, A. Foley, D. Wallace.
Replacements:	J. Staunton for Crotty, J. O'Neill for Mullins, D. Hegarty for Prendergast, M. Cahill for Clohessy, D. O'Callaghan for Galwey, C. McMahon for Williams, J. Blaney for O'Gara.
Scorers:	J. Holland, F. Sheahan, a. Foley, D. Crotty, M. Galwey, A. Quinlan tries; R. O'Gara five penalties, three conversions.

v:	Castres
Venue:	Stade Pierre-Antoine
Result:	Lost 13–21
Munster:	D. Crotty, J. Kelly, M. Mullins, J. Holland, A. Horgan, R. O'Gara, P. Stringer, P. Clohessy, F. Sheahan, M. Horan, M. Galwey (captain), M. O'Driscoll, J. Williams, A. Foley, A. Quinlan.
Replacements:	J. Staunton for Crotty, R. Henderson for Holland, J. Hayes for Horan, P. O'Connell for O'Driscoll, D. Wallace for Foley, D. Hegarty for Staunton.
Scorers:	D. Wallace try; R. O'Gara two penalties, conversion.

Quarter-final

v:	Stade Français
Venue:	Stade Jean Bouin
Result:	Won 16–14
Munster:	D. Crotty, J. Kelly, R. Henderson, J. Holland, A. Horgan, R. O'Gara, P. Stringer, P. Clohessy, F. Sheahan, J. Hayes, M. Galwey (captain), P. O'Connell, J. Williams, A. Foley, D. Wallace.
Replacement:	M. Horan for Clohessy.
Scorers:	A. Horgan try; R. O'Gara 2 penalties, drop goal, one conversion.

Semi-final

v:	Castres
Venue:	Beziers
Result:	Won 25–17
Munster:	D. Crotty, J. Kelly, R. Henderson, J. Holland, A. Horgan, R. O'Gara, P. Stringer, P. Clohessy, F. Sheahan, J. Hayes, M. Galwey (captain), P. O'Connell, A, Quinlan, A. Foley, D. Wallace.
Replacements:	M. Mullins for Henderson, M. Horan for Clohessy, D. O'Callaghan for Foley.
Scorers:	J. Kelly try; R. O'Gara six penalties, conversion.

Final

v:	Leicester
Venue:	Millennium Stadium
Result:	Lost 9–15
Munster:	D. Crotty, J. O'Neill, R. Henderson, J. Holland, J. Kelly, R. O'Gara, P. Stringer, P. Clohessy, F. Sheahan, J. Hayes, M. Galwey (captain), P. O'Connell, A. Quinlan, A. Foley, D. Wallace.
Temporary replacement:	J. Blaney for Sheahan.
Scorer:	R. O'Gara three penalties.

2002/2003

v:	Gloucester
Venue:	Kingsholm
Result:	Lost 16–35
Munster:	J. Staunton, J. Kelly, M. Mullins, R. Henderson, M. Lawlor, R. O'Gara, P. Stringer, M. Horan, F. Sheahan, J. Hayes, M. Galwey, M. O'Driscoll, J. Williams (captain), A. Foley, A. Quinlan.
Replacements:	J. Holland for Henderson, E. Halvey for Galwey.
Scorers:	P. Stringer try; R. O'Gara three penalties, conversion.

v:	Perpignan
Venue:	Thomond Park
Result:	Won 30–21
Munster:	D. Crotty, J. Kelly, M. Mullins, J. Holland, M. Lawlor, R. O'Gara, P. Stringer, M. Horan, F. Sheahan, J. Hayes, M. Galwey, M. O'Driscoll, J. Williams (captain), A. Foley, A. Quinlan.
Replacement:	K. Keane for Crotty.
Scorers:	J. Kelly, A. Quinlan, J. Hayes tries; R. O'Gara three penalties, three conversions.

v:	Viadana
Venue:	Musgrave Park
Result:	Won 64–0
Munster:	J. Staunton, M. Lawlor, M. Mullins, J. Holland, A. Horgan, R. O'Gara, P. Stringer, M. Horan, F. Sheahan, J. Hayes, P. O'Connell, D. O'Callaghan, J. Williams (captain), A. Foley, A. Quinlan.
Replacements:	S. Kerr for Horan, M. O'Driscoll for O'Callaghan, E. Halvey for Foley, C. McMahon for Lawlor, J. Fogarty for Sheahan, K. Keane for Staunton,
Scorers:	R. O'Gara try, eight conversions, penalty; A. Foley (two), A. Horgan, F. Sheahan, P. O'Connell, J. Holland, M. Prendergast, tries; penalty try.

v:	Viadana
Venue:	Stadio Luigi Zaffanella
Result:	Won 55–22
Munster:	J. Staunton, J. Kelly, M. Mullins, J. Holland, A. Horgan, R. O'Gara, P. Stringer, M. Horan, F. Sheahan, J. Hayes, P. O'Connell, D. O'Callaghan, J. Williams (captain), A. Foley, A. Quinlan.
Replacements:	S. Kerr for Horan, M. O'Driscoll for O'Connell, M. Lawlor for Mullins, J. Fogarty for Sheahan, K. Keane for Staunton, M. Prendergast for Stringer.
Scorers:	J. Holland (two), A. Quinlan (two), F. Sheahan (two), M. Mullins, J. Kelly, A. Foley tries, R. O'Gara, five conversions.

v:	Perpignan
Venue:	Stade Aimé Giral
Result:	Lost 8–23
Munster:	J. Staunton, J. Kelly, M. Mullins, J. Holland, M. Lawlor, R. O'Gara, P. Stringer, M. Horan, F. Sheahan, J. Hayes, D. O'Callaghan, M. O'Driscoll, J. Williams (captain), A. Foley, A. Quinlan.
Replacements:	D. Leamy for Quinlan, M. Galwey for O'Driscoll.
Scorers:	A. Foley try; R. O'Gara penalty.

v:	Gloucester
Venue:	Thomond Park
Result:	Won 33–6
Munster:	J. Staunton, J. Kelly, M. Mullins, J. Holland, M. Lawlor, R. O'Gara, P. Stringer, M. Horan, F. Sheahan, J. Hayes, D. O'Callaghan, M. O'Driscoll, J. Williams (captain), A. Foley, A. Quinlan.
Scorers:	J. Kelly (two), M. Lawlor, M. O'Driscoll tries; R. O'Gara three penalties, two conversions.

Quarter-final

v:	Leicester
Venue:	Welford Road
Result:	Won 20–7
Munster:	J. Staunton, J. Kelly, M. Mullins, R. Henderson, A. Horgan, R. O'Gara, M. Horan, F. Sheahan, J. Hayes, D. O'Callaghan, P. O'Connell, J. Williams (captain), A. Foley, A. Quinlan.
Replacements:	J. Holland for Henderson, M. O'Driscoll for O'Connell.
Scorers:	R. O'Gara try, two penalties, two conversions; P. Stringer try.

Semi-final

v:	Toulouse
Venue:	Stade de Toulouse
Result:	Lost 12–13
Munster:	J. Staunton, J. Kelly, M. Mullins, R. Henderson, A. Horgan, R. O'Gara, P. Stringer, M. Horan, F. Sheahan, J. Hayes, D. O'Callaghan, P. O'Connell, J. Williams (captain), A. Foley, A. Quinlan.
Replacement:	J. Holland for Henderson.
Scorer:	R. O'Gara two drop goals, two penalties.

2003/2004

v:	Bourgoin
Venue:	Stade Pierre Rajon
Result:	Won 18–17
Munster:	J. Staunton, J. Kelly, M. Mullins, J. Holland, S. Payne, R. O'Gara, P. Stringer, M. Horan, F. Sheahan, J. Hayes, P. O'Connell, D. O'Callaghan, J. Williams (captain), A. Foley, D. Wallace.
Replacements:	R. Henderson for Holland, M. Lawlor for Staunton.
Scorer:	R. O'Gara six penalties.

v:	Benetton Treviso
Venue:	Thomond Park
Result:	Won 51–0
Munster:	J. Staunton, J. Kelly, M. Mullins, R. Henderson, S. Payne, R. O'Gara, P. Stringer, M. Horan, F. Sheahan, J. Hayes, D. O'Callaghan, P. O'Connell, J. Williams, A. Foley, D. Wallace.
Replacements:	M. Lawlor for Staunton, J. Holland for Mullins, E. Reddan for Stringer, J. Blaney for Sheahan, G. McIllwham for Hayes, D. Pusey for O'Connell, S. Keogh for Williams.
Scorers:	A. Foley (two), J. Holland (two), J. Staunton, s. Payne, P. O'Connell, D. O'Callaghan tries; R. O'Gara four conversions, penalty.

v:	Gloucester
Venue:	Kingsholm
Result:	Lost 11–22
Munster:	S. Payne, J. Kelly, M. Mullins, R. Henderson, A. Horgan, R. O'Gara, P. Stringer, M. Horan, F. Sheahan, J. Hayes, D. O'Callaghan, P. O'Connell, J. Williams (captain), A. Foley, D. Wallace.
Replacements:	G. McIllwham for Horan.
Scorers:	A. Horgan try; R. O'Gara two penalties.

v:	Gloucester
Venue:	Thomond Park
Result:	Won 35–14
Munster:	S. Payne, J. Kelly, M. Mullins, R. Henderson, A. Horgan, R. O'Gara, P. Stringer, M. Horan, F. Sheahan, J. Hayes, D. O'Callaghan, P. O'Connell, J. Williams (captain), A. Foley, D. Wallace.
Replacements:	G. McIllwham for Horan, S. Keogh for Williams.
Scorers:	M. Horan (two), F. Sheahan, J. Kelly tries; R. O'Gara three penalties, three conversions.

v:	Treviso
Venue:	Stadio Communale di Monigo
Result:	Won 31–20
Munster:	S. Payne, J. Kelly, M. Mullins, R. Henderson, A. Horgan, R. O'Gara, P. Stringer, G. McIllwham, J. Blaney, J. Hayes, P. O'Connell, D. O'Callaghan, J. Williams (captain), A. Foley, D. Wallace.
Replacements:	J. Staunton for Payne, J. Holland for Henderson, E. Reddan for Stringer, F. Roche for McIllwham, S. Kerr for Hayes, D. Pusey for O'Callaghan, S. Keogh for Wallace.
Scorers:	M. Mullins, J. Blaney, A. Foley, J. Williams, J. Staunton tries; R. O'Gara three conversions.

v:	Bourgoin
Venue:	Thomond Park
Result:	Won 26–3
Munster:	J. Staunton, J. Kelly, M. Mullins, R. Henderson, A. Horgan, R. O'Gara, P. Stringer, M. Horan, J. Blaney, J. Hayes, D. O'Callaghan, P. O'Connell, J. Williams (captain), A. Foley, D. Wallace.
Replacements:	J. Holland for Henderson, G. McIllwham for Horan, D. Pusey for O'Connell, M. Lawlor for Horgan, S. Keogh for Wallace.
Scorers:	M. Mullins, P. Stringer, P. O'Connell tries; penalty try, R. O'Gara three conversions.

Quarter-final

v:	Stade Français
Venue:	Thomond Park
Result:	Won 37–32
Munster:	C. Cullen, J. Kelly, R. Henderson, M. Mullins, S. Payne, R. O'Gara, P. Stringer, M. Horan, F. Sheahan, J. Hayes, P. O'Connell, D. O'Callaghan, J. Williams (captain), A. Foley, D. Wallace.
Replacements:	A. Horgan for Mullins, J. Holland for Kelly.
Scorers:	S. Payne, R. Henderson, M. Mullins, M. Horan tries; R. O'Gara three penalties, four conversions.

Semi-final

v:	London Wasps
Venue:	Lansdowne Road
Result:	Lost 32–37
Munster:	C. Cullen, J. Kelly, R. Henderson, M. Mullins, S. Payne, R. O'Gara, P. Stringer, M. Horan, F. Sheahan, J. Hayes, P. O'Connell, D. O'Callaghan, J. Williams (captain), A. Foley, S. Keogh.
Replacements:	J. Holland for O'Gara, A. Horgan for Kelly.
Scorers:	A. Foley, J. Williams tries, J. Holland three penalties, two conversions; R. O'Gara three penalties.

2004/2005

v:	Harlequins
Venue:	Thomond Park
Result:	Won 15–9
Munster:	C. Cullen, M. Lawlor, J. Kelly, R. Henderson, A. Horgan, R. O'Gara, P. Stringer, M. Horan, F. Sheahan, J. Hayes, T. Hogan, P. O'Connell, J. Williams, A. Foley (captain), D. Leamy.
Replacement:	A. Quinlan for Williams.
Scorers:	A. Horgan, D. Leamy tries; R. O'Gara penalty, conversion.

v:	Neath Swansea Ospreys
Venue:	St Helens
Result:	Won 20–18
Munster:	C. Cullen, J. Kelly, S. Payne, R. Henderson, A. Horgan, R. O'Gara, P. Stringer, M. Horan, F. Sheahan, J. Hayes, D. O'Callaghan, P. O'Connell, J. Williams, A. Foley (captain), D. Wallace.
Scorers:	P. Stringer try; R. O'Gara five penalties.

v:	Castres
Venue:	Stade Pierre-Antoine
Result:	Lost 12–19
Munster:	C. Cullen, M. Lawlor, S. Payne, R. Henderson, A. Horgan, R. O'Gara, P. Stringer, M. Horan, F. Sheahan, J. Hayes, D. O'Callaghan, P. O'Connell, J. Williams, A. Foley (captain), D.Wallace.
Replacements:	A. Quinlan for Williams, M. Mullins for Lawlor.
Scorer:	R. O'Gara four penalties.

v:	Castres
Venue:	Thomond Park
Result:	Won 36–8
Munster:	C. Cullen, S. Payne, M. Mullins, R. Henderson, A. Horgan, R. O'Gara, P. Stringer, M. Horan, F. Sheahan, J. Hayes, D. O'Callaghan, P. O'Connell, A. Quinlan, A. Foley (captain), D. Leamy.
Replacements:	T. Hogan for O'Callaghan, G. McIllwham for Horan, M. Prendergast for Stringer, P. Burke for O'Gara, J. Williams for Quinlan, J. Blaney for Sheahan, M. Lawlor for Horgan.
Scorers:	A. Foley, D. Leamy, P. O'Connell, F. Sheahan, C. Cullen tries; R. O'Gara penalty, three conversions; P. Burke conversion.

v:	Neath Swansea Ospreys
Venue:	Thomond Park
Result:	Won 20–10
Munster:	C. Cullen, M. Lawlor, S. Payne, M. Mullins, A. Horgan, P. Burke, P. Stringer, M. Horan, F. Sheahan, J. Hayes, D. O'Callaghan, P. O'Connell, A. Quinlan, A. Foley (captain), D. Leamy.
Scorers:	C. Cullen, A. Foley tries; P. Burke two penalties, two conversions.

v:	Harlequins
Venue:	Twickenham
Result:	Won 18–10
Munster:	C. Cullen, S. Payne, M. Mullins, R. Henderson, A. Horgan, P. Burke, P. Stringer, M. Horan, F. Sheahan, J. Hayes, D. O'Callaghan, P. O'Connell, A. Quinlan, A. Foley (captain), D. Leamy.
Replacements:	J. Williams for Quinlan, J. Holland for Henderson.
Scorers:	A. Horgan, D. Leamy tries; P. Burke penalty, conversion.

Quarter-final

v:	Biarritz
Venue:	San Sebastian
Result:	Lost 10–19
Munster:	S. Payne, J. Kelly, M. Mullins, R. Henderson, A. Horgan, P. Burke, P. Stringer, M. Horan, F. Sheahan, J. Hayes, D. O'Callaghan, P. O'Connell, A. Quinlan, A. Foley (captain), D. Wallace.
Replacements:	P. Devlin for M. Mullins, J. Williams for Quinlan, J. Holland for Burke.
Scorers:	D. Wallace try; P. Burke penalty, conversion.

2005/2006

v:	Sale Sharks
Venue:	Edgeley Park
Result:	Lost 13–27
Munster:	S. Payne, J. Kelly, B. Murphy, G. Connolly, A. Pitout, R. O'Gara, T. O'Leary, M. Horan, F. Sheahan, J. Hayes, D. O'Callaghan, M. O'Driscoll, A. Quinlan, A. Foley (captain), D. Leamy.
Replacements:	P. Stringer for O'Leary, J. Flannery for Sheahan, F. Pucciariello for Hayes, T. Hogan for Quinlan, D. Wallace for Leamy.
Scorers:	F. Sheahan try; R. O'Gara two penalties, conversion.

v:	Castres
Venue:	Thomond Park
Result:	Won 42–16
Munster:	S. Payne, J. Kelly, G. Connolly, T. Halstead, A. Horgan, R. O'Gara, P. Stringer, M. Horan, J. Flannery, J. Hayes, D. O'Callaghan, M. O'Driscoll, D. Leamy, A. Foley (captain), D. Wallace.
Replacements:	B. Murphy for Connolly, J. Manning for O'Gara, T. O'Leary for Stringer, D. Fogarty for Flannery, F. Pucciariello for Hayes, T. Hogan for O'Driscoll, S. Keogh for Foley.
Scorers:	T. Halstead, D. O'Callaghan, J. Flannery, A. Horgan, J. Kelly tries; R. O'Gara two penalties, four conversions; J. Manning penalty.

v:	Newport Gwent Dragons
Venue:	Rodney Parade
Result:	Won 24–8
Munster:	M. Lawlor, J. Kelly, G. Connolly, T. Halstead, A. Horgan, R. O'Gara, P. Stringer, M. Horan, J. Flannery, J. Hayes, D. O'Callaghan, M. O'Driscoll, D. Leamy, A. Foley (captain), D. Wallace.
Replacements:	B. Murphy for Connolly, J. Manning for O'Gara, F. Roche for Horan, D. Fogarty for Flannery, T. Hogan for O'Callaghan, S. Keogh for Leamy, T. O'Leary for Foley.
Scorers:	D. Leamy, M. Horan tries; R. O'Gara two penalties, drop goal, conversion; M. Lawlor drop goal.

v:	Newport Gwent Dragons
Venue:	Thomond Park
Result:	Won 30–18
Munster:	S. Payne, J. Kelly, G. Connolly, T. Halstead, A. Horgan, R. O'Gara, P. Stringer, M. Horan, J. Flannery, J. Hayes, D. O'Callaghan, M. O'Driscoll, D. Leamy, A. Foley (captain), D. Wallace.
Replacement:	B. Murphy for Halstead.
Scorers:	M. O'Driscoll, A. Foley, J. Flannery tries; R. O'Gara three penalties, three conversions.

v:	Castres
Venue:	Stade Pierre-Antoine
Result:	Won 46–9
Munster:	S. Payne, J. Kelly, B. Murphy, T. Halstead, I. Dowling, R. O'Gara, P. Stringer, M. Horan, J. Flannery, J. Hayes, D. O'Callaghan, P. O'Connell, D. Leamy, A. Foley (captain), D. Wallace.
Replacements:	T. O'Leary for Kelly, G. Connolly for Halstead, J. Manning for O'Gara, F. Pucciariello for Horan, D. Fogarty for Flannery, M. O'Driscoll for O'Connell, S. Keogh for Foley.
Scorers:	P. O'Connell (two), T. O'Leary (two), M. Horan, S. Payne, J. Kelly tries; R. O'Gara penalty, three conversions; J. Manning conversion.

v:	Sale Sharks
Venue:	Thomond Park
Result:	Won 31–9.
Munster:	S. Payne, J. Kelly, B. Murphy, T. Halstead, I. Dowling, R. O'Gara, P. Stringer, M. Horan, J. Flannery, J. Hayes, D. O'Callaghan, P. O'Connell, D. Leamy, A. Foley (captain), D. Wallace.
Replacements:	M. Lawlor for Payne, T. O'Leary for Stringer, F. Pucciariello for Horan, D. Fogarty for Flannery, M. O'Driscoll for O'Connell, S. Keogh for Foley, G. Connolly for Halstead.
Scorers:	A. Foley, I. Dowling, B. Murphy, D. Wallace tries; R. O'Gara four conversions, penalty.

Quarter-final

v:	Perpignan
Venue:	Lansdowne Road
Result:	Won 19–10
Munster:	S. Payne, J. Kelly, T. O'Leary, T. Halstead, I. Dowling, R. O'Gara, P. Stringer, M. Horan, J. Flannery, J. Hayes, D. O'Callaghan, P. O'Connell, D. Leamy, A. Foley (captain), D. Wallace.
Replacements:	C. Cullen for Dowling, J. Manning for O'Gara, M. O'Driscoll for Leamy.
Scorers:	P. O'Connell try; R. O'Gara four penalties, conversion.

v:	Leinster
Venue:	Lansdowne Road
Result:	Won 30–6
Munster:	S. Payne, A. Horgan, J. Kelly, T. Halstead, I. Dowling, R. O'Gara, P. Stringer, F. Pucciariello, J. Flannery, J. Hayes, D. O'Callaghan, P. O'Connell, D. Leamy, A. Foley (captain), D. Wallace.
Replacements:	R. Henderson for Kelly, T. O'Leary for Stringer, D. Leamy for Foley.
Scorers:	R. O'Gara try, three penalties, three conversions; T. Halstead, D. Leamy tries.

Final

v:	Biarritz
Venue:	Millennium Stadium
Result:	Won 23–19
Munster:	S. Payne, A. Horgan, J. Kelly, T. Halstead, I. Dowling, R. O'Gara, P. Stringer, M. Horan, J. Flannery, J. Hayes, D. O'Callaghan, P. O'Connell, D. Leamy, A. Foley (captain), D. Wallace.
Replacements:	F. Pucciariello for Horan, M. O'Driscoll for O'Connell, A. Quinlan for Foley.
Scorers:	T. Halstead, P. Stringer tries; R. O'Gara three penalties, two conversions.

2006/2007

v:	Leicester
Venue:	Welford Road
Result:	Won 21–19
Munster:	S. Payne, J. Kelly, B. Murphy, T. Halstead, I. Dowling, R. O'Gara, P. Stringer, M. Horan, F. Sheahan, J. Hayes, D. O'Callaghan, P. O'Connell (captain), D. Leamy, A. Foley, D. Wallace.
Replacements:	A. Quinlan for Foley, L. Mafi for Murphy, F. Pucciariello for Hayes.
Scorers:	D. O'Callaghan, D. Wallace tries; R. O'Gara, two penalties, drop goal, conversion.

v:	Bourgoin
Venue:	Thomond Park
Result:	Won 41–23
Munster:	S. Payne, J. Kelly, B. Murphy, T. Halstead, I. Dowling, R. O'Gara, P. Stringer, M. Horan, F. Sheahan, J. Hayes, D. O'Callaghan, P. O'Connell (captain), A. Quinlan, D. Leamy, D. Wallace.
Replacements:	F. Pucciariello for Horan, M. O'Driscoll for Quinlan, A. Kyriacou for Sheahan, L. Mafi for Halstead, J. O'Sullivan for O'Connell, T. O'Leary for Stringer, J. Manning for O'Gara.
Scorers:	F. Sheahan, I. Dowling, B. Murphy, D. O'Callaghan, J. Kelly, A. Kyriacou tries; R. O'Gara four conversions, penalty.

v: Cardiff Blues
Venue: Cardiff Arms Park
Result: Won 22–12
Munster: S. Payne, T. O'Leary, L. Mafi, T. Halstead, I. Dowling, R. O'Gara,
                     P. Stringer, F. Pucciariello, F. Sheahan, J. Hayes, D. O'Callaghan,
                     P. O'Connell (captain), A. Quinlan, D. Leamy, D. Wallace.
Replacements: D Hurley for Pucciariello.
Scorers: D. Leamy try; R. O'Gara five penalties, conversion.

v: Cardiff Blues
Venue: Thomond Park
Result: Won 32–18
Munster: S. Payne, J. Kelly, B. Murphy, T. Halstead, I. Dowling, R. O'Gara,
                     P. Stringer, D. Hurley, F. Sheahan, J. Hayes, D. O'Callaghan,
                     P. O'Connell (captain), A. Quinlan, D. Leamy, D. Wallace.
Replacement: F. Pucciariello for Hurley.
Scorers: D. Leamy (two), A. Quinlan, B. Murphy tries; R. O'Gara two
                     penalties, three conversions.

v: Bourgoin
Venue: Stade de Genève
Result: Won 30–27
Munster: S. Payne, J. Kelly, B. Murphy, L. Mafi, I. Dowling, R. O'Gara,
                     P. Stringer, M. Horan, F. Sheahan, J. Hayes, D. O'Callaghan,
                     P. O'Connell (captain), M. O'Driscoll, D. Leamy, D. Wallace.
Replacements: J. Flannery for Sheahan, T. O'Leary for Kelly, a. Foley for Leamy,
                     F. Pucciariello for Horan.
Scorers: M. Horan, L. Mafi tries; penalty try; R. O'Gara three penalties,
                     three conversions.

v: Leicester
Venue: Thomond Park
Result: Lost 6–13
Munster: S. Payne, J. Kelly, B. Murphy, L. Mafi, I. Dowling, R. O'Gara,
                     P. Stringer, M. Horan, F. Sheahan, J. Hayes, D. O'Callaghan,
                     P. O'Connell (captain), M. O'Driscoll, D. Leamy, D. Wallace.
Replacements: T. O'Leary for Kelly, J. Flannery for Sheahan, A. Foley for
                     O'Driscoll, J. Coughlan for Foley
Scorer: R. O'Gara two penalties.

Quarter-final
v: Llanelli Scarlets
Venue: Stradey Park
Result: Lost 15–24
Munster: C. Cullen, J. Kelly, L. Mafi, T. Halstead, I. Dowling, R. O'Gara
                     (captain), P. Stringer, M. Horan, J. Flannery, J. Hayes,
                     D. O'Callaghan, M. O'Driscoll, A. Quinlan, D. Leamy, D. Wallace.
Replacements: B. Murphy for Kelly, T. O'Leary for Dowling, D. Ryan for
                     O'Driscoll, F. Pucciariello for Horan.
Scorers: I. Dowling, D. Ryan tries; R. O'Gara penalty, conversion.

2007/2008

v:	London Wasps
Venue:	High Wycombe Lost 23–24
Munster:	S. Payne, B. Carney, R. Tipoki, L. Mafi, A. Horgan, R. O'Gara (captain), P. Stringer, M. Horan, J. Flannery, J. Hayes, D. O'Callaghan, M. O'Driscoll, A. Quinlan, D. Leamy, D. Wallace.
Replacements:	T. O'Leary for Payne, J. Paringati for Leamy, A. Foley for Quinlan, T. Buckley for Horan.
Scorers:	S. Payne, R. Tipoki tries; R. O'Gara three penalties, two conversions.

v:	Clermont Auvergne
Venue:	Thomond Park Won 36–13
Munster:	S. Payne, B. Carney, R. Tipoki, L. Mafi, I. Dowling, R. O'Gara (captain), P. Stringer, M. Horan, J. Flannery, J. Hayes, D. O'Callaghan, M. O'Driscoll, A. Quinlan, D. Leamy, D. Wallace.
Replacements:	F. Sheahan for Flannery, T. Buckley for Hayes, A. Foley for Quinlan, J. Paringati for Wallace, G. Hurley for Stringer, P. Warwick for O'Gara, K. Lewis for Tipoki.
Scorers:	S. Payne, B. Carney, R. Tipoki, A. Quinlan, M. Horan tries; R. O'Gara four conversions, penalty.

v:	Llanelli Scarlets
Venue:	Stradey Park
Result:	Won 29–16
Munster:	S. Payne, B. Carney, R. Tipoki, L. Mafi, I. Dowling, R. O'Gara (captain), P. Stringer, M. Horan, J. Flannery, J. Hayes, D. O'Callaghan, M. O'Driscoll, D. Leamy, A. Foley, D. Wallace.
Replacements:	F. Sheahan for Flannery, P. Warwick for Payne, J. Coughlan for Wallace.
Scorers:	M. Horan, D. Wallace tries; R. O'Gara five penalties, two conversions.

v:	Llanelli Scarlets
Venue:	Thomond Park
Result:	Won 22–13
Munster:	S. Payne, B. Carney, R. Tipoki, L. Mafi, I. Dowling, R. O'Gara (captain), P. Stringer, F. Pucciariello, J. Flannery, J. Hayes, D. O'Callaghan, M. O'Driscoll, D. Leamy, A. Foley, D. Wallace.
Replacements:	M. Horan for Pucciariello, D. Ryan for O'Driscoll.
Scorers:	B. Carney, J. Flannery tries; R. O'Gara four penalties.

v:	Clermont Auvergne
Venue:	Parc Marcel-Michelin
Result:	Lost 19–26
Munster:	S. Payne, B. Carney, R. Tipoki, L. Mafi, D. Howlett, R. O'Gara (captain), P. Stringer, M. Horan, J. Flannery, J. Hayes, D. O'Callaghan, M. O'Driscoll, D. Leamy, A. Foley, D. Wallace.
Replacement:	T. Buckley for Hayes, A. Quinlan for Foley.
Scorers:	L. Mafi try; R. O'Gara four penalties, conversion.

v:	London Wasps
Venue:	Thomond Park
Result:	Won 19–3
Munster:	S. Payne, B. Carney, R. Tipoki, L. Mafi, D. Howlett, R. O'Gara (captain), P. Stringer, M. Horan, J. Flannery, J. Hayes, D. O'Callaghan, M. O'Driscoll, D. Leamy, A. Foley, D. Wallace.
Replacements:	F. Sheahan for Flannery, T. Buckley for Hayes, A. Quinlan for Foley.
Scorers:	D. Leamy try; R. O'Gara four penalties, conversion.

Quarter-final

v:	Gloucester
Venue:	Kingsholm
Result:	Won 16–3
Munster:	D. Hurley, D. Howlett, R. Tipoki, L. Mafi, I. Dowling, R. O'Gara, T. O'Leary, T. Buckley, J. Flannery, J. Hayes, D. O'Callaghan, P. O'Connell (captain), A. Quinlan, D. Leamy, D. Wallace.
Replacements:	F. Pucciariello for Buckley, A. Foley for Leamy, M. O'Driscoll for Wallace.
Scorers:	D. Howlett, I. Dowling tries; R. O'Gara two penalties.

Semi-final

v:	Saracens
Venue:	Ricoh Arena
Result:	Won 18–16
Munster:	D. Hurley, D. Howlett, R. Tipoki, L. Mafi, I. Dowling, R. O'Gara, T. O'Leary, M. Horan, J. Flannery, J. Hayes, D. O'Callaghan, P. O'Connell (captain), A. Quinlan, D. Leamy, D. Wallace.
Replacements:	D. Ryan for O'Callaghan
Scorers:	R. O'Gara try, two penalties, conversion; A. Quinlan try.

Final

v:	Toulouse
Venue:	Millennium Stadium
Result:	Won 16–13
Munster:	D. Hurley, D. Howlett, R. Tipoki, L. Mafi, I. Dowling, R. O'Gara, T. O'Leary, M. Horan, J. Flannery, J. Hayes, D. O'Callaghan, P. O'Connell (captain), A. Quinlan, D. Leamy, D. Wallace.
Replacements:	T. Buckley for Horan, M. O'Driscoll for O'Connell.
Scorers:	D. Leamy try; R. O'Gara three penalties, conversion.

2008/2009

v:	Montauban
Venue:	Thomond Park
Result:	Won 19–17
Munster:	K. Earls, D. Howlett, R. Tipoki, L. Mafi, I. Dowling, R. O'Gara, P. Stringer, M. Horan, J. Flannery, J. Hayes, D. O'Callaghan, P. O'Connell (captain), A. Quinlan, J. Melck, D. Wallace.
Replacements:	F. Pucciariello for Hayes, D. Ryan for Quinlan, J. O'Sullivan for Melck, P. Warwick for Tipoki, B. Murphy for Dowling.
Scorers:	B. Murphy try; R. O'Gara four penalties, conversion.

v: Sale Sharks
Venue: Edgeley Park   Won 24–16
Munster: P. Warwick, D. Howlett, K. Earls, L. Mafi, I. Dowling, R. O'Gara, T. O'Leary, M. Horan, J. Flannery, J. Hayes, D. O'Callaghan, P. O'Connell (captain), A. Quinlan, D. Wallace, J. O'Sullivan.
Replacements: D. Ryan for Quinlan, J. Melck for O'Sullivan, B. Murphy for Earls.
Scorers: R. O'Gara two penalties, drop goal, conversion; P. Warwick try, drop goal; D. Wallace try.

v: Clermont Auvergne
Venue: Parc Marcel-Michelin
Result: Lost 19–25
Munster: K. Earls, D. Howlett, B. Murphy, L. Mafi, I. Dowling, R. O'Gara, T. O'Leary, M. Horan, F. Sheahan, J. Hayes, D. O'Callaghan, P. O'Connell (captain), A. Quinlan, D. Wallace, N. Ronan.
Replacements: D. Fogarty for Sheahan, T. Buckley for Horan, D. Ryan for Ronan, J. Coughlan for Quinlan.
Scorers: M. Horan try; R. O'Gara four penalties, conversion.

v: Clermont Auvergne
Venue: Thomond Park
Result: Won 23–13
Munster: K. Earls, D. Howlett, B. Murphy, L. Mafi, I. Dowling, R. O'Gara, T. O'Leary, M. Horan, J. Flannery, J. Hayes, D. O'Callaghan, P. O'Connell (captain), A. Quinlan, D. Wallace, N. Ronan.
Replacements: D. Fogarty for Flannery, T. Buckley for Hayes, D. Ryan for Quinlan, J. Coughlan for Wallace, P. Stringer for O'Leary, P. Warwick for Murphy.
Scorers: M. Horan, N. Ronan, D. Wallace tries; R. O'Gara two penalties, conversion.

v: Sale Sharks
Venue: Thomond Park
Result: Won 37–14
Munster: P. Warwick, D. Howlett, K. Earls, L. Mafi, I. Dowling, R. O'Gara, T. O'Leary, M. Horan, J. Flannery, J. Hayes, D. O'Callaghan, P. O'Connell (captain), A. Quinlan, D. Leamy, D. Wallace.
Replacements: D. Fogarty for Flannery, F. Pucciariello for Hayes, D. Ryan for Quinlan, N. Ronan for Leamy, P. Stringer for O'Leary, B. Murphy for Earls, D. Hurley for O'Gara.
Scorers: P. Warwick try, penalty; I. Dowling, T. O'Leary, J. Flannery, P. O'Connell, D. Wallace tries; R. O'Gara two conversions

v: Montauban
Venue: Stade de Sapiac
Result: Won 39–13
Munster: P. Warwick, D.Howlett, K. Earls, L. Mafi, I. Dowling, R. O'Gara, T. O'Leary, M. Horan, J. Flannery, J. Hayes, D. O'Callaghan, P. O'Connell (captain), A. Quinlan, D. Leamy, D. Wallace.
Replacements: D. Fogarty for Flannery, F. Pucciariello for Hayes, D. Ryan for O'Connell, N. Ronan for Leamy, P. Stringer for O'Leary, B. Murphy for Earls, D. Hurley for O'Gara.
Scorers: L. Mafi (two), B. Murphy (two), T. O'Leary tries; R. O'Gara two penalties, three conversions; P. Warwick conversion.

Quarter-final

v:	Ospreys
Venue:	Thomond Park
Result:	Won 43–9
Munster:	P. Warwick, D. Howlett, K. Earls, L. Mafi, I. Dowling, R. O'Gara, T. O'Leary, M. Horan, J. Flannery, J. Hayes, D. O'Callaghan, P. O'Connell (captain), A. Quinlan, D. Leamy, D. Wallace.
Replacements:	D. Fogarty for Flannery, T. Buckley for Hayes, M. O'Driscoll for O'Callaghan, N. Ronan for Leamy, P. Stringer for O'Leary, B. Murphy for Magi, D. Hurley for O'Gara.
Scorers:	P. Warwick try, two drop goals; K. Earls (two), P. O'Connell tries; R. O'Gara four conversions, three penalties.

Semi-final

v:	Leinster
Venue:	Croke Park
Result:	Lost 6–25
Munster:	P. Warwick, D. Howlett, K. Earls, L. Mafi, I. Dowling, R. O'Gara, P. Stringer, M. Horan, J. Flannery, J. Hayes, D. O'Callaghan, P. O'Connell (captain), A. Quinlan, D. Leamy, D. Wallace.
Replacements:	D. Fogarty for Flannery, T. Buckley for Hayes, M. O'Driscoll for O'Callaghan, N. Ronan for Leamy, M. Prendergast for Stringer, B. Murphy for Earls, D. Hurley for Warwick.
Scorer:	R. O'Gara two penalties.

APPENDIX 2

IRFU
Senior Interprovincial Championship winners

1946 – Ulster
1947 – Munster
1948 – Leinster
1949 – Leinster
1950 – Ulster
1951 – Ulster
1952 – Munster
1953 – Ulster
1954 – Leinster/Munster
1955 – Ulster/Connacht
1956 – Leinster/Ulster/Connacht
1957 – Munster
1958 – Leinster
1959 – Munster
1960 – Leinster
1961 – Leinster
1962 – Munster
1963 – Leinster
1964 – Leinster
1965 – Munster
1966 – Munster/Ulster
1967 – Ulster
1968 – Munster
1969 – Ulster
1970 – Ulster
1971 – Leinster
1972 – Leinster/Ulster/Munster
1973 – Munster

1974 – Ulster
1975 – Leinster/Munster/Ulster
1976 – Ulster
1977 – Leinster/Munster/Ulster
1978 – Munster
1979 – Leinster
1980 – Leinster
1981 – Leinster
1982 – Leinster/Ulster/Munster
1983 – Ulster/Leinster/Munster
1984 – Ulster
1985 – Ulster
1986 – Ulster
1987 – Ulster/Munster
1988 – Ulster
1989 – Ulster
1990 – Ulster
1991 – Ulster
1992 – Ulster
1993 – Leinster/Ulster/Munster
1994 – Munster
1995 – Leinster
1996 – Munster
1997 – Leinster
1998 – Munster
1999 – Munster
2000 – Munster

The official Irish Interprovincial Championship was discontinued at the end of the 2000/2001 season.

INDEX